ENCHANTED CREATURES

Also by Natalie Lawrence

Planta Sapiens: Unmasking Plant Intelligence
(with Paco Calvo)

ENCHANTED CREATURES

OUR MONSTERS AND
THEIR MEANINGS

NATALIE
LAWRENCE

W&N
WEIDENFELD & NICOLSON

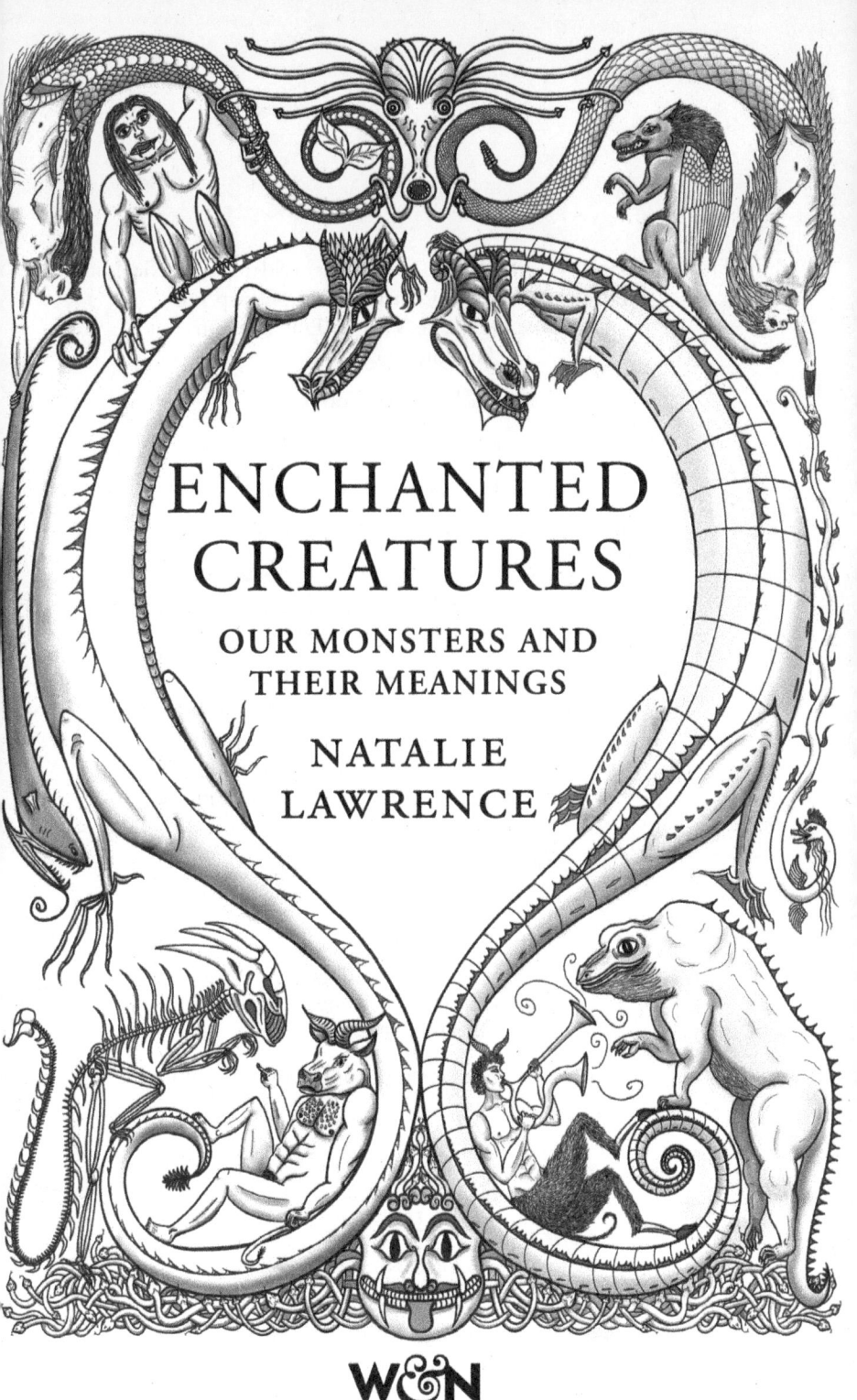

First published in Great Britain in 2024 by Weidenfeld & Nicolson,
an imprint of The Orion Publishing Group Ltd
Carmelite House, 50 Victoria Embankment
London EC4Y 0DZ

An Hachette UK Company

1 3 5 7 9 10 8 6 4 2

Copyright © Natalie Lawrence 2024

Illustrations copyright © Natalie Lawrence 2024

The moral right of Natalie Lawrence to be identified as
the author of this work has been asserted in accordance
with the Copyright, Designs and Patents Act of 1988.

All rights reserved. No part of this publication may be
reproduced, stored in a retrieval system, or transmitted
in any form or by any means, electronic, mechanical,
photocopying, recording, or otherwise, without the
prior permission of both the copyright owner and the
above publisher of this book.

A CIP catalogue record for this book is
available from the British Library.

ISBN (Hardback) 978 1 4746 1901 1
ISBN (Export Trade Paperback) 978 1 4746 1902 8
ISBN (eBook) 978 1 4746 1904 2
ISBN (Audio) 978 1 4746 1905 9

Typeset by Input Data Services Ltd, Bridgwater, Somerset

Printed in Great Britain by Clays Ltd, Elcograf, S.p.A.

www.weidenfeldandnicolson.co.uk

www.orionbooks.co.uk

To my parents,
for raising a little monster

'All things in this world were born from the minds of men and since all men were mad, they were mad creatures, madly running'

Robert Holdstock, *Lavondyss*

'We don't see things as they are; we see them as we are'

Anaïs Nin, *Seduction of the Minotaur*

Contents

Introduction: Making Beasts ... 1

Part One: Monsters of Creation ... 19
1: The Horned Sorcerer ... 21
2: Dragons of Chaos ... 49
3: The Minotaur and the Labyrinth ... 75

Part Two: Monsters of Nature ... 99
4: Snake Women ... 101
5: Grendel ... 131
6: Leviathans ... 163

Part Three: Monsters of Knowledge ... 195
7: Scaly Devils ... 197
8: Terrible Lizards ... 227

Conclusion: Titans of Gaia ... 255

Acknowledgements ... 277
Bibliography ... 281
Notes ... 317
Index ... 353

Introduction

Making Beasts

'We are unfashioned creatures, but half made up'
Mary Shelley

Have you ever been scared by a monster? Real fear, I mean – the kind that spikes your heart rate and prickles up the back of your neck. In spite of your conscious mind telling you not to be silly, there's nothing there. I bet that you have, at least once in your life. It might have been some long-fingered presence crouched under your childhood bed or biding its time behind a closet door. It may have been a scaly predator that writhed invisibly under the water while you swam, eyeing up your unprotected ankles. Or a gruesome creature implanted in your mind by a film, that managed to accompany you home from the cinema and slide into a shadowy corner. We've all been there, at some point: jumping into our beds and pulling the covers up; braving a dark corridor and quickly turning on the lights after watching a horror film – just to prove to ourselves that there is nothing *really* there.

I know I have. During sleepovers with friends when I was about eight years old, we made up scary stories for each other. We revelled in the thrills of fear stirred up by each melodramatic conclusion, delivered in voices as ominous as little girls could manage. One night, we conjured a character that would haunt us for months: a wolf that had black ink running in its veins, that could slide like a shadow through the cracks in doorframes to devour you in your bed. Someone came up with the idea that the creature lived in the shrubbery at the bottom of my friend's garden. That got us really worked up. None of us slept properly for weeks, for fear of seeing the liquid beast slip into our bedrooms. We set about devising ways that it could be overcome. All monsters need an Achilles heel: there has to be an escape clause to the fear. Vampires have their garlic and stakes, werewolves their silver bullets. And the Ink Wolf had a stopper in his back heel that, if unplugged, would drain his ink away and kill him – if you could get to it in time. With that plan, we started to feel a bit better about it, though the creature still lingered in our minds.

Thinking back on it, it's an odd fantasy. The wolf's peculiar vital fluids probably had something to do with the fact that we were constantly refilling our fountain pens as we ground through our schoolwork. You might remember some similarly off-beat inventions from your own childhood, monsters that were terrifying at the time but seem silly from the perspective of adulthood. One of the joys of childhood is that you don't care what anyone thinks, though. Your fantasy world is your own; it can be as strange and nonsensical as you like. That's also the point of monsters. They're not meant to be acceptable. They're meant to be extreme, ridiculous, repulsive things – and all the more captivating for it. The stranger the better.

Despite being abhorrent, monsters are deeply persistent. The unselfconscious freedom of childhood might slip away as we age and our fantasy worlds recede, but monsters stay with us. From the manticores and hydras of the ancient world to the alien Predators and Facehuggers of modern films, our imaginations have always produced monsters and we've always been entranced by them. Palaeolithic humans crafted strange hybrids on cave walls, from Europe to Southeast Asia. Dragons appear in different guises in almost every culture. Creature films gross hundreds of millions of dollars in cinema box offices. Monsters have been, and continue to be, so prolific in human imaginations that they must be deeply significant.

So, what exactly *are* monsters? Pinning this down isn't easy. Monsters, by their nature, resist definition. They are as varied and shifty as any group collected together under the same name can be. They have none of the physical similarities or shared origins that we use to group things in nature, like rocks or trees or songbirds. They can be unsightly creatures in distant lairs, magical exotic beasts, parasitic aliens, giant enveloping blobs of slime, or humanoid science experiments gone awry. That's a very mixed crowd to be summed up by a single word.

Very different definitions of monsters have been suggested over history. If you consult a Classical author such as Pliny in the first century, he would wave at anything in Creation that was bizarre or extreme. St Augustine, in the fourth century, might have said that monsters were irrational, non-human beings (he was quite certain that humans were rational beings). The learned seventh-century archbishop, St Isidore of Seville, defined monsters as portents, signs from God that something bad was about to happen. Today, the Oxford English Dictionary (OED) offers two definitions of monsters: 'a large, ugly, and frightening imaginary creature' and 'an inhumanly cruel or wicked person'. How can one word mean so many things? Describing both a person and a non-person, things that exist and that don't exist. Not all monsters are especially large or frightening, either. What ties all of these ideas together?[1]

We do have an instinctual sense of what a monster is, which we can demonstrate with a thought experiment. Picture a large, predatory animal like a grizzly bear, something terrifying and deadly if you get too close to it. Is that a monster? Most people would probably say it wasn't. The grizzly needs something extra for that, to be given some imaginative flair, like gigantic size, the ability to breathe fire, or the freakish addition of an unnatural body part – a scorpion tail or eagle wings. You can build your own bear-manticore in your mind. Compare this to another kind of animal, such as a deep-sea angler fish with its hellish toothy grimace and glassy eyes. Many people might look at a picture of one of those and say it qualified as a monster, even though it couldn't do much to you if you encountered one. It's a matter of perspective. The grizzly is a familiar beast, associated with cuddly animals and children's cartoons. The angler fish isn't at all familiar: its horrible appearance shocks and repels us. It seems bizarre, almost supernatural, as if it's been made up.

Monstrousness, then, is in the eye of the beholder. To be a monster, something has to go beyond the boundaries of familiar nature, to confound our expectations in some way. That's why we think of monsters as 'large, ugly and imaginary' because gigantic, horrible and unnatural are all qualities that shock. The boundaries of what is 'normal' and 'natural' are moveable, though. They depend on what we're familiar with, the particular view of the world that we have. A deep-sea marine biologist might protest at the idea that an angler fish is a monster, for example. One reason that so many monsters exist is that they have been created in different times and places, emerging from the wide array of worldviews that humans have held.

It's easier to see how this works from the vantage point of a few hundred years' distance. During my PhD in History and Philosophy of Science at the University of Cambridge, I went hunting for exotic monsters from the early modern period, spanning from the sixteenth to the eighteenth centuries. On the well-thumbed pages of ancient natural history books, I found malevolent scaly devils, miniature dragons, gargantuan dodos and walruses with very poor sleep hygiene. These were real animals that had been brought to Europe – as body parts or in travellers' tales – via the trade networks snaking around the globe from European ports such as Amsterdam and Antwerp. People who described these creatures turned many of them into monsters. Some were used as evidence of monsters from ancient myths: the shrivelled skin of a bird of paradise could be a phoenix or a fallen angel, for example. Others were crafted into bizarre, new monsters: the beak and femur of a dodo were evidence of a bird that was so fat it couldn't even walk, never mind fly. Pangolin skins became the bodies of devilish lizard-pigs. Walrus pelts were the spoils taken from terrible sea monsters.

These ideas seem ridiculous to us now. Why did they make these new creatures into monsters? Why not just odd animals? Were the people who described them delusional? Absolutely not. You don't get halfway around the world on a ship or write erudite encyclopaedias and philosophical treatises by being gullible or irrational. They didn't know much about these new things, but they were doing something very rational with the evidence that they did have. They were trying to put together all the new things that they were encountering with their existing view of the world.

These new animals didn't fit neatly into the traditional picture of the cosmos. They posed a taxonomic problem to naturalists – a dodo or a bird of paradise was not anything

ENCHANTED CREATURES

like what a bird was meant to be, for example. A walrus made a rather shoddy whale, and a pangolin was a very odd lizard. As the world was explored and expanded, more novel things poured in and more misfits appeared. They started to undermine accepted ancient knowledge from Classical texts and the Bible. So, naturalists matched up what they could with familiar monsters that were already thought to exist in distant places – such as griffons and dragons. They turned other creatures into less extravagant, new monsters. These things 'beyond nature' did not really *need* to fit into what nature was meant to be. As we shall see in Chapter Seven, making a holding-bay of oddball monsters offered some breathing space to decide what to do with them. Over time, new structures for organising the world were built. The accepted picture of nature was reshuffled into something that could comfortably include these beasts. Eventually, they were no longer monsters at all.

By studying the careers of exotic creatures in early modern Europe, I learnt a lot about the European imagination at this time (though almost nothing about walruses or pangolins). As we'll explore later, the monsters they created were the products of a worldview infused with theological and magical thinking, one that seems alien to us now. New creatures unlike anything that had been encountered before seemed like monsters, and monsters were *expected* to exist. It's a good example of the complex relationship between reality and our experience of it. We are not data machines, what we confront in the outside world interacts with what exists in our culturally infused minds. The products of these interactions can show us a great deal about ourselves and how our minds work. Like art or poetry, the monstrous products of our imaginations hold truths.

The word 'monster' itself hints at the revelatory quality that monsters have. It comes from the Latin *monstrare* (to demonstrate) or *monere* (to warn). As mysterious and shadowy as they might be, monsters are illuminating. They're signs from the deep that erupt to reveal hidden things about our inner worlds and how we deal with reality – if we dare look hard enough. The boundaries of what is seen as natural and normal to us today are very different to those several hundred years ago. We don't believe in manticores or sea monsters, and we don't think a walrus or a pangolin is out of step with nature. But monster-making continues in many other ways. So, what do the monsters we have created over history, and still create today, reveal about us? This is what this book explores: the important part that monsters play in human experience and how we deal with being us. It is an (un)natural history of monsters which is, really, a history of ourselves.[2]

Storytelling animals

How can we understand what it was like to be human long ago? We can look at objects left behind – the remains of buildings, tools, weapons and ornate jewellery. These can tell us something about how people lived, what they *did* in the world. In contrast, the stories that have survived the centuries are windows into how they experienced the world. Many myths and legends don't need to be unearthed; they persist, alive in our memories, transmitted from person to person over time, changing as they go. They give us insight into the minds that have carried them in a way that physical objects cannot. Stories reach much further back in time than formal recorded history does.

Like many other children, I was captivated by the myths of ancient Greece, Egypt and Scandinavia when I was young. I still am – they're not just for children. These stories conjure landscapes rippling with gods and heroes, magic and monsters. They connect our imaginations with those of people long ago. Some of the monsters we recognise today, such as hydras, sphinxes and dragons, have been kept alive over the centuries in these ancient tales. The monsters always seem more interesting than the heroes that battled them. They have mysterious, wild lives driven by visceral desires and extravagant backstories.

Stories persist because they create meaning from the world. We are, as Jonathan Gottschall described in 2013, 'storytelling animals'. 'We are, as a species, addicted to story', he says. 'Even when the body goes to sleep, the mind stays up all night, telling itself stories'. Dreams, myths, fairy tales or scriptural allegories aren't just frivolous fantasy. They use the world as a flexible mirror, revealing truths about our individual and shared humanity. The characters in these tales play out subjective realities in a make-believe landscape. As a deeply social primate species, communal mythologies express and build our shared values. The monsters of stories, therefore, are representations of what a society collectively rejects and fears – there's nothing like a common enemy to bind people together.[3]

The psychoanalyst Bruno Bettelheim described the importance of fairy tales in *The Uses of Enchantment* (1978): 'If one takes these stories as descriptions of reality, then the tales are indeed outrageous in all respects – cruel, sadistic, and whatnot. But as symbols of psychological happenings or problems, these stories are quite true'. For Bettelheim, classic fairy tales, with all their nasty, gritty impact, give children a place to work through the melee of emotions and fantasies they experience as they mature. Stories mutate over time, of course. The modern versions of fairy tales in books and Disney films are relatively watered-down. They don't deal with the psychological realities of childhood so brutally and directly. But the stories made it to the cinema screen in the first place because they had power. They do not need to represent objective reality to be 'real': they reveal psychological realities.[4]

The monsters in these stories are some of the most important characters. They are formed from elements of ourselves that are as powerful and horrible as the monsters appear. Not all monsters are scary, of course – my early modern pangolins and birds of paradise were quite benign.

ENCHANTED CREATURES

But the most potent monsters are created from things in ourselves that we don't like: aggression, cruelty, fear, grief, anxiety. Elements of human nature and experience which we disown or shy away from. Our imaginations package up these aspects into fantastical, horrible beings that can be banished far away, or comfortably slain by heroes and gods. An even more cunning trick is to label them as *other* and also *imaginary*. They're not us and they were never real in the first place.

It's an illusion, though. Once we have created monsters, we can't escape or erase them, because they are parts of ourselves – and they'll be back. When the scientist in Mary Shelley's *Frankenstein* creates a patchwork human out of dead bodies, he tries to escape his monster, but ends up spending the rest of his life locked in a cat-and-mouse chase with his creature, trying to kill it or avoid being killed. As much as we want to get rid of monsters, they draw us in – fascinating and horrifying us at the same time. We can push them into the deep seas, the dark of the wildwoods, the barren emptiness of outer space – far away from our cosy living rooms and dinner parties. But we can't *really* escape them. They constantly return: in the dark of night, from under the bed, in the unruly spaces of our dreamscapes.

That's really why monsters are scary. Not because they're big and ugly, but because they're exactly the parts of us we've pushed away and that threaten to burst violently back in. They're as big and ugly as the bits of us that they are created from. Monsters are many things, but they are not imaginary: their forms are fanciful, but what they *are* is very real. This is why understanding how monsters work is part of understanding how we work, and why it is so important to do so. That's what we're going to explore in the chapters of this book, along with the many ways it has shaped the Western relationship with the world.

Beastly natures

In one of his notebooks, the fifteenth-century polymath Leonardo da Vinci advised artists: 'if you wish to make one of your imaginary animals appear natural – let us suppose it to be a dragon – take for its head that of a mastiff or setter, for its eyes those of a cat, for its ears those of a porcupine, for its nose that of a greyhound, with the eyebrows of a lion, the temples of an old cock and the neck of a water-tortoise'. Da Vinci's recipe is a timeless one, many monsters are collages of animals. Dragons, the primary 'Ur' monsters, combine the qualities of reptiles, birds, felines and fish. The Xenomorphs in the film *Alien* (1979) are predators with mammalian elegance, insect-like joints and moist amphibious skin. They will eat your face and use you as a brooding chamber at the same time – just like a botfly or a Guinea worm would, were they a thousand times the size. The natural world is already full of barely imaginable beings. Take a macro photograph of an ant's face, all blade-like hairs, implacable compound eyes and industrial jaws. Or watch a ribbon worm feed, suddenly shooting out a sticky thread-like proboscis as big as its body, to grab prey. We don't need to go far beyond what exists to create monsters.

Our lives are intimately connected with other animals. We've always hunted, feared, eaten, observed, mimicked, teamed up with and been fascinated by them. So, of course, they inhabit our fantasies, making up so much of the matter from which we create. They're living, breathing comparators to our own existence and we use them as symbols for qualities in ourselves: a lion is brave, a donkey is stubborn, a peacock is vain. To borrow a well-known phrase from the anthropologist Claude Lévi-Strauss, animals are 'good to think [with]'. But monstrous creatures are even better.[5]

We call other animals *creatures* and *beasts* – but these words don't literally mean 'animals'. They betray so much more about our relationships to other species. The Latin verb *creare* (to create) became the Middle English *creature* (something created). The OED defines a creature as 'an animal, as distinct from a human being'. The Cambridge Dictionary suggests: 'a life form that is unusual or imaginary'. Merriam-Webster lists: 'something created either animate or inanimate, being a lower animal, a human being, or a being of anomalous or uncertain aspect of nature' and 'one that is the servile dependent or tool of another'. To be 'creaturely' is to be conceived by and indentured to human whims.

The word *beast* is interesting, too. The OED traces how the word *bestia* in Latin became *beste* in Old French and remained *beast* since Middle English. It can be some kind of animal 'as opposed to humans', either 'domestic' or a 'large or dangerous four-footed one'. The second layer of meaning attaches moral values: someone with 'brutish or untamed' qualities, or an 'objectionable or unpleasant' person or thing, even 'inhumanly cruel, violent or depraved'. Beasts are defined by what we do not want to be.[6]

As much as we don't like to admit it, we're beastly creatures too, with the ability to be cruel, violent and depraved like any other – perhaps more so. We're animals among animals, organic beings with all the inevitable limitations. This worries us, which is one reason why monstrous creatures have run riot through our imaginations. The cultural anthropologist Ernest Becker described how our animal state has motivated our culture: 'The real world is simply too terrible to admit. It tells man that he is a small trembling animal who will someday decay and die'. Cultural 'illusions' give us an escape, making 'man seem important, vital to the universe, immortal in some ways'. Culture allows us to create mythologies for living which make existence easier; to structure the world to make it manageable. We make gods to reach for, to give us the hope of immortality on the one hand. We make and eject monstrous beasts, to push our beastly natures away, on the other.[7]

Many of our most important monsters have been created from the other animals which we both kill and fear being killed by. The American writer David Quammen points out that 'every once in a while, a monstrous carnivore emerged like doom from a forest or a river to kill someone and feed on the body', which meant that 'among the earliest forms of self-awareness was the awareness of being meat'. The wolves, tigers, crocodiles, bears, lions and all the other animals that will kill and consume humans on occasion are more than just dangerous, they're reality checks. A human body can very quickly become food. We have dealt with threatening 'alpha predators', as Quammen calls them, by mythologising them into gods and denigrating them as monsters. We've also killed most of them off.[8]

Western scholars and theologians have spent thousands of years trying to distinguish the 'human' from the 'animal'. The answers to 'what makes us special?' have changed over history: from divine priority and the possession of a soul to complex language, self-awareness and abstract thought. We have created codes of civilised conduct to firmly repress the wilder parts of our minds and behaviours. We placed ourselves at the top of a hierarchy above all other living things and wove elaborate myths of Divine Order to reinforce the idea. From Aristotle onwards, the *Scala Naturae* or 'Great Chain of Being' shaped the way the West saw the natural world. It placed man just below God and the Angels, with other lifeforms arranged below in order of increasing simplicity, from birds and mammals, to reptiles and amphibians, to insects and shelled things. Poised in a lonely position between God and a pile of lowly beasts, the only sensible way was up: to differentiate ourselves from 'lower beings' and reach for the divine.[9]

The result of 'ten thousand years of modernity' has been, as natural philosopher Melanie Challenger puts it, to deliver 'an animal that doesn't think it's an animal'. Or, we could say, an animal that hasn't *liked* to think it's an animal, but has constantly worried about the difference. We have emphasised the qualities such as self-consciousness that we think are distinctly human, to separate ourselves from nature while trying to suppress the parts of ourselves that tug towards animality. But, severing our connection to our creatureliness also alienates us from the organic world and all it vitally gives us. It turns us into partial beings fending off beastly 'others'. The history of our monstrous creatures reveals our ambivalence towards, and need for, our animal natures. They're the shrapnel in the wounds of this vexed relationship. They might also be key to healing it.[10]

There is far more to be said than I intend to say about the monsters that straddle the uneasy boundaries between the human and the animal. These include the bearded ladies and other fairground exhibits; horrible caricatures of race and nationality; people vilified because of their developmental disorders and even our relationships with great apes and other primates. It is an area wrought with political and social complexity, often tied to the operation of power and empire, which requires its own handling.

This book investigates the wider menagerie of monstrous beasts that have helped shape our minds, our societies, and our understanding of our place in nature: the creatures we think with. We begin with stories of chaos and creation, coming full circle to our fantasies of Apocalypse and its catastrophic beasts. Moving from our earliest art through to recent media, we'll trace the history of our monstrous imaginings. We'll see that human nature has not changed much across the millennia, as much as we have changed the world around us. Now, when our relationship to nature is on a precipice, we need to understand our monsters more than ever.

Beware: it's not for the faint-hearted.

PART ONE

Monsters of Creation

The Horned Sorcerer

Chapter 1

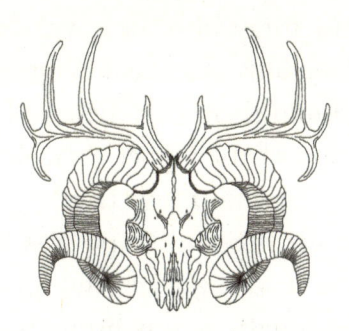

'These images are memories of long-forgotten dreams'
Werner Herzog

Two years before the outbreak of the First World War, brothers Max and Louis were on an autumn adventure together. They made their way between rocks, tracing along the small Volp River that passed by the town of Montesquieu-Avantès in the French Pyrenees. Approaching a hill, they could see the river disappearing into a tangle of branches that framed a deep, black mouth. This was the entrance to Tuc d'Audoubert, a mysterious cave which had fascinated the brothers since they had come across it several months earlier. Their father, Comte Henri Bégouën, had always talked to them about the times before written history began, the traces of which could still be found if you were lucky. Max and Louis had the same insatiable appetite for adventure and discovery as their father. They were sure that this cave held ancient secrets. It was the sort that giant bears and sabre-tooth cats might have made their lairs in. They were intent on exploring it.[1]

On a previous foray into the cave, the brothers had found the faint remains of ancient paintings on the walls. Their father had told them that these had been drawn by people in the time of the Upper Palaeolithic (beginning about 50,000 and ending about 12,000 years ago). These artists lived when the landscape was extraordinarily different, covered in vast glaciers and inhabited by a cast of spectacular animals. It was home to giant elk with wide-spreading antlers, steppe mammoths, sharp-horned woolly rhinos, cave bears and heavy-shouldered aurochs. The large animals that we are familiar with today – such as red deer, European bison and wolves – are but traces of the Ice-Age menagerie that once was.[2]

The Bégouën brothers had ventured only a little way into the blackness of the tunnel before. They were both in their late teens now, nineteen and sixteen years old – too grown up to be frightened, they thought. They came prepared with lights, a homemade raft and the determination to unearth the tunnel's deeper secrets. The boys punted the narrow vessel along the Volp's shallow waters and the cool darkness of the hill enveloped them. It was a welcome relief from the summer heat. Moving further in, they had to lie flush with the raft to avoid grazing themselves on the low tunnel ceiling. They used a staff to nudge themselves along the cave walls and the unstable, stony floor of the river until they reached the place where the Volp gushed underground. When the last of the sunlight disappeared, the brothers turned on their lamp. They caught sight of a small opening to a dry upper chamber, the entrance they had not dared to break their way into last time. They tethered their raft on a rock and clambered up to the opening, hefting rubble out of the way so they could squeeze through. Inside, the cave narrowed further, so they slid and crawled over crunching scree, their gangly teenage limbs fitting awkwardly in the passage. The dim lamplight bounced skittishly off the sides of the tunnel – it didn't seem to have an end.

The sound of water echoed faintly. Their route was more challenging than the Volp's well-worn slipstream which ran somewhere nearby. The boys had to shimmy themselves up through rock shafts several metres high and inch their bodies along narrow passages. They contorted around protrusions in the rock, sometimes using a chisel to knock nodules out of their way. Eventually, scratched and coated with dust and sweat, Max and Louis smashed through a thin film of rock and clambered out into a small gallery. They had lost all sense of direction, any awareness of where the river was or where they had come from – they must have come hundreds of metres from the entrance. At least they could now walk around, as long as they crouched a little.

What the boys saw took their breath away. There were finger-smeared waveforms on the walls and footprints in the clay floor – some large and adult-like, others that had to be those of children. Stalactites and stalagmites reached to each other across the cave space until their tips touched. Gigantic pawprints and deep claw-scrapes surrounded the skeletons of cave bears with their skulls smashed open.

The boys walked on, skirting around boulders and crawling under deep bows in the cave roof. The gallery widened and they reached what looked like an altar. On it were two great beasts shaped from clay: bison standing nearly upright. Their flanks had been smoothed by an ancient sculptor, who had rendered their humped backs, bristling napes and the ridges of their faces with precise, fine lines.

Max and Louis were ecstatic. They flung themselves back down the tunnels and galleries, covering themselves in bruises, wriggling through the narrow gaps as fast as they could. Their father had to see what they had found before nightfall. They dashed home and relayed their adventure with infectious excitement. A few hours later, having ripped his shirt, lost his trousers and a little dignity – it had taken more help with the chisel to get him through some openings – Henri was standing in the bear cave with his sons. As he stepped carefully behind them, he gasped at the sight of the bison. Henri examined every detail: the slight cracks in the dried clay skins; the lost tip of a horn or tail; the ball of clay on the floor that was indented with human fingerprints; the half-formed ghost of a third animal below.[3]

That night, Henri composed an excited letter to his friend, the prominent French prehistorian Émile Cartailhac, who might help them study the cave and its treasures. Max, as the eldest son, added an afterword, filled with the enthusiasm that would inform his life's work:

> You can imagine, Dear Sir and Master, my feelings on penetrating a sanctuary that none had entered for so many centuries. One had the feeling that the magicians had just left and that they were coming back at any moment to take up their lumps of clay and knead statuettes once again! I am wild with happiness . . . I can't wait to show them to you!!!!

They did not know it yet, but the Bégouëns would go on to discover a whole treasure-trove of far stranger cave beasts that had emerged from our ancestors' creature-filled imaginations. We'll see how these monsters helped fulfil deep human needs – ones that we still have, even today.

The Cave of the Trois-frères

As if one major archaeological finding was not enough, two years later, on the brink of the First World War, Max and Louis made another discovery with their brother Jacques. Trailing through the rough summer grass about a mile and a half from the entrance to Tuc d'Audoubert, the young men spotted what looked like an animal's den.

The closer they got, the deeper the opening seemed to get. When they stood at its lip, they could see it was not an animal den at all, but a tunnel. It was a sinkhole, perhaps another entrance to the black heart of the hill.

This tunnel led to more than the brothers could have imagined. It was an entirely separate cave complex, carved out by the Volp River in its younger days. Scattered along the walls of these caves they found images of beasts that the cave's prehistoric visitors must have known: aurochs, cave bears, great stags, horses and prowling lions. There was a gallery filled with red dots; another with handprints. There was a chamber dominated by the image of a vast lioness flanked by several others; and a space overlooked by the eerie engravings of three owls and a mammoth.[4]

After the First World War ended, Henri Bégouën and his sons began to survey this new cave complex with professional archaeologists, including the eminent Abbé Henri Breuil. They named it Caverne des Trois-frères or 'Cave of the Three Brothers', in honour of its discoverers. So few people have been allowed to visit these caves that they remain largely unchanged. Breuil's chair still sits at the bottom of a pit at the entrance to the complex, and the same rope he used to climb up is still the only aid for visitors making the steep initial ascent (it's so old and dilapidated now that it probably wouldn't pass an official health and safety check).[5]

Exploring the caves further, the Bégouëns and other archaeologists discovered more astounding images. They found that the cave paintings came to a climax in a gallery half a kilometre into the cave, now known as The Sanctuary. Animals sprang out of every rock crevice – scimitar-horned woolly rhinos, bison, onagers, ibexes, mammoths – bumps and cracks in the rock incorporated into their lively forms. A bear pierced with many spears vomited what seemed to be blood. There were strange creatures scattered around: wolf-headed bears, bison-tailed bears, reindeer-haunched bison, duck-footed reindeer. A prowling lion guarded the end of the gallery.

On the very end wall of this large chamber, a sea of beasts ran amok. Above them, neither leaping nor quite standing, was a figure now called the 'Sorcerer', engraved into the rock and painted with dark pigment. The Sorcerer was located four metres up, a spot that could only have been reached through some acrobatic spread-eagling between the narrowing cave walls. The Sorcerer was another impossible creature – feline-limbed and horse-flanked, possibly stag-horned – yet unmistakeably human in aspect. It was certainly a male, because a phallus emerged from under the swishing horse's tail. He was a 'therianthrope' – meaning a transitional human-animal form – looking over the beasts below.

Breuil dated most of these cave paintings to about 13,000 years ago and the clay bison of Tuc d'Audoubert to 14,500 years ago. But some of the paintings might have been made millennia before: the caves must have been visited repeatedly over vast swathes of time. Images overlaid on one another spanning several thousand years are not unusual in the painted caves around Europe. It is a striking contrast to our own art, locked tightly in history and context. Even condensing several hundred years of distance – say, overpainting a Renaissance masterpiece with a Banksy – is unthinkable today. Prehistoric artists collapsed time in a way inconceivable to us now, combining creatures envisioned thousands of years apart on the same rock canvases. It seems that people made the arduous journey into the cave for reasons that remained the same across millennia. They shared an unchanging desire to enter the earth and create cave monsters there.[6]

Empirical magic

The magic of cave paintings is a subtle one, but once it catches you it's hard to escape the enchantment. In 2010, I went to see Werner Herzog's film, *The Cave of Forgotten Dreams*, about the art of Chauvet Cave in Southern France. I was lulled into a dreamlike state by Herzog's intonations as he describes the unknowability of the past and the fantasies of its peoples lost in time. He suggests that 'Stone Age man might have had a similar sense of inner landscapes' to the Romantics of the nineteenth century. In Romantic art and writing, landscapes such as precipitous mountains and lonely, windswept moors were used to portray subjective states. Herzog suggests that prehistoric mindscapes were of a more intimate sort: chambered spaces where the concrete world dissolved and the depths of the mind could be accessed. In a wacky sci-fi postscript, Herzog imagines some 'mutant crocodiles' (actually imported albino alligators) escaping from their enclosures and gazing up in awe at the Chauvet paintings, asking 'are we today, possibly, the crocodiles who look back into an abyss of time'. I would like to think that, despite the passage of time, we can still understand the meaning of cave art better than mutant reptiles.

The Trois-frères cave is one of around four hundred cave art sites that have been found globally, the majority of which are located in France and Spain. Trois-frères is not the largest or most exceptional but it has a particular allure. When I came across the story of the Trois-frères caves, I was first hooked by the adventure of the discovery, and then by the enigmatic Sorcerer and his horde. Why make images in caves, and what purpose did the fantastical creatures serve? Their meaning seemed *almost* possible to grasp intuitively, as if these ancient images speak to some visceral, unchanging part of us. This intuition is not wrong: cave artists lived a long time ago, but they were *Homo sapiens*, as we are. Archaeologists agree that people 40,000 years ago had brains and bodies just like ours. We have not changed significantly since – we have just domesticated ourselves and altered the world around us. Our imaginations have always bristled with the forms of other animals, so it's no surprise that the shades of our ancestors' entanglements with cave beasts still fascinate us.[7]

We can't know exactly what motivated the painters of the Trois-frères caves. However, it does seem possible that the Sanctuary over which the Sorcerer watches was a sacred place for Palaeolithic peoples. They made great efforts to reach it and were well prepared to create art in the dark caverns. These caves were not places of safety and shelter, nor were they an easy canvas. *Entering* them and the *process* of making images, to abandon in the cave depths, were important too. Sometimes images were made in tiny recesses into which only one person could crawl, other times artists used large expanses of rock that might have been viewed by many people. This was probably not art for art's sake, nor just flippant doodling.[8]

There's a contradiction between the realistic images of animals and the impossible monsters among them. The artists were keen observers, closely acquainted with the species they depicted, able to capture their nature with minimal, elegant marks. A carved piece of mammoth bone found in the Trois-frères caves, for example, bears what is the earliest known representation of an insect. It depicts a cricket, so anatomically accurate that the species has been identified by specialists as a camel cricket, *Troglophilus*. Using bone and stone, these people could represent animals clearly enough to communicate to modern scientists. The more bizarre creatures on the cave walls, such as the Sorcerer, cannot have been just the products of delusion or ignorance.

The hybrid beasts in the cave must have had a purpose. The archaeologist Henri Breuil had some ideas while studying the Trois-frères caves. He saw the Sorcerer and his animal minions as an example of 'sympathetic magic' – akin to that still practised by some modern hunter-gatherer societies today. This magic relies on a link between image and object: acting on one affects the other. Paintings of animals dying from clubs and spears, for instance, should bring about successful hunts. Painting plenty of game in the caves might cause them to multiply on the tundra. By the end of the Pleistocene, there is evidence that the really *big* animals were becoming more scarce, perhaps due to the combined effects of climate change as the Ice Age waned and hunting by humans. Were these people using images of cave beasts to increase the stocks of game through a kind of magic?[9]

Breuil's idea of sympathetic magic doesn't quite hold up, though. If these cave monsters were part of 'hunting magic' rituals, we might expect to see the species that the Palaeolithic peoples hunted appearing most often. Or, plenty of images of their successful capture. But we don't: there is little correlation between the animals pictured in the caves and those most often eaten or hunted by humans at this time, as evidenced by cooking remains. Even fewer animals are shown being killed by hunters. Many are predators, such as lions or bears, or species that were rarely killed, such as woolly rhinos. And a significant number are hybrid creatures that only existed in the cave.

There is also no evidence to support the need to multiply game at the times these paintings were made. The Ice Age steppes were teeming with animals in a way that our ecologically depleted world makes it difficult to imagine. When the giant animals did start to die out as the ice receded, it looks like deer, fish and other meat sources multiplied. The Ice Age landscape was a tough physical environment but it had an abundance of animals, in part because there weren't that many people yet. Palaeolithic humans were not going hungry as a result of a biodiversity crisis. So, it seems that these paintings were not two-dimensional voodoo-dolls or magical invocations of successful hunts, they served some other purpose. What we can tell is that, as humans became the dominant mammals in the landscape, they dreamed of fading giants.[10]

Fear of the dark

To understand more about what motivated these cave artists, I had a video call with Jill Cook, Keeper of the Department of Britain, Europe and Prehistory at the British Museum, one crisp January morning. I was sitting in a cabin surrounded by woodland, part of a rewilding project in Norfolk. As we spoke, over my laptop I could see the dark forms of water buffalo grazing across the lake. They were miniature replacements for the hefty aurochs that disappeared from Britain about 3,000 years ago, mulching up the soil with their hooves in much the same way aurochs used to, keeping the land fertile and ecologically diverse.

Jill has been studying cave paintings for decades. Unlike some more traditional archaeologists, she argues that, as humans looking at human artifacts, we should use

ENCHANTED CREATURES

ourselves as part of the evidence. The greatest thing we have in common with people long ago is our humanity, so we can cautiously use the insights that arise from this connection. With energising humour, Jill took me on a virtual tour of some mysterious Palaeolithic remains, threading them together with three essential human traits: fear, imagination and the ability to symbolise. These qualities, she argues, underpin much of the figurative art that was created since about 40,000 years ago in Europe.

During our conversation, Jill asked me, 'Doesn't the dark make you afraid?' The universal power of fear seems self-evident. Fifteen thousand years ago, we were skinny apes in a landscape inhabited by cave lions with teeth like daggers. Never mind the other dangers, such as cave bears or trampling mammoths. This was a life in which fear was close to the surface. Through most of our evolutionary history, the dark of night was only kept back by a ring of firelight. With the bright morning sun streaming through my cabin windows, I agreed with Jill's question on an intellectual level: of course, we still fear the dark and what might emerge from it. Later on, walking back to my cabin in the moonless night after dinner, twitching at every odd sound and startled by muntjac deer crashing through bushes, I knew it at a visceral level. I tried not to think what might be hiding among the trees.

Many modern humans live without dangerous predators, but our brains are still shaped by this history. Neurological studies show that the amygdala, the fear centre of the brain, has a specific response to animal forms. In one study, patients experienced a distinct spike in neurons in the amygdala when shown pictures of animals as opposed to landscapes, objects or people. Derek Hodgson, a neuropsychologist at the University of York, suggests that our visual system was shaped by the need to detect mammalian predators in the tundra landscape of Ice-Age Europe. It was prepared to create beasts from the merest shapes, or to pick out creatures in the flickering shadows on cave walls. A false negative is far more dangerous than a false positive, so we tend to see *something* where there is any chance at all there might be an animal. As Jill put it, 'You don't really want to be running away from a mouse, but you *definitely* want to run away from a lion'. Even the sign of a predator – a footprint or spoor – would be enough to conjure it in the mind. Images of beasts are woven into our neural networks; our brains are primed with the fear of them. As we will see in Chapter Four, predatory mammals aren't the only animals that have shaped our vision and brains.

How did we go from perceiving beasts to creating them on cave walls? At some point in history, Jill argues, the amygdala became linked with the imagination and creativity in the human pre-frontal cortex. The ability to think, symbolise and imagine allowed us to process raw fears. It resulted in the drive to depict what we feared, and the need to express artistically – though this likely did not happen first in Europe. The rock of a cave wall became a giant Rorschach inkblot exercise: a surface onto which mental images could be spilled. It was the predatory or dangerous species that were most often depicted. The artists did not just daub creatures arbitrarily onto the cave walls. The relief and features of the rock itself were part of the images: a small nodule could become an eye; a slight ridge might denote a back or tail. Sometimes these textures were marks made by animals themselves, such as the scratch of a cave bear's claws. The artist had only to breathe life into the image with a few minimal lines to bring the beast into being.

The shadows cast by flames would have given dynamism to these creatures. In many cave images, the beast is only present through the right interplay of light, rock and painting. The artists gave the animals no terrain to cross, no sense of scale or context – these were free-floating troglodytes. Only when light is held at a particular angle are some cave images fully visible, casting just the right amount of shadow on a bump or ridge in the cave wall to complete an animal. As soon as a lamp is moved the form disappears, like a creature melting back into a dark forest."

Certainly, in many traditional tales of dragons and monsters fought by heroes, the evil beast is faced in its cavernous lair or in the gloom of tangled woods. The environmentalist George Monbiot suggests that tales of heroic battles with monsters might be mythic versions of our ancestral combats with gigantic Ice-Age creatures. These stories may be cultural memories of fear transmitted through the ages. There could be something to it. Cave paintings show that imagined beasts have been important to us for as long as we could create art, not just in Europe but further afield. These creatures must have been deeply significant to those that depicted them, part of the stories that people wove around their lives. The combination of fear and symbolic imagination in the caves might have resulted in a common mythology which joined people together to make life more liveable. The Sorcerer and his strange creatures can show us more about how this might have happened.

The Sorcerer's riddle

Getting a handle on the Sorcerer is difficult – even the image itself is elusive. During his study of the caves, Henri Breuil made a sketch of the Sorcerer, which has become an iconic image in books and papers. Comparisons between this sketch and modern photographs of the Sorcerer throw up strange contrasts, however. The antlers and face in Breuil's Sorcerer sketch don't show up in photographs, for example. Was Breuil using his imagination to elaborate on a suggestive image? Archaeologists still debate what the 'real' image was. Modern imaging methods, which allow us to visualise everything from the galaxy to molecular structures, can't quite capture it. It is as if the image only exists woven into the fabric of the rock and disintegrates in the cold light of day.

The Sorcerer is unusual too. There are more than 360 sites of prehistoric rock art across Europe. While they contain an array of detailed images of beasts, hybrid creatures and animal montages, there is a surprising lack of humanoid figures. When humans do appear, they're usually minimal stick figures. Early humans don't seem to have had the same intense interest in self-representation that we do. Or perhaps humans didn't need to be painted: their images were created by the shadows in the firelight. These silhouettes danced on the cave walls and melted into darkness as soon as the fire died.

Even rarer are therianthropes, transitional human-animal forms, like the Sorcerer. They're only found in a handful of sites. Those that we do know of seem to have been of great importance, placed at key positions in caves or carefully crafted. One of the oldest known pieces of figurative art, the Lion-man of the Hohlenstein-Stadel, was carved from mammoth bone between 39,000 and 41,000 years ago. He has the legs of a man, a narrow leonine waist, the shoulders of a lion with arms tapering to human hands, topped by a majestic lion's head. It would have taken incredible artistic skill and about 400 hours to carve him. This effort was probably made because the Lion-man was an important ceremonial object. The figure combines elements of the three apex mammals of the tundra world: the bulk of the mammoth, the ferocity of the lion and human ingenuity. Perhaps creating hybrids was a way to absorb animal powers, mitigating their threat. Making a monster like the Lion-man might have been a way of wielding a kind of magic.[12]

What the Sorcerer image is meant to represent is ambiguous: is he a supernatural creature? Or a man dressed in skins and antlers, adopting an animal stance? Some have suggested the Sorcerer might be a deity, or a shaman in the throes of a trance-like connection with the spirit world. Perhaps becoming a hybrid creature was a way to access altered states of reality. Positioned above a tangle of creatures on the cave wall, he might have ruled this monstrous assembly.

We have some concrete clues as to what the Sorcerer might have been. Hundreds of miles from the Trois-frères, in North Yorkshire, there is an archaeological site called Star Carr. It dates to 12,000 years ago, in the Mesolithic period, when the ice retreated across Europe and left a new landscape in its wake (about 5,000–15,000 years ago). Archaeological excavations at Star Carr have uncovered twenty-four headdresses from the remains of the lakeside encampment there. Each headdress was precisely shaped from the antlered skulls of red deer and preserved in the acidic lake silt. One of these headdresses now sits in a glass case in the British Museum in London, staring back defiantly as you try to decode its meaning. Could our Trois-frères Sorcerer have been wearing headwear like this?[13]

The people of the Mesolithic were intimately engaged with the bodies of deer; they were essential to existence in the increasingly forested landscape. To be human was also to be partially deer: people's arms were extended by deer-bone spear-throwers, their deerskin clothing was sewn with antler awls and deer sinews, they adorned themselves with deer tokens and their bodies were fed by deer meat. Where beast ended and human began was likely not so distinct for Mesolithic peoples as it is for us today. Humans hadn't cordoned themselves off from nature and drawn the hard line between the human and 'non-human' that we have. Taking on the form of the deer, fusing human and animal spirits, might have represented the consummation of an important relationship.

The Evens people of Siberia and the Russian Far East or the Evenk in North Asia herd reindeer on the open steppes and used to practise shamanism. Until most of these people were forcibly settled in the twentieth century, male and female shamans would don ritual antler headdresses very similar to those found at Star Carr. Their shamanistic dress often involved the matching of animal body part to garment: the skin of the head to make a cap, or trousers fashioned from leg pelts. Given that deer were important game for Palaeolithic hunters, our Sorcerer might have been a shaman swathed in deer skins and antlers, dissolving his humanity to travel into realms beyond immediate experience. This is no incidental thing, as we shall see. He and his cave monsters were part of a barely tangible history which has shaped humanity.[14]

The cave of the mind

We can only guess what exactly Palaeolithic shamans might have been doing in the caverns of Trois-frères. The word 'shaman' originates from Siberia and Northeast Asia, from the Manchu-Tungus word *šaman* meaning 'one who knows'. It's since been used as a general term for spiritual practices in hunter-gatherer societies centred around figures who can communicate with spirit realms. But 'shamanism' is an artificial category that includes widely different practices over time and space, each with their own particular qualities. Using the word in its broadest sense for convenience, shamanism has been one of the most globally widespread and historically persistent forms of spiritual experience. These practices have been a vitally important part of life for most of human history, drawing on fundamental elements of human nature and biology.[15]

Shamanistic rituals use different ways of hijacking the neurochemistry of the brain to enter different states of consciousness. Trance states can be induced by psychedelic drugs, breathing practices, ritual drumming and chanting or fasting, for example. Such states are thought to allow shamans to access alternate spirit worlds, existing above or below everyday reality. These rituals often occur at specific sites, believed to be the physical entrance to these other planes of existence. Different cultures have imagined these alternate realities as a variety of watery, chthonic underworlds or transcendent heavenly realms.

If Palaeolithic peoples entered the Trois-frères caves for these types of rituals, the caves themselves must have shaped their experiences. As the Bégouën brothers found when they first explored the caves, reaching the inner galleries was like a rebirth, squeezing through long and difficult tunnels. The process of entering these spaces might have helped in the creation of trance states: a place of quiet dark where the tangible world fell away and the realm of imagination yawned open. The South African archaeologist David Lewis-Williams and French prehistorian Jean Clottes describe how caves might have been seen as 'the entrails of the underworld, and their surfaces – walls, ceilings and floors – were but a thin membrane between those who ventured in and the beings and spirit-animals of the underworld'. There's evidence of people trying to reach beyond these fragile boundaries in Trois-frères. Artists merged with their materials as they sprayed their hands with paint. They left finger traces along the walls or pressed small fragments of tooth and flint into crevices, perhaps as messages for the spirit world beyond the rock.

Different levels of trance state have been reported to create different types of visual, which suggest origins for our cave monsters. Light trance states produce geometric shapes – cross-hatches, concentric circles, dots – that emerge from the inherent properties of the visual and nervous system. Deeper states have been described as producing emotive visions of animals, spirits and monsters. Some of these can be animal spirit guides or familiars that aid the shaman on their quest. Passing through these states is like entering a tunnel or vortex, which Lewis-Williams describes as leading to 'a new realm inhabited by its own beings'. The monsters conjured from the rocks might have been the beasts that emerged from trance visions, that inhabited Palaeolithic imaginations.

Lewis-Williams describes how 'all this is wired into the human nervous system. There is a cave in the mind'. The physical cavern led to a psychological underworld.[16]

Why venture into the deep recesses of the mind? Perhaps it was for the same reason that humans have always explored new places: to know what they did not yet, to better understand themselves and experience life differently. Perhaps trance states were places of power, where the fears of everyday life could be made bearable and given meaning. When people came together in the caves, they created something irreplaceable. Hunter-gatherers lived most of their lives dispersed across the landscape in small groups. By sharing in a communal ritual, they journeyed together to an alternate world filled with monsters that haunted and hunted them. Ordinary concerns and differences fell away and bonds were reinforced. As we shall see, these wild, underworld experiences were fundamental to building larger civilisations.

Beasts of the otherworld

In late 2019, just before the pandemic shut the world down, I went to an extraordinary event under some old railway arches in London. It was a party attended by the kinds of people who go to Burning Man and raves. The theme was 'Religion'. I arrived early, and watched the space fill up with people in elaborate costumes, wearing gilded antlers and headdresses fanned with peacock feathers or encrusted with shells. A stilt-walker swathed in a tapestry of moss and leaves strode slowly around like some primal creature, tree-branch antlers reaching up strangely in the haze of the lights. It was accompanied by a nymph-like girl in white lace and glitter who reached up to stroke the creature's long skull face. These pagan figures cavorted among the faux-priests and high priestesses, gods, goddesses and monsters, layering manifestations of belief and ritual in a carnival celebration. Such alter egos evoked the power of shamanic magic. People made themselves other-than-human, an act of collective therianthropy. They attempted to reach an alternate consciousness together as hybrid, hedonic beasts on waves of melodic techno.

Throughout our history, humans have entered cavernous spaces to access these alternate realities. When we moved away from natural caves, it is likely that we recreated them with vast stone megaliths or wooden halls, as humans began to live in larger and more settled societies. The towering masses of Stonehenge in Southern England still attract Pagans today for Solstice celebrations filled with songs and drumming. We still seek the sense of unity and wider connection with nature. As Jill Cook also pointed out, over winter 'when it's dark and there's food that will go off, everyone enjoys a good feast and a knees-up – it's also good for outbreeding'. Later, we had the transcendent spaces of churches and cathedrals. Now, for the secular, there are majestic baroque concert halls or laser-filled warehouse raves. Womb-caves of stones or branches or brickwork still do something to our imaginations.[17]

Collective experiences of elevated states have always had intense value for us – they allow humans to gather in increasingly large groups, to put up with the difficulties of living together and forget strife. When we meet to sing, make music or dance, when we gather to share spiritual experiences, we still enter something akin to these altered states our ancestors did. Robin Dunbar is Emeritus Professor of Evolutionary Psychology at the University of Oxford and has spent many years trying to understand the role of collective transcendence in human evolution and history. In his recent book, *How Religion Evolved* (2022), he argues that group trance states have been foundational to human society and the development of religion. Rituals and altered states surge endorphins, creating collective bonding and a sense of unity. This euphoric sense of togetherness is social glue. We put up with discomfort – of sitting in stuffy opera seats, church politics, being pushed up against strangers in a dark venue, overpriced drinks or waiting in queues – all to be part of something large and transcendental, just for a little while.[18]

Our animal nature is essential for these experiences: communing with our inner beasts helps us to escape the confines of civilised human consciousness. The creatures of our mind-caves today might differ from those of our Palaeolithic ancestors, though. A friend of mine described to me his recent experience taking the South American psychedelic Peyote in Ibiza: 'I was suddenly all gone – I was this animal being that *had* to seek the moon. I raced off and was just my beastly self alone in the dark, wondering at the night sky'. It sounded both ridiculous and totally believable. The immediacy of the animal, the sense of profound wildness on these kinds of drugs is there even for modern, urban humans. Perhaps that's why so many people in Ibiza think they're shamans.

The magic of the cave beasts is still alive. It's part of our evolutionary history, predating religious dogma and theism. Over time, though, strange things happened to the antlered shamans who led transcendental experiences for small groups of humans. As people settled into larger farming communities, these magical figures might have become gods, like the Celtic Cernunnos, a horned, torqued deity, 'lord of the wild things', who could pass to and from the spirit world. There was also Cocidius, the Romano-British god of war and hunting. And Pan, the Classical god of the wild, and his rowdy attendant Satyrs. The individual shaman for a few might have become a deity known by many, whose power was channelled in wider spiritual rituals and shared belief. These hybrid gods have been part of animistic belief systems, where every element of the physical world was thought to have a spirit. They could unleash the creaturely power of the unconscious.

Eventually, when large organised religions such as early Christianity took over, these wild hybrid gods were ousted from the spiritual experience. As societies grew and became more complex, the mind's appetite for connecting with the animal and capacity for transcendence was co-opted by new rituals. Spirituality was dominated by monotheism in many places. The wild spirits were only worshipped at the margins, as remnants of ancient beliefs. Transcendence became instead reaching for a state of purity, free from lowly animal nature – even human nature. We were no longer creatures within a network of beasts, we were set apart. Something special and better.[19]

The ancient horned gods became shadow beings. As mainstream religion pulled us away from our connection to the natural world, fear and imagination still combined to produce these strange creatures. But they weren't spirit guides that helped us to handle our fears and limitations. They became evil forces luring us into beastly darkness and causing chaos. In Europe, they might have become feared devils, such as the Judeo-Christian Satan, with his cloven hooves and horns. In the next chapter, we will explore how we have used myths of vanquished dragons to explain the chaos of life and the need for order in the human world.

Dragons of Chaos

Chapter 2

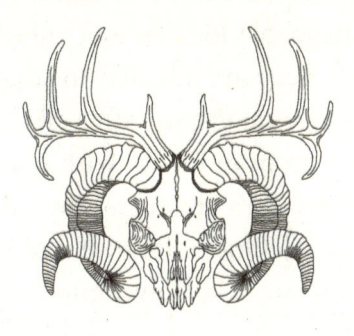

*'They viewed the vast immeasurable abyss,
Outrageous as a sea, dark, wasteful, wild'*
John Milton

Cosmic troubles

How did the universe begin? How did everything we know come into being? Most people today might answer: 'The Big Bang' – a pithy summary of the most inconceivable event in the history of the universe. It is a good shorthand for our current understanding of how everything came to be, a primordial explosion of matter from an initial state of extreme density and temperature. The theory doesn't explain all that we can observe about the universe but it's our best working hypothesis.[1]

The name 'Big Bang' was coined in the mid-twentieth century by opponents of the theory, dismissing what they saw as a silly idea. The name stuck, even after the Big Bang was generally accepted. There probably wasn't a 'bang' *per se*, but the idea of a big 'explosion' of energy and matter is a manageable idea for our minds and language to get a hold of. They are adapted to small-scale, organic life rather than cosmic events, after all. The Big Bang is, for most people, an origin story within a scientific world view. We are not God's creatures these days. Instead, as astrophysicist Neil deGrasse Tyson has put it, 'the universe is in us. And, we are not only figuratively, but literally stardust'.

In some ways, the Big Bang echoes many ancient creation myths, describing universes emerging from violent upheavals. In the late nineteenth century, the German scholar, Hermann Gunkel, described a common theme across creation myths which he called *Chaoskampf*, meaning literally, 'struggle against chaos'. It refers to battles between gods and primordial chaos in the formation of the cosmos (a word derived from the Greek word *kosmos*, meaning 'order' or 'world'). Chaos and the forces that tamed it were pictured as monsters and gods at loggerheads with each other. Assyriologist JoAnn Scurlock notes 'monster bashing is a feature common to all mythologies of the ancient world', especially creation myths. Across cultures and times, human imaginations have used monstrous creatures to embody cosmic turmoil. These Ur-monsters are massive and flamboyant – dragons or giants with ten heads, flaming maws, terrible calls, long talons, scythe like teeth, the list goes on.[2]

Take the battle between the Gods of Olympus and the monstrous Titans of Classical myth, called the 'Titanomachy'. Before Zeus and the other Olympian gods could rule the cosmos, they had to battle the ancient, brutal beings that had dominated since time began – who had a habit of swallowing their own offspring. When the gods had overcome the older Titans, Mother Earth, known as Gaia, birthed a fresh clutch of monsters. Their leader was Typhon, whose 'shoulders grew an hundred heads of a snake, a fearful dragon' with 'dark, flickering tongues, and from under the brows of his eyes in his marvellous heads flashed fire', according to the ancient Greek poet, Hesiod. Zeus and his sibling gods vanquished these horrible young Titans, locking them up with their predecessors in a hellish prison called Tartarus. The gods then took charge of Olympus and ruled a more-or-less organised world.

Less present in our minds now – perhaps because they haven't made it into many film adaptations and children's books – are the Levantine Canaanite tales of the sea god Yam and his serpent servant, Lotan, who were overcome by the sky god Ba'al-Hadad. There's also the Norse god Thor and his battle with the Midgard Serpent, Jörmungandr. And, my focus for this chapter, the myth of the dragoness Tiamat and the storm god, Marduk, who killed Tiamat and her monster army to reign supreme. This story was told in ancient Babylon two millennia ago, one of a cluster of myths we know from Ancient Mesopotamia. All of these different creation stories involve monsters that dominate a formless world, sky gods and often some ugly young troublemaker that has to be vanquished.[3]

Chaoskampf myths do not all function in the same way, even if their ingredients look similar. Myths will always be laced with the political and social resonances of the times and places in which they were told. These stories essentially describe how chaos was shaped into an ordered world. Not only the physical world: these stories can be understood as dramatisations of the development of the human mind and the formation of collective human experience. They can even be read as stories about the nature of creativity itself. Here, we'll look at how the battle between the Mesopotamian dragoness Tiamat and the storm god Marduk allowed the blood of chaos monsters to run through our lives, making us the complex, inventive creatures that we are. The myth speaks to us of the unavoidable losses that occur as we come fully into being; of how both creation and destruction are essential parts of being alive.

The Ishtar Gate

In 2019, just before the first wave of Covid took hold in Europe, I visited a monument to this ancient fight between gods and monsters. It sits in Berlin's Pergamon

Museum, among the city's Eastern Bloc architecture. A long, blue-tiled walkway leads to the Gate of Ishtar, the Mesopotamian goddess of love and war. As you walk up the corridor, life-sized bas-relief lions stride the passage alongside you. The gate itself is stunning – covered in dragons with delicate necks and heads, leonine forelimbs and snaky tongues. They were called *mušḫuššu* and were Ishtar's divine pets. The gate was made in New Babylon in the sixth century BCE, roughly where modern-day Iraq is now. Contrasting with the grimy city full of business and techno, the serene setting of the museum masks the real meaning of this monument. Two thousand years ago, before the gate was moved to Berlin, it was the centre of a yearly festival called *Akitu* which re-enacted the cosmic drama between chaos and order. As I walked through the Ishtar Gate, I was retracing the path taken by ancient Babylonians as they processed during these celebrations, carrying statues towards a golden temple.[4]

The stories of the Mesopotamians are not as familiar to us as those of ancient Greece or Rome, in part because they were lost for millennia. Many were recorded in the largest library of ancient Mesopotamia, created at Nineveh by King Assurbanipal. It contained clay tablets inscribed with 'cuneiform', a balletic script of wedges and lines that is even older than Egyptian hieroglyphics. The tablets preserved text in a way that paper or parchment never could: when Nineveh was sacked in the sixth century BCE, the library buildings collapsed and became natural kilns that fired the clay tablets so they didn't disintegrate.

In the 1800s, 30,000 of these fragmented tablets were found in Assurbanipal's library under the remains of the ruined city. Archaeologists carted them off to European museums and laboriously reassembled them. Once the mysterious cuneiform script could be read, they revealed a lost world. Among the official trading registers and ledgers were tales of battles with cosmic dragons, flights into the underworld, elemental sex, apocalyptic floods and heroic quests for immortality.[5]

Across seven of these clay tablets was scribed the Epic of Creation, or *Enūma Eliš*. It described the beginning of the Mesopotamian world and was infused with the flood-plain landscape that surrounded the city. The Tigris and Euphrates rivers flowing out into the Persian Gulf were lifelines for the Mesopotamians. The word 'Mesopotamia' itself means 'the land between two rivers'. Their estuary waters deposited rich, fertile silt that allowed farming to flourish and created new land: it was thought by the Mesopotamians to have given rise to the whole world.[6]

The *Enūma Eliš* is named after the opening phrase of the poem, which means 'When on high'. It begins before the world was made, at the watery birth of being itself. Because it's unfamiliar to most, let's enter the dreamlike world of the myth before we dissect its monsters. I have changed the original verse form into prose and left out some details to make it more readable, but have tried to retain as much of the spirit of the original as possible. As you read, let the distinctions between character and landscape dissolve in your mind. Imagine this story being recited in a clay-walled city surrounded by wide floodplains overhung with thick, dense cloud banks that could suddenly erupt with thunder and flooding rains. Imagine the clay formed into tablets, imprinted by scribes with reed styluses, baked and buried in the sun, holding the story safe.[7]

Enūma Eliš

Before the world was formed, all of existence was liquid shapelessness. Nothing more. All things were nameless and without purpose. Only the sweet water and the salt were distinct: the god of subterranean fresh water, called Apsu, flowed into the salted deeps of his lover Tiamat, the sleeping dragon-goddess of the seas. Their swirling chaos mingled together to create beings for the very first time. From this divine union came the next generation of gods, Lahmu and Lahamu, meaning 'mud' and 'silt'. They were the gods of the fertile sediments that settled in the stillness which followed their parents' watery passion. They instantly combined with one another and birthed the next gods, Anshar and Kishar, the twin deities of the horizon – the meeting point of the sky and the earth. They moved slowly together day and night, eternally approaching each other until, in the soft glow of sunrise, they birthed the god Anu, who would rule the sky.

Anu was the greatest god yet, but he created a son who was greater still. This was Ea, the trickster, who cunningly flowed through the streams and riverways. Sometimes he dived into the underground waters of his great-grandfather Apsu and flowed out into the salty ocean embrace of his great-grandmother Tiamat. Ea was a young god and full of energy, always pushing the limits of his powers. He gathered with other new divinities in the vault of heaven, to cavort as only young gods could at the very dawn of the universe.

Their clamour riled up the briny waters of Tiamat's belly, churning and frothing her insides till she writhed in discomfort. Their commotion rattled the scales of her flanks and assailed her ears, but she could not bring herself to chastise them. For they were her beloved, gifts that had risen from her deep birth waters. She kept silent, despite the pain they caused. Apsu was far from patient, though. He plotted to put an end to this clan of unruly offspring, to cleanse the chaotic rabble from the world and return to peace. He would not listen to Tiamat's protests: the rage boiled inside him as she begged him to stop.

Ea was too canny and too quick to be taken unawares, though. He was drunk on fresh powers – but his senses were not dulled. The fast-running streams and rivers that flowed through the underworld carried whispers of Apsu's hidden plan to him. So, Ea created a spell and tipped magic into Apsu's waters. It gushed through the old god, drenching the sweet waters with stupor. As Apsu slept, Ea cut his throat and killed him.

There was no time for victory celebrations. Ea built a palace over Apsu in which to dwell with his wife,

ENCHANTED CREATURES

Damkina. Its splendid chambers, halls and towers were decorated with the intricacies of Ea's wily thoughts. In this cool water oasis, Damkina gave birth to their son, Marduk. The boy-god grew vigorously, nursed by milk from the breasts of goddesses. He was perfectly formed and had not two eyes, but four far-seeing ones; four large ears that could hear all and a mouth that blazed heaven's fire. There was nothing he did not perceive or know. Anu, his grandfather, created four serpent-tailed winds for him to play with. Marduk spun them into action, shaping dust into whirlwinds and whipping up tempests from Tiamat's belly.

Tiamat could not forgive her children for the death of Apsu, and nursed her vengeance. She plotted what would be the first great battle of the universe. Rending her watery belly open, she poured forth monstrous forms, more horrible than anything that had yet been created. She birthed an army to punish the evil done to her, seeded by the waters of her dead lover Apsu. There were serpents, filled with venom instead of blood; sharp-fanged demi-gods that reared their dragon heads; and weapon-bearing demons: scorpion men, rabid dogs, fish-men, bull-men. Over these, she made her terrible son and consort, Quingu, the leader.

News of the dark army mustering reached the ears of Ea through the inlets and slipstreams of the underworld. He tried to reach Tiamat, to call off her fury, but was turned back by the horrible ranks of creatures broiling in her waters. Ea gathered a council of gods and told them of the fearsome chaos about to descend upon them under Quingu and his dragon queen. One by one the gods attempted to still Tiamat's waters, but each returned shaking in terror at what they saw. Then Ea spoke up: 'My son Marduk will be his father's champion.' The gods cheered, drank wine and feasted, their bodies swelling with pride. They agreed that Marduk's word would be law, crying, 'Marduk is King!'

The young Storm God, clothed in splendour, prepared for battle. He was armed with a mace, a feathered bow and a net to trap Tiamat. He carried a herb to counter poison, and a terrible spell sat on his lips. Anu added to the four serpent-tailed winds some tempestuous gusts that trailed behind Marduk. The young god rode on his storm-chariot, drawn by four venom-spitting steeds. Crowned and armoured, his ancestral gods thronging about him, Marduk went to cut off Tiamat's power.

The dragoness of the salt waters stirred as Marduk approached. She saw the gods, her children, massed behind him and spat dark bile. 'How glorious you look, Marduk, with your gods assembled around you', Tiamat taunted. He looked sternly at her: 'Your surface waters are calm, Tiamat, but you plot malice in your deeps. You have schemed against your own children-gods, and crowned Quingu, your dreadful son. This must be righted. Leave your hordes, fight me in single combat'. Tiamat was enraged. She screamed – a high, piercing keening – filled with betrayed passion. She drew back, rearing up into a great wall of black water that sparkled darkly with the fire of Marduk's eyes. Her scaly head bared white-flecked teeth as she lunged down to swamp the young god. But he took his net and encircled her body with it, catching her with her own engulfing magic. He blew Anu's winds into her open mouth, swelling her monster-filled womb and bloating her angry waters.

One arrow was all it took to pierce her, straight through her distended belly. It rent her heart, quelling the storm rage and the currents of pain circling within. Her writhing power was instantly deflated, the hybrid horrors she had created in her grief were ejected and scattered in the winds. Marduk had no mercy. He splintered Tiamat's dragon skull with his mace and slit open the arteries of Tiamat's deeps until salty blood flooded from them. He threw down her body and stood astride it while he cowed her army, tethering them like cattle. Then the Storm God sat back and looked at her vast corpse, thinking what to do: this monster could be made into marvels.

Like a fish split on the drying rack, Marduk sliced the dragon queen's body in half. One part he made into the sky, studded with bright star-shrines for each of the gods, their gates bordered by Tiamat's ribs. He divided up the formless expanse of the cosmos into a measured rhythm of time and space. Three stars were given to each of the twelve months. Their passage was marked by the cycle of the moon, a crescent formed from Tiamat's dragon horns. He conjured clouds and rain – setting the winds running in their paths. From Tiamat's other half, he made the Earth. Her foetid udders formed mountains that Marduk pierced to release streams flowing down their rough sides. He tied her long, scaly tail as an anchor-rope between the sky and heaven. Finally, Marduk set Tiamat's head on high and punctured her eyes, from which the rich waters of the rivers Tigris and Euphrates would flow forever.

After Marduk had shaped the formless world, he told the gods to build a city where he would rule: Babylon, its gates decorated with images of Tiamat's vanquished monsters. Finally, the gods took Quingu – Tiamat's son-consort – and sliced him open so that his blood spattered the Earth. Ea wrenched bones from the bodies of the rebel monsters and made small skeletons from them. From these dark materials, Ea shaped men, little creatures like gods, but only part divine – the other part black as the sea's deeps. These creatures would labour forever in the gods' stead and pay tribute to them throughout their short lives.

Order from chaos

It's an intense story, full of baroque details: a dynasty of elemental gods kills their patriarch and battles their vengeful mother's monster army. On the surface, *Enūma Eliš* describes how the physical and human worlds came to be, and why Marduk – the Storm God of the most powerful city state at the time – should rule it. The characters of the story certainly reflect the particular natural forces that the Mesopotamians experienced: silt, clay, flooding and storms. But this myth was not just a fantasy conjured by pre-scientific minds. The story is about the origins of *human* experience, and the bittersweet nature of life's passage. The Big Bang is the origin myth for the modern age, but the ancient *Enūma Eliš* explains more from a human perspective, as we shall see.

The *Enūma Eliš* says something essential about the nature of creation: that it requires both productive chaos as well as an ordering force for anything at all to emerge. And, that creation involves division and loss. In this story, the chaos is a terrible female dragoness, while the organising power is an imposing male sky god. But Tiamat was not just a monster. She was both fecund and destructive: a nurturing mother and a passionate lover, a breeder of horrors and a fearful avenger. She was all the powerful, enveloping forces that motivate life and animate nature. Just like Gaia of Classical myth, she created things without boundaries or separation – silty proto-gods that flowed into one another; gnarly hybrid monsters; a son whom she took as an incestuous boyfriend.

To get things into shape, this potent, swirling melee has to be turned into something. Lines have to be drawn and violence has to be done. Marduk brings this in spades. He penetrates Tiamat's belly, the cradle of fertility, with his weapons. Then he takes a breather and gathers his thoughts – he's not a hothead. There is a cruelty in how

Marduk stands coolly above Tiamat's corpse, wondering what to do with it. As he butchers chaos into parts, he cuts off Tiamat's fertile power. She can no longer create; she is just material. There's a great loss in Marduk's creation: of potential, possibility, continuity. Making *something* out of *anything* means that it's not anything anymore.

As you have probably noticed, from a modern perspective, the story is a feminist nightmare. The power of creation being wrested from the female goddess by an inexorable male force. The dragon queen fills the universe with rich, elemental chaos; Marduk rides gloriously into battle, cheered on by his father figures, to take violent charge of Tiamat's fecund waters and churlishly chop her into pieces. This wasn't the way in all Mesopotamian myths. In the story of Ishtar and Tammuz, it is a goddess who creates order in the world and makes the rhythmic cycles of nature turn. But the *Enūma Eliš* was also a sly piece of propaganda. The myth justified the growing political power of Old Babylon in the region by placing the city's patron god in the top cosmological spot, above the deities of all the other cities. In some earlier versions, such as one found in the city of Ashur, the city's patron god Assur played the starring role. Who the Storm God was depended on who was telling the story. As Babylon gained power and became a deeply patriarchal and misogynistic state, Marduk rose from a provincial farming deity to become the supreme king of the gods. In the *Enūma Eliš*, he turned a fluid, universal matriarchy into an ordered, political patriarchy.[8]

The oceanic mind

The *Enūma Eliš* reaches deeper than political history though. The mythographer Joseph Campbell described how 'Shakespeare said that art is a mirror held up to nature. And that's what it is. The nature is your nature, and all of these wonderful poetic images of mythology are referring to something in you'. Myths describe our inner worlds; they are guides to the truths of life – and to living it well. The psychoanalyst Carl Jung posited a similar relationship between myth, landscape and psyche which is useful when thinking about the *Enūma Eliš*: 'Mythologized processes of nature, such as summer and winter, the phases of the moon, the rainy seasons, and so forth, are in no sense allegories of these objective occurrences; rather they are symbolic expressions of the inner, unconscious drama of the psyche'. And there is a great deal of drama in the processes that our minds undergo.

Mythological realms are stories of the human condition enacted in the theatre of nature. One of Jung's students, Erich Neumann, argued that myths about the world's origins are also stories about the birth of human consciousness. The characters are drawn from the physical landscape – a Storm God, a god of underground rivers, an ocean dragon – but they play out psychic events. The *Enūma Eliš* is a story of the formation of the psychological world, from boundless to delineated. It tells how mental order is carved from chaos monsters; how chaotic, infantile experience is shaped into an organised, mature consciousness capable of interacting with reality.[9]

Water is the most widespread symbol of the unconscious: primal waters and apocalyptic floods occur throughout the mythologies of the world, a relationship we will explore further in Chapter Six. At the beginning, Tiamat's oceans mingled with Apsu's freshwaters are like the cushioned water world of the womb which we imagine that babies experience. The psychoanalyst Sigmund Freud wrote about the 'oceanic feeling' – a boundless sense of the self being continuous with the world around. There is no separation from the external world or awareness of other persons as distinct beings. In this state, there is no time, nor any borders. There is even possibly a feeling of perfect continuity between the mother and child. According to another psychoanalyst, Melanie Klein, this illusion of union is rent violently asunder by being weaned off breast milk, a tragic loss that lingers only in the deepest memories.

The events of the *Enūma Eliš* could be seen to track this psychological development – it's an interesting thought experiment at the very least. First, primal water deities are divided up: they fractionate into the demigods of seas and clouds, lakes and rivers, like the mind discerning basic distinctions in the world as the eyes gain focus and noises start to have meaning. Then, Tiamat becomes angry and vengeful against her offspring, bringing a violence to the dreamlike oceanic feeling. The loving mother Tiamat turns into a hateful dragon. From a psychic perspective, she's turning from an ideal providing mother to a cruel withholding one. She produces monsters, embodiments of all the difficult, overwhelming experiences a child might have of absence and deprivation. All the frustrating, terrible things in the world that an infant encounters become her fault. Mothers, it is well known, get blamed for everything.

Alongside this loss, the Sky God, the airy, rational part of the mind, takes charge. He's a father figure who creates an ordered psychological landscape from the subconscious chaos. The loss of unity leads to a sense of individuality, boundaries and structure. Marduk sets stars to measure time, puts the winds in their different tracks and makes laws. As he splits Tiamat into parts, he divides one all-encompassing, watery entity into dualities: inertia and action, liquid and solid, earth and sky, ruler and subjects. This division, between the order and the monsters of chaos, allows our minds to develop, so that they can eventually handle the terrible things outside. These become part of ourselves, just as Marduk makes humans from Quingu's blood. Humans are part god, part monster and part earth. This combination of the divine and monstrous makes for a balanced, nuanced view of the world.

In the same way, our parents and societies impose structures on our experiences, giving meaning to the overwhelming streams of stimuli pouring into our early consciousnesses. The wide expanse of sensation is given defined routes down which to flow. Our minds become able to logically divide the world up into manageable chunks as we develop and grow up. We lose some of our fluid creativity, but we can – just about – function. This balance between order and chaos is what leads to all the astounding things that humans can do. As long as the monsters are kept in check.

Entropy

Another inescapable feature of creation is that things fall apart. In the scientific universe, we know this as entropy: in simple terms, all matter is continually moving towards a state of increasing disorder. In a similar way, the monster world of the *Enūma Eliš* seethed with the threat of dissolution. If you build the foundations of a world from the broken body of a dragon and populate it with men made from monsters, you had best make sure that everything continues to run smoothly. After Marduk created the world and started the metronome of time, all living things became vulnerable to decay and death Without his watchful eye, nothing would just stay the same.[10]

This transience was an ever-present feature of the Mesopotamian city states such as Babylon, Uruk and Assur. They were cities built from clay: from their architecture and art to their official state documents. Farming on the surrounding land was governed by a yearly cycle between dry and wet seasons, when the soil fertility was refreshed by flooding and storms. These could be ruthless tempests that wreaked havoc on the world below, but a temporary return to watery chaos was necessary. The drying forces of the sun and wind, the Storm God's agents, calmed these elements so farming could resume. It was a volatile balance: the hand of the Storm God was needed to keep things running, to hold creation in tenuous order and maintain these cycles. The world could always return to water and silt.[11]

The stuff from which humans were made also had serious consequences. The gods fashioned the first men out of betrayal, earth and the blood of monsters. Humans were deeply flawed and had to be wary of the chaos in themselves and in each other. This is a different kind of chaos to the serene, formless Nirvana which Apsu and Tiamat represented. It is the constant threat of upheaval in the divine world order, called 'kratogenic' chaos. Anyone who has played the PlayStation game *God of War* will recognise the name of the main character, 'Kratos'. He crosses mythic realms on a cruel vendetta driven by his hatred for the gods. Kratos wants to mess things up.

Very sensibly, Marduk puts safeguards in place to avoid the threat of uprisings. Before he defeats Tiamat, Marduk demands loyalty from the other gods: if they want him to deal with chaos, they have to be part of his hierarchy. In the same way, for civilisation to exist, we each have to play by society's rules so that kratogenic chaos is kept at bay. Many of us might not think much of our rulers and politicians these days but most of us submit ourselves to society: we care about what other people think of us, we usually abide by laws and we do what our jobs require of us. We might have religious beliefs or other moral structures that guide our actions. Because we rely on a bustling civilisation to supply our needs, we choose what roles to play and make sacrifices to become part of it, like specialised cells within an organism working together to stay alive.

Letting go of parts of our own potential is a price that we each pay for keeping the monsters of chaos at bay. In order to get really good at something, you have to be devoted to it and neglect other aspects of yourself. Nobody can be good at *anything* and do *everything*. So, we direct our prolific, creative energies towards things which fulfil us, make us money, add to the world – whichever we value most highly. It's one way in which we try to overcome the finite nature of things. By continually creating, we keep the cycles of life going in a disorderly world, replacing what falls apart.

Looking into the abyss

A few years ago, I was standing with a friend of mine who is an actor, composer and writer in the smoking area of an artists' club in central London. It's one of those crazy places where the creative and eccentric congregate. I'd already hit a well-known comedian in the face by mistake while gesturing too enthusiastically (he apologised to me in a very British way). It was drizzling slightly, and we were both in one of those moods where we wanted to put the world to rights. As we huddled away from the rain under a narrow awning, I asked him to describe what it's like being a creative.

'Well . . . most people, they exist in the middle, where it's reasonably familiar and safe. They're a bit bored but they have a steady job and they get on with life. It's nice there. We . . . well, we're all the way over *here*, staring into the abyss. We see stuff that they can ignore. We come to understand important things. But we might fall in.'

I thought back to this conversation many times when writing this chapter. My friend is someone who has many things going for him – from looks to talent. But he exists in a state of constant effort. He both loves his abilities, and suffers for them, because being a very creative person is a call that cannot be ignored. It requires you to constantly wrestle with the chaos monsters that writhe beneath the ordered world, and in your own psyche. You have to face them, feed them, and know how to harness them. They can take over, if you are not careful.

It's no surprise that chaos was imagined as an oceanic dragoness by the Mesopotamians: dragons are all creatures and none, wielding all the powers of nature. Tiamat was as all-encompassing as the oceans, the being from which everything came. She was the vital, volatile stuff of life that fuels creativity. In Nietzsche's philosophical fiction, *Thus Spoke Zarathustra* (1883), the protagonist Zarathustra proclaims, 'one must still have chaos in one, to give birth to a dancing star'. In order to create something magical, we need the impetus of inner chaos. In the introduction to *Frankenstein* (1831), Mary Shelley argued: 'Invention, it must be humbly admitted, does not consist in creating out of void, but out of chaos; the materials must, in the first place, be afforded: it can give form to dark, shapeless substances, but cannot bring into being the substance itself'. We can't make something out of nothing. We need a raw mass of material that can be wrestled into a work of art. Whether that be monstrous body parts, or a glut of human experience to write a book, paint a canvas or carve a sculpture.

To be deeply creative we have to know how to plumb our oceanic depths and titrate them out carefully. William Wordsworth described poetry as 'the spontaneous overflow of powerful feelings', originating from 'emotion recollected in tranquillity'. He described how a poet has to peel back their calm exterior and contemplate what's underneath until 'an emotion, kindred to that which was before the subject of contemplation' is 'gradually produced, and does itself actually exist in the mind'. Then writing can begin. For Wordsworth, poetry was the journey between deep, careful thought and raw, powerful feeling. T. S. Eliot called this core of emotion 'the dark embryo', like a primordial dragon egg.

This process needs the violence of Marduk because to truly create, the profusion of possibility had to be dismembered and rearranged. When we create art, we use the intellect to harness our raw emotion and ideas, ruthlessly moulding them into something. A (possibly apocryphal) comment by the artist Pablo Picasso described art as 'chaos taking shape'. He's also quoted as saying that 'every act of creation is first an act of destruction'. Chaos is not enough: you need the tools to face it and battle it into becoming something, to turn chaos into cosmos.

This is true in science too. The American philosopher Eric Hoffer described creativity as 'the ability to introduce order into the randomness of nature'. The natural world is incredibly complex and frustratingly mutable. Natural phenomena, especially biological ones, don't always adhere to the rules we sift out from anomaly-filled data. Shaping a taxonomy to describe the organic world involves dealing with the fact that species and groups aren't really the neat categories we like to think they are. But we willingly do violence to nature in order to make it into something that feeds the appetite for meaning in our minds, dissecting the dragons and dividing them up into their component beasts. We lose some appreciation of the real diversity of nature, but it's worth it – we're very uncomfortable with the meaninglessness of chaos.[12]

The modern world is geared to remove chaos rather than shape it, though: we have screens to show us the weather, the train times or where our rapid food delivery is. We're fed reductive messages through news and social media channels. When the world feels too regimented, people seek ways to commune with their monsters. These modern routes to escaping everyday life and finding chaos can also consume us: playing violent video games, dancing at techno raves, plunging down rabbit holes on online internet forums, or dissolving the mind with illicit substances.

Many exceptionally creative people have been overwhelmed by these shortcuts to chaos. Flirtations with the abyss are always risky. Jumping head-first into Tiamat's waves, where the Storm God can't reach, means there's nothing to keep the monsters at bay, so creativity can be overwhelmed by consumption. No wonder many people want to avoid the project entirely, to sit comfortably in the middle of the ordered and known. Others are driven to brave the abyss and drag back the bodies of monsters from which marvels can be made that speak to all of us. What the myth of Tiamat and Marduk shows us is that we are made of potent, monstrous matter and that we have the ability to control it. We need to harness both of these elements – embracing the inevitable losses of life – in order to lead the fullest and most creative lives we can.

The Minotaur and the Labyrinth

Chapter 3

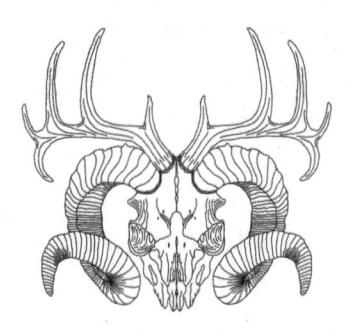

'The Minotaur more than justifies the existence of the Labyrinth'
Jorge Luis Borges

Minotaurs and matadors

One of the most monstrous things I have ever seen was on a family holiday to Southern France when I was about twelve years old. After days spent swimming and playing fractious family tennis matches, we decided to experience some local culture. It was a short drive to see a bullfight in the nearby town of Arles. We filed into the wooden amphitheatre seats and felt the energy mount as the matadors strutted around the ring in their bright brocade tailoring. An announcer roused the crowd in Spanish.

Then the first fight began – a cage door opened and the bull skittered out across the sand. I had expected it to be far larger, for some reason. Its shoulder barely reached to the matador's chest, slender legs finishing in neat, cloven hooves. Its horns looked lethal, though.

What followed was a game of cat and mouse, which the matador wanted to play and the bull didn't so much. Every time the bull attempted to slope off to the side of the arena to mind its own business, the matador would pursue it with a flourish. The first spear was a shock, delivered ostentatiously to the nape of the bull's neck, drawing applause from the audience. The blue and pink frills of the *banderillio* spear shaft bobbed up and down as the bull bucked in irritation and blood began to seep down its sides.

After about ten minutes, the animal was pin-cushioned with lances and dripped a trail of blood in the sand. All I could think about was the pain of them twisting in its flesh as it moved. The matador, buoyed by the crowd's cheering, pressed his pirouetting attack harder. Between the fervour of the locals and the tourists shifting uncomfortably in their seats, I began to feel like this was something I did not want to see. We left before the final deadly act.[1]

Unsurprisingly, this *corridas* style of bullfighting, in which the bull is eventually killed, has come under attack over time. Blood sports don't sit well with modern sensibilities. Arles is one of a handful of places where deadly bullfights still happen, one end of a very long cultural thread. The ritualised slaughter of the bull carries too much meaning to erase, so locals put up strong resistance when bans are proposed. After watching his first bullfight in 1923, Ernest Hemingway commented: 'bullfighting is not a sport. It is a tragedy, and it symbolizes the struggle between man and the beasts.' It dramatises our vexed relationship with other animals, and with the beasts in ourselves.

To heighten the spectacle of this struggle, bulls are bred carefully. Hemingway described one bull he saw as 'absolutely unbelievable. He seemed like some great prehistoric animal, absolutely deadly and absolutely vicious.' In the world of the *corrida*, Hemingway added, 'a good fighting bull is an absolutely incorrigible bad bull'. The matadors, on the other hand, strive for perfection, to fight flawlessly. Hemingway commented that 'the worst criticism the Spaniards ever make of a bullfighter is that his work is "vulgar"'. The dance between the 'beast' and the 'hero' must be elegant in order to be meaningful art.[2]

The bullfight may be an opposition of man and beast but it is not quite the same as hunting, which is a simpler case of man facing and overpowering nature. A bullfight is a choreographed battle, a moral story played out for an audience which needn't involve death. The style of bullfight my parents had *meant* to take their daughters to was the one local to Arles, in which *raseteurs* jump over the bull and dance around, evading it without actually harming the animal. Further afield, rodeos in the United States serve much the same purpose, as cowboys sit astride bucking steers for as long as they can, risking a trampling. Even small children can try their might against animal power. Once, in Colorado, I saw the minors' segment of the rodeo, called 'mutton bustin''. Intrepid children clung for dear life onto the backs of panicking sheep, who were let loose to micro-gallop across the sandy enclosure, eventually flinging their riders off like unwieldy sacks of potatoes. The kid who held onto their woolly juggernaut steed the longest was the champion mutton buster.

Why do people need to fight bulls? Why the struggle between man and beast that Hemingway described? We've always lived *with* beasts and *on* beasts, so we've theatrically demonstrated dominance over the creatures close to us. A skilful fight is a very intimate thing. But it's even more than that. We *are* beasts. The bullfight is a struggle between man and his beastliness. It's an eruption of violence, a pressure valve for the eternal problem of what to do with the animal inside, locked in a civilised world. The heroic matador slays a sacrificial bull, representing this inner beast, and the crowd gets a catharsis. This display has created a powerful mythology in bullfighting towns in Southern Europe. Even for those of us who don't live anywhere near blood-sport arenas, bull monsters still stalk through our imaginations.

The artist Pablo Picasso had watched bullfights while growing up in Southern France, experiences which embedded the bull and the cult of the matador in his mind. Picasso took the beast in and made it part of himself. He painted not just men fighting bulls, but bull-men.

As Europe felt the ravages of war in the early twentieth century, Picasso produced a series of works linking bull-fighting culture with the Minotaur of the ancient world, woven through with his personal mythology. This theme was explored in an exhibition in The Gagosian Gallery in London, *Picasso: Minotaurs and Matadors* (2017). One of the most famous images, the devastating *Minotauromachie* (1935), shows a minotaur knotted with muscle looming menacingly above a prone, naked woman. He's held at bay by a small girl wielding a candle. In some of Picasso's other paintings, the Minotaur is a protective male force, delicately lifting a limp maiden into a boat; or a wretched one, curling in foetal position, pierced by an arrow, watched by sailing naiads.[3]

The eminent art historian John Richardson, a friend of Picasso's who died soon after curating the Gagosian exhibition, spoke about the artist's darker instincts in 2008. He described Picasso's early mistreatment by art critics, which gave Picasso a taste for torturing them. The artist would etch elaborate designs on a sandy beach, relishing the distraught looks on the faces of the critics as they watched the sea wash the priceless art away. Picasso was filled with a consuming energy: he wanted to draw out raw emotions from people around him, 'a bit like a vampire'. He notoriously wrought havoc on the women in his life, through strings of intense partnerships and philandering. But, like some of the pitiful minotaurs Picasso painted, he was also a 'victim of misfortune and tragedy' Richardson pointed out.[4]

Picasso's minotaurs were a mirror hall of images through which he could look at himself. Oscar Wilde's Dorian Grey had a painting in his attic to age for him as he indulged his baser instincts. Picasso had a clutch of burly taurine creations to embody the powerful qualities that his small form couldn't. Sometimes he donned one of the bull headdresses that matadors wore for training to pose for photographs – literally becoming a minotaur. Picasso said himself in 1960: 'If all the ways I have been along were marked on a map and joined up with a line, it might represent a Minotaur'. Picasso's journey as a man left the footprint of a beast.[5]

Not many people think of themselves as half-beasts trapped in human guise, but there's an echo of the animal in everyone. A beast we each have to struggle with, large or small, trapped and subdued by a maze of modern life. This chapter investigates how we handle our minotaurs, locked carefully in the labyrinths of our minds, and the cost of keeping them at bay.

Asterion

Not long before Picasso was painting his bull-men, the ruins of an ancient palace were being unearthed at Knossos, just outside Heraklion in Crete. The young archaeologist, Arthur Evans, was not the first to excavate there – he followed in the footsteps of several Greek archaeologists. But their origins didn't suit the heroic twentieth-century narratives of archaeological discovery as well as Evans's, so he still receives the retrospective limelight.

Evans was familiar with the idea that Knossos might be the site of King Minos's palace and its Labyrinth. It was a link dreamed up by ancient Roman writers, revived many times over the centuries and widely assumed to be true in early twentieth-century Europe. Evans was initially sceptical of this connection – he knew that it wasn't even mentioned by Classical Greek texts. But, when he uncovered a set of winding passageways and chambers at Knossos, he couldn't help himself. In Evans's imagination, the ruins conjured up the Labyrinth and the palace of King Minos. He named the newly discovered civilisation 'Minoan', after the mythical king.

This association would become Evans's obsession and captivate the minds of archaeologists after him. But visiting Knossos looking for signs of the Labyrinth is a fool's errand. While the idea is a major source of income for the Cretan tourist industry, no trace of a physical maze has actually been found at Knossos. I knew this when I went to visit. The hilltop site juts into the sky, surrounded by pale carunculated peaks studded with dark trees. It *feels* like a mythical place. Deep down, I secretly hoped to encounter minotaur spoors and tracks to inspire this chapter. But I might as well have traipsed through the overpriced shopping streets of Capri looking for sirens or sea nymphs.[6]

There is no doubt that the soul of ancient Crete was entangled with bulls, though, just like that of Arles today.

The palace was decorated with frescoes and statues of bulls and balletic human figures vaulting over their writhing, muscular forms. These tokens stoked the flames of Evans's Labyrinth-hunting. He began to flesh out the story of one of the earliest civilisations of Europe, which had flourished until about 1450 BC. Crete had traded through the Aegean, Mesopotamia – even as far as Northern Europe – becoming so rich that it dominated all the nearby Mediterranean islands. In early texts, this growing power was credited to the ambition and force of King Minos, but whether or not he existed as an individual, we shall never know.[7]

These ancient stories also mention a dark secret under the King's palace. A mass of stony passageways winding round and round, folding back on themselves and tangling with one another. From a single entrance, they led to the very centre of a maze. It had been built by the cunning craftsman Daedalus, who was the only man capable of making a truly inescapeable maze. This Labyrinth housed a creature whom King Minos never wanted to see the light of day, nor to hear spoken of in the palace: his stepson.[8]

The boy's name was Asterion, which means 'the starry one' – ironic given that he had barely seen the skies. He had been born to Minos's wife, Pasiphaë, the offspring of her fervent lust for a shining white bull. This animal had emerged from the salt-foam of the sea, a gift from the sea-god Poseidon for Minos to sacrifice to him. But Minos had greedily sequestered the bull away in his herds, offering another fine animal to Poseidon instead. As a punishment, Poseidon filled Minos's wife with insatiable desire for the white bull. She lingered by the bull's enclosure, watching his glossy white flanks and sighing with longing. Frustrated by the impossible logistics of inter-species relations, she begged the craftsman Daedalus to help her. He built her a lifelike model cow – hollow and upholstered with cowhide. He took it to the centre of a field, helped her into it, and left her to her dubious bliss with her bovine suitor.[9]

The baby she birthed from this union was a monster, a bull-headed child. But he grew quickly, hidden away, becoming violent and inhumanly powerful. So, Minos plunged the monstrous youth into the dark of the Labyrinth. Only the rumbling reminders of his bellows could be faintly heard through the palace floor. The creature had to be fed, though. Every nine years, a tribute of fourteen young men and women arrived by ship from Athens, a tax extracted by Minos's armies. The tributes were feasted and adorned with garlands, showered with splendour for one night. The next day, they trembled as they faced the stone slab of the Labyrinth door. They would only see it once, before the dark swallowed them up for good.

I imagine that Asterion could sense the tributes entering through the twisting passageways. Years of waiting in the crooked dark had sharpened his senses to every small change: the achingly slow growth of cracks in the stone, or the small plumes of dust sent up by the feet of fleeing rats. His eyes were not suited to the dark, but his soft black ears caught the faint echoes of their terror. His wet nostrils drew in each faint scent. The entrance of the young men and women set the stagnant air ablaze with the noxious sweat of fear. He did not need to hunt them down – they would come to him. Each path in the Labyrinth led to its centre, disorientating the victim as they fled – drawing them straight to what they feared.

Twenty-one years after he was locked away, the Minotaur heard a third grinding slam of the Labyrinth door. He smelt the familiar terror. Yet amidst the fear was something else: intent. He felt rage tinged with foreboding for the first time. Something was coming for him.

It was Theseus, son of Poseidon, stepson to the King of Athens, set on freeing his people from Minos's tyranny. He held a prize that would save him from the Labyrinth – a simple clew of blood-red thread given to him by Asterion's beautiful half-sister, Ariadne. She had fallen for the young prince as he danced at the feast the night before, and had resolved to save Theseus from his bloody fate. Pressing herself close to him, as drunken revellers cavorted around them, she had wrapped him in her warm scent and folded his fingers around the clew. A promise of freedom – as long as Theseus took her far away with him.

As the other Athenians cowered by the door the next morning, flinching from the shadows of the maze, Theseus tied the end of the thread tight and unwound the clew beside him, pacing into the dark. The bright filament traced his steps to the beast's lair and – blood-soaked and victorious – led him back out into the light again. The youths wrenched the door slowly open, and the fourteen figures stole off into the night to the harbour. In the dark of the maze, a black heap lay still on the sandy floor in the centre of the Labyrinth. Asterion's eyes clouded over and slowly dulled.[10]

Hoof prints

You know a story is a myth when it can be retold over millennia and doesn't lose its essence. It's the same for mythical beasts: they can be repeatedly remade and still be recognisable over the ages. The Minotaur is probably over three thousand years old – an appreciable age for a monster. He has lived a long and florid life since the first millennium BC, when he was described in the poems and histories of Greek writers such as Plutarch and Diodorus. Modern retellings embellish the brusque descriptions of Classical authors, but the beast remains essentially the same. There is something about the bull-man in the maze which gripped our attention and never let go.[11]

The Minotaur was part of a wider obsession with Minoan Crete that began in the nineteenth century after Evans's findings, according to Professor of Aegean Archaeology Nicoletta Momigliano. This fascination – which caught artists, writers and thinkers, like Picasso and Sigmund Freud – was dubbed 'Cretomania'. Momigliano points out that this interest was driven more by the *fantasies* about Minoan Crete than the actual evidence of it.

This is because the myth offers more than any history. As Momigliano describes: 'the story of the Minotaur, like many other ancient Greek narratives (and not just Greek narratives) can be and has been endlessly re-imagined to address different aspects of the human condition at different times and in different contexts'.

There have been many attempts to weave historical reality into the myth of Minoan Crete. When you hear a myth, do you want to know what it was based on? The tangible realities that might have seeded it? Explanatory breadcrumb trails are alluring, as we will see in Chapter Six for tales of sea monsters. Some historical links for the Minotaur's story rest on word associations: 'Minos' might have been a word meaning 'king', rather like 'pharaoh', for example. Likewise, the 'labyrinth' might be a word play: the double-axe symbol, or *labrys*, is commonly found above the doorways of Knossos palace, making it the 'house of the *labrys*'. Momigliano dismisses this idea, as the *labrys* mark made by masons was hardly unique to Knossos.[12]

Links between aspects of the myth and Minoan religion are also possible, though very difficult to prove. The mythographer Joseph Campbell suggested that Queen Pasiphaë and her bull-lover might be a mythological reworking of Minoan religious traditions, perhaps a coupling of a moon goddess and a cosmic bull. As with the rest of Minoan life, we have slim evidence of the spiritual rites they practised, so we can't know if this was the case. Campbell was superbly able at making highly plausible extrapolations, but it is possible.[13]

Alternatively, it has been suggested that the Minotaur's bellows might have been the rumble of geological activity under the island, imagined as a creature buried in an animate landscape. The Minotaur could also have been a beast of a man. The Greek philosopher Plutarch described a General Taurus, who was having an illicit affair with Queen Pasiphaë. The Athenian youths and maidens were slaves given as prizes for games held on Crete, which the General invariably won. Taurus treated his captives with the kind of hedonistic cruelty that would have impressed Emperor Caligula. He was finally bested in wrestling – as Plutarch's story goes – by the young hero Theseus.

There are no images of minotaurs *per se* in the Minoan ruins, only a few bull-men pictured on seals and coins found there. So it seems that this monster was created at some distance from his mythical home. What might have motivated the ancient Greeks to create him? He could represent the fall of tyrannic powers: the Minoans had long exploited the resources of the Aegean, perhaps represented by the blood-tribute of Greek youths in the myth. Weakened by the effects of a volcanic eruption, Minoan Crete was overrun by Mycenaean forces from the Greek mainland around 1450 BCE. The death of the Minotaur at the hands of a young Athenian hero might have represented the fall of ancient Crete to forces from the Greek mainland.[14]

Whether one or all of these is true is not really possible to tell. Historical events survive time more poorly than myth. If anything, these historical clues lead away from the timeless power of the Minotaur. More suggestive are his symbolic uses in literature. In his *Metamorphoses*, Ovid used Asterion's bull head as a shameful pantomime mask mocking Minos. Ovid described how Minos's 'Disgrace had grown; the monstrous hybrid beast / Declared the queen's obscene adultery'. The uptight Roman philosopher, Seneca, wrote how Pasiphaë's sin was 'greater than that of' her 'monster-bearing mother' and that she 'defiled only herself with debauchery . . . a mother's wickedness betrayed by her hybrid baby's bestial features'.[15]

Much later, in the fourteenth century, Dante Alighieri had the Minotaur guarding the seventh circle of Hell in Canto Twelve of his *Inferno* from the *Divine Comedy* (1308–20). This creature watches over a fiery river of blood, where sinners who have committed violent crimes burn for eternity. Dante and Virgil, on their grand tour of Hell, break off their erudite discourse when they see him. They manage to sneak past the mountain of muscle and horns by irritating him so much that he begins to gnaw his own flesh and roar with incoherent fury, entirely forgetting about the intruders.

The Minotaur's enduring power comes from his ability to mean many things at the same time: lust, rage and anger, as well as the disgrace and shame that follow them. We all have these impulses, but must find ways to restrain them in order to live with each other and with ourselves. The maze offers one solution to this problem.

ENCHANTED CREATURES

The clew of thread

The Labyrinth opens a path to understanding what's behind the Minotaur's inscrutable muzzle. Labyrinths have had mystical meanings for as long as humans have been creating images. They are natural forms, like the coiled guts of animals, or networks of spider's webs. Whorls and spirals have been found in prehistoric cave paintings, like those we saw in Chapter One, that might be representations of shamanic visions. Elaborate mazes can be found everywhere: from mandalas and alchemical symbols, to the hedge mazes of country houses and the rose window of Notre Dame in Paris. They lead through winding convolutions, removing the linearity of logical thought. But they always reach the centre, whichever path you take. Labyrinths are not really mazes, but manifold paths to one point.

There are numerous books on the spiritual and meditative uses of labyrinths. Artist Liz Simpson writes: 'the labyrinth is a universally imprinted archetype or theme illustrating our life's journey towards spiritual development and completion'. They can represent surrender to the unknown or the shifting paths of life. They can mirror explorations of the mind's depths to find the self, recovering a lost past from childhood or reconnecting with our place in the web of nature. Tracing the path of a labyrinth is a way to undergo a journey, and emerge changed in some way. This change comes from reaching the interior, and encountering what is there.

The Minotaur's Labyrinth is not just a meditative tool for self-transformation – it contains a man-eating monster. The craftsman Daedalus constructed it as an inescapable prison, somewhere to keep the monster alive but out of sight. As clever as he was said to be, Daedalus almost got lost in the Labyrinth's passages as he built it. When Theseus entered, he had no guarantee of returning: all paths led in, but they didn't lead out.

The Labyrinth's twisting passages reflect the contortions of the mind's psychological depths. Freud often likened the subconscious mind to the disorienting corridors of a labyrinth, mental defences masking the monstrous things at the centre. As writer Ruth Padel puts it, the labyrinth is 'a maze which conceals its own shame, its subterranean bull violence'. Daedalus's Labyrinth was a metaphorical folly in a psychological landscape; a shield against a subconscious beast. The ingenious craftsman represents the conscious mind – the intellect creating rational defences around a dark core. Deep in that inner mental space, civilised humanity cedes to something primitive and animalistic that is too threatening to be allowed out.[16]

How effective are these defences? Emotions such as lust or rage are despotic forces in the mind: they cannot just be shut up and ignored, they have to be fed or faced. Minos tries to sate the appetite of his monster by sending human prey, rather than meeting the monster himself. The Minotaur terrifies these youths and maidens before ripping them apart, he's the tyrant of the Labyrinth – but is also a captive in it. He's walled in with his own bestial impulses, making him even more monstrous. This is where events such as the *corrida* are necessary, venting the power of the beast and subduing it again. Bullfights indulge visceral instincts, momentarily, but these bloody tributes are only a makeshift solution.[17]

The cost of imprisoning and avoiding these parts of ourselves is to make them more terrifying and consuming. This is played out in Stanley Kubrick's 1980 adaptation of Stephen King's novel *The Shining*. Jack Nicholson plays Jack Torrance, a struggling writer who takes his family away to the isolated Overlook Hotel in Oregon. His job as winter caretaker is an escape from his banal everyday existence, where Jack ignores his failures as both writer and father. The hotel is warren-like, with impossible physical dimensions, and is bordered by a large hedge maze. But in this winding, ice-bound prison, Jack feels like he might really '*achieve* something'. He revels in the isolation, tapping feverishly away on his keyboard and becoming increasingly feral, while his wife and young son struggle to keep the building running.

While King's book was a horror story, Kubrick's film was even more sinister, a psychological thriller filled with archetypes from Jungian psychoanalysis. Ghosts haunt the Overlook: the iconic twin girls in the hallway; canny barmen and opulent parties from past decades; a former caretaker who murdered his family; a beautiful naked woman in the bath of room 237 who turns into a cackling corpse. In the film, these emerge from the minds of the hotel inhabitants. The 'shining' ability of Jack's son, a telepathic insight that reveals visions of murdered girls and rivers of blood, is borne of trauma. When Jack's wife finds the streams of repetitive nonsense that he has typed out instead of a manuscript – 'all work and no play makes Jack a dull boy' – it becomes clear that writing is not what Jack wants to achieve. His real ambition is to plunge into the depths of his internal labyrinth and be a monster. He wants to stay here 'for ever and ever'.[18]

He will do. The characters are trapped in the bewildering passages of the hotel – but it becomes Jack's domain, the place that releases something inside him. He stands over a model of the hedge maze, both surveying it and lost in it. Jack's insanity creeps up slowly over the weeks, leading to savage outbursts – anger, confusion and frothing at the mouth. The culmination is in the final encounter with the beast, unleashed on his family. In the film's most iconic scene, Jack hacks at a bathroom door with an axe while his terrified wife screams inside. He then kills the hotel chef who comes to save them and frenziedly chases his own son through the snow-covered maze. The boy evades Jack by tricking him with footprints in the snow. In the morning, Jack's rigid body grins up at the sky, the minotaur-man frozen forever in his labyrinth.

Kubrick's film has many interpretations. But for me, it shows that the maze makes the monster. The labyrinth is crafted by the intellect to keep our beastly parts under control so we can live a civilised life. The maze can become more elaborate as we develop and age, burying the monsters deeper and even making them stronger. But wouldn't it be nice if we could be free of both?

Beastly conditions

In *The House of Asterion* (1947), one of several stories on labyrinths by Argentinian writer Jorge Luis Borges, the eloquent but illiterate Minotaur is not trapped – the maze is home. When he tries venturing out once, he terrifies everyone he encounters, so he hurries back to the safety of his Labyrinth. There, the Minotaur is a lordling, decorating his palace idly with corpses. In the light, he's a freak. There is no place for him in polite society, but his solitude and his incessant inner monologue are wearying. The contemplative monster remains hopeful, though: 'my loneliness does not pain me, because I know my redeemer lives . . . I hope he will take me to a place with fewer galleries and fewer doors. What will my redeemer be like? I ask myself. Will he be a bull or a man?'

For Borges, the bull in the maze was an image of the human condition. It reflects the experience of each person alone in their own mental labyrinths, both distanced and protected from the bewildering world. Who the Minotaur's saviour is remains unclear. It might be only himself, yet he remains waiting.[19]

How can we escape our mental mazes and the monsters inside them? One solution is to make them more impenetrable, to bury the monsters deeper. The other is to dive into the labyrinth and meet the monster within. This is a dangerous task – encountering your beastly self can be a scary thing. Theseus needed the help of the bright thread that Ariadne gave him; without it, he would have perished in the confusion of passages, like any other captive. To explore the intricacies of the mind and face what is there takes careful, patient guidance and some way of finding the upperworld again. Freud had an answer for the ordinary person: psychoanalysis. In an interview in 1927 he described how 'Psychoanalysis simplifies life. We achieve a new synthesis after analysis. Psychoanalysis reassorts the maze of stray impulses, and tries to wind them around the spool to which they belong. Or, to change the metaphor, it supplies the thread that leads a man out of the labyrinth of his own unconscious'. You might have to fight some minotaurs along the way, though.

In *Seduction of the Minotaur*, Anaïs Nin's autobiographical novel, a woman called Lilian undertakes a process of self-discovery. Though rich and insightful, it wasn't one of Nin's most popular novels, being as complex as the process of self-analysis is. Lilian travels to Mexico in order to escape herself, and falls in love with a troubled doctor. Through the pains and difficulties of this love, she is forced to confront herself and her past: to enter into her own labyrinth. What she discovers is that 'the detours of the labyrinth did not expose disillusionment, but unexplored dimensions. Archaeologists of the soul never returned empty handed'. Until then she had been scared of 'meeting the Minotaur who would devour her'. But 'now that she had come face to face with it, the Minotaur resembled someone she knew. It was not a monster. It was a reflection upon a mirror . . . the hidden masked part of herself unknown to her, who had ruled her acts'. By undertaking this journey, she had come home to herself. She had befriended her monster: 'She extended her hand towards the tyrant who could no longer harm her'.

Entering the labyrinth can be a necessary part of growing up. When you're young, the monsters of the subconscious are not yet securely locked away. Shame and intellect haven't wrapped their stone corridors around powerful emotions and appetites. These butt heads with the hard facts of the world, which seems strange and unjust. Jim Henson's 1986 cult film *Labyrinth* explores how the inner monsters are reconciled with adult realities in adolescence. The world seems distinctly 'not fair' to sixteen-year-old Sarah. She has to stay home and look after her baby brother, when she wants to be out with her friends. She wishes he would disappear. The Goblin King Jared, played by David Bowie, answers her wish and spirits him away. He's a seductive, nylon-sporting substitute for the Minotaur, indulging her selfish fantasies. Sarah has to struggle through the nonsensical monsters and obstacles of Jared's Labyrinth to find her brother. The Goblin King tempts her with the promise of eternal devotion, if she can give up her baby brother. She chooses to leave the Labyrinth and return to the safety and responsibility of everyday life instead, but the monsters she met inside remain her friends.

For most of us, forays into our psychological labyrinths aren't one-off adventures. Through the long process of shaping ourselves, we have to return many times and face the monsters in different states. Sometimes these journeys are triggered by periods of crisis – a breakup, a death, a betrayal or some other catastrophe. Such events make the world seem unbearable and they drive us into our interiors to face what's there. Life throws these things at us repeatedly and each time, as terrifying as it is, we can have another go at untangling the labyrinth inside and bringing our minotaurs up to the light. We can prove to ourselves that we are far less monstrous than we thought.

PART TWO

Monsters of Nature

Snake Women

Chapter 4

'The serpent lurks in the reflected image of every daughter of Eve'
Marina Warner

Ophidiophobia – a crippling fear of snakes – is the most common of all phobias, affecting two in every hundred people. For those who suffer from it, snakes can affect their daily lives, even when there are no snakes around. I remember teasing one of my childhood friends when she admitted that she avoided baths, lest a snake emerge from the plughole and attack her (we lived in London). For plenty of others, snakes are repellent, even when encountered on a screen. The 2016 documentary series *Planet Earth II* included a nail-biting scene of a young marine iguana evading predatory racer snakes on its first sprint to the sea. The empty beach erupted into a writhing mass, as hundreds of snakes suddenly came out of nowhere. The clip rattled everyone who saw it, even those without ophidiophobia.

While such fears seem irrational in modern urban life, snakes were the deadliest predators of early primates. The fear of snakes is embedded deep in our evolutionary history: they were our first monsters. If you suffer from ophidiophobia, you're following in a long-standing family tradition reaching all the way back to when our distant ancestors were something like tarsiers. This long relationship caused us to create a special group of hybrid monsters: the snake-women. In this chapter we will explore why snake women are some of the most powerful and pervasive monsters of all, and how we have used them to handle the cruel realities of nature. Some will be well known, such as the Gorgon Medusa or the Biblical Eve; others might be less familiar to you – such as the hybrids Lamia and Melusine.

When scientists want to scare monkeys in an experiment, they use snakes. Pictures of snakes will do, but rubber snake puppets are more effective. They have been used to study the role of fear in primate behaviour, and how primates balance the desire for safety against the desire for food. These decisions are affected by the connections between two brain regions, the amygdala and the orbitofrontal cortex. The amygdala, which I mentioned in Chapter One, is an almond-shaped nugget nestled on top of the mammalian brain stem, and generates our instinctual responses to threats. The orbitofrontal cortex sits at the front of the primate brain and controls subjective decision making. When you wonder what type of cheese to buy while shopping, for example, your orbitofrontal cortex will weigh up what tastes best, how much money you feel like spending, whether you're trying to cut down on your saturated-fat intake or which packaging appeals to you most. The outcome won't be a perfect computation but a largely subjective one.

Some unpalatable experiments using brain lesions have been carried out on macaque monkeys to understand how these two brain areas interact. A normal macaque will hold back from going after a tasty treat if a snake is within sight. The orbitofrontal cortex compares the appeal of food with the warning alarms from the amygdala, so the monkey chooses caution. But monkeys with obliterated amygdalas don't seem to feel fear: they will go after a treat, even with a snake present. Destroy a monkey's orbitofrontal cortex, however, and fear dominates – even when there aren't any snakes around. Food will not seem sufficient reward for the animal to venture away from safety. These two brain areas determine how humans and other primates perceive the risks and rewards of life.[1]

The gastronomic benefit of being able to spot the ripest fruit and freshest leaves is thought to have driven the evolution of primates' characteristic trichromatic or 'three-colour' vision. But snakes have had a more dramatic impact on our evolutionary history. Professor Lynne Isbell, who works in the Department of Anthropology at the

University of California Davis, has spent years looking into our long relationship with snakes. While working on primate social systems in the early 2000s, she had the kernel of an idea which became a key theory of primate evolution. Her Snake Detection Theory describes how the primate brain was shaped by the urgent need to avoid predatory snakes. Evolving alongside snakes caused the hyper-development of our sensory systems and our large, visually dominated brains.[2]

The threat of being suddenly enveloped in constricting coils or stabbed with venom caused primates to develop specialised snake-responsive neurons in their visual cortexes. These allow primates to react far more rapidly to snakes than to other threatening objects. Their stress hormone levels rise when they see something snake-like, too, but it is much better to be a neurotic monkey than a dead one. Researchers recently found that these neuronal responses are also present in the brains of human babies, even if they've never seen a snake before. And, like other primates, babies fixate on snakes in a way they don't with frogs or caterpillars.[3]

Isbell wanted to know what exactly it was about the appearance of snakes that activated these neurons. It could have been their limbless shapes, their winding movements or perhaps their scales. She tested vervet monkeys using the cured skin of a gopher snake, which she covered with grass, leaving just a small patch exposed. It turned out that the monkeys could rapidly spot even a few square centimetres of motionless snake skin among complex vegetation. The shape and pattern of these scales is very unusual in nature – lizard, crocodile or fish scales have a different visual effect. 'They also remembered where they saw snakes,' Isbell added; 'they knew to watch out where they had seen a snake before.' Females were quicker than males to spot the skins: if you have young offspring, the dangers of snakes multiply. Again, from an evolutionary standpoint, it is better to be a neurotic mother than a bereft one.[4]

Snakes have been an evolutionary albatross around primate necks, forcing our ancestors to invest in high-spec visual hardware and jittery mental software. But this shared evolutionary heritage can tell us a lot about ourselves and our relationship with nature. Our brains evolved in an ancient Eden filled with colourful ripe fruit, interlaced with scaly threat. Nature has been both bountiful and deadly – the ambivalent muse that has inspired the creation of the snake women, who embody some of our deepest and most fundamental fears.

Scales and apples fall

Most of us don't live with snakes anymore, and those that do don't face the terrors of the small early primates clinging to tree branches in the night. But our coexistence with snakes has left a fearful genetic memory. They wind through our imaginations, generating phobias, myths, stories, fascination and disgust. Ever since humans started making art, snake-like creatures have been created from nothing but curves and scaly crosshatches. They are the first animals that children can draw before their manual dexterity affords them a crayon cat or a dog. Even the sinuous bends of an 's' susurrate with a serpentine hiss as it hits the eye or ear.[5]

Serpent coils reach into the mythologies of most human cultures. The half-human Naga and Naginis of Southeast Asian mythology lived in jewel-encrusted underworld caverns and the Rainbow Serpent was a primordial creation deity of Australian Aboriginal myth. The evil Nordic serpent Nidhogg gnawed greedily at the roots of the Tree of Life, Yggdrasil, and the West African snake-god, Danh, encircled the world, stopping it from breaking apart into splinters.

In the realm of altered consciousness, snake-like things are said to slide through the visions generated by powerful psychotropic substances such as ayahuasca. The Swiss-Canadian anthropologist Jeremy Narby found this to be the case when he went to live in the Amazon with the Peruvian Indians in the 1980s. He wanted to explore their claims that they received botanical and biochemical knowledge directly from the vines used to produce ayahuasca. According to Narby, even the winding shape of the DNA double helix was said to have been known to the Peruvian Indians well before it was discovered by twentieth-century Western science.

During his personal ayahuasca experiences in the Amazon, Narby had the kinds of snake-infused visions which he had been told conveyed knowledge from the powerful forest vines. Beginning as a sceptic, Narby eventually came round to the idea that the serpentine shapes wove images of DNA's double helix, and that these altered states of consciousness could confer deep understanding of nature. He searched avidly for connections between the snake images, traditional helical imagery and the use of hallucinogens that appear in numerous cultures. Though his quest didn't fit neatly into a Western way of thinking, it demonstrates the cultural resonance of snakes and their effects on our imaginations.[6]

Supra-naturally knowledgeable snakes and plants sit at the centre of Judeo-Christianity too. Professor Isbell wrote a book about our evolutionary relationship with snakes, called *The Fruit, the Tree and the Serpent*. The title evokes one of the founding myths of the West: the Garden of Eden and the Fall, from the Old Testament Book of Genesis. In doing so, she links primate evolution with a core origin story of human consciousness. Isbell's Christian childhood had made the connection self-evident to her, but it was a quietly brilliant one. Her scientific theory of the origins of primate vision and awareness resonates deeply with the mythic representation of how humans gained self-knowledge: evolving alongside snakes and fruit caused us to see better, to be hyper-aware of danger; the Biblical snake showed the woman the forbidden apple, and naïve innocence was lost.

The implications of this are profound. It's an example of where our deep evolutionary roots might permeate through our culture. Early primates could not only select the sweetest fruits of the primordial Earth, they could see the serpents that hunted them. Their brains conjured predators from the slightest signs – an elongated shape, a patch of scales, a rustle of leaves. We can imagine that, as the primate brain developed, layered with systems primed for seeing snakes, self-awareness and fear emerged entangled together. Scaled danger existed all around and was pre-programmed into primate awareness, because pre-emption is the most effective way to avoid death. The discomforting nest of mental snakes was the evolutionary cost of being better at staying alive.

Picturing our ancestors as a bunch of tweaky marmosets hyped up on fructose and paranoid fantasies is a slight exaggeration, of course. The primates are a very social bunch, and have many other things going on in their lives which have contributed to their well-developed brains. But the essential duality of life-giving fruit and death-dealing serpents persisted into the world of *Homo sapiens*. Our hyper-developed prefrontal cortex, with our capacity to symbolise and imagine, turned these two sides of nature into cultural abstractions. The swelling of ripe fruit, echoing the fecund roundness of pregnant female bodies, symbolised the allure of fertility and life. Snakes, on the other hand, became a concept that meant more than just predation. They could mean death or harm, and all the sinister connotations that follow from that.[7]

This imagery underpins the story of the Garden of Eden and the Fall. Consisting of only a few short passages in the Book of Genesis, it has been represented, analysed and argued over far more than most other texts. It tells the story of our ejection from the womb of the world after Adam and Eve tasted the fruit of the Tree of Knowledge of Good and Evil at the behest of a snake. A woman listened to the serpent, ate the fruit with Adam, and the world was never the same again. The Fall caused innocence to be replaced with awareness, and immortality to be traded for a meaningful life. They woke up: their eyes 'were opened', and they could not be closed again. Adam and Eve then knew that they were vulnerable: they could do harm and harm could be done to them. They realised that they could suffer and die – that they were essentially alone in the world. This same awareness comes crashing in as a baby is born; when it is weaned off the breast; through the awkward changes of the teen-ages; or in facing all the difficulties that life throws at people. With that knowledge comes the stepwise loss of Eden, the painful entry into the world and a growing vision of the end. The stages of being fully alive and facing death arrive together.[8]

The woman and her snake caused a great deal of trouble that day in the Garden of Eden, and that wasn't the last of it.

The draconopede's gaze

For Christian theologians and scholars, the Fall determined the human condition. Original Sin had initiated death and suffering – so it was important to know exactly what this woman had done wrong. Over the long centuries since the Biblical stories were assembled, the sin committed by Eve was reworked numerous times. The historian of science Stephen Greenblatt has traced these changing interpretations. Scholars flung a litany of charges against Eve; she was weak and stupid, tricked into forgetting God's rules. She might have been depraved, seeking sensual fulfilment; or vain, lured by her own self-image. She may have been proud, neglecting what the men in charge told her. She may have been Satan's whore. For some Medieval theologians, Greenblatt suggests, this made Eve 'not merely Satan's ally' but 'his lover, joining her body to his in filthy rites'.

In many late Medieval and Renaissance images, rather than a snake in the tree, it is a serpent with a human face or body, called a draconopede. Michelangelo's serpent in the Sistine Chapel, for example, is a woman down to the groin, tapering into a pale, fleshy, yellow tail. Sometimes the serpent has Eve's face, or is a mirror image of Eve herself balancing on a serpent tail. In a woodcut by Lucas Cranach the Elder made around 1500, the serpent is an armless, nubile twin of Eve whispering in her ear, standing on a short, scaly stub. In some, the snake was omitted entirely; the representation of Eve herself was enough to suggest the snake. She *was* the snake. Rather than seeing out into the world with open eyes, Eve sinned by gazing into her own mirror image. Her crime was one of vanity and sensuality – a pretty poor reason to cause a rift in existence. But, according to some Renaissance thinkers, women were just like that.[9]

Even more damning: if Eve and the snake were one, she was not a victim of the Fall, but the root cause. Greenblatt suggests that for many scholars the temptation was really woman's own flesh, rousing male desire and deceiving man into his own destruction. All daughters of Eve, sharing this inexorable, treacherous allure, were just as snakey as she was. For St Peter Damian in the eleventh century, for example, women were all 'harlots, prostitutes, with your lascivious kisses, you wallowing places for fat pigs, couches for unclean spirits, demi-goddesses, sirens, witches ... the victims of demons, destined to be cut off by eternal death'. It seems that St Peter Damian might not have liked women very much.[10]

Eve had a rebellious doppelganger too, the notorious Lilith. Her precursors might have been the *lilitu* of Mesopotamian legend: barren, owl-winged demons with poison-filled breasts and impossibly long hair who haunted the night. These succubi stole men's semen and murdered pregnant women and babies. There is also one reference to a *lilith* creature in the Hebrew version of the Bible, dwelling with the 'wild beasts' and the 'satyrs' of the desert lands. In another collection of little-known texts are references to a woman called Lilith, who was the very first monstrous woman. In Jewish folklore, she was Adam's first wife: seductive, voluptuous and vain. In one text, she coupled with Adam and birthed many demons. In another, she was the companion to the archangel Samael and spawned innumerable horrors.[11]

Over time these threads were woven together into the notorious Lilith, Adam's headstrong first wife who had shimmering long hair and refused to lie beneath her husband. Banished from the Garden of Eden for this insolence, she fled to live wild in the desert – a witch, a demon, a whore. One Renaissance Jewish mystic described Lilith as the 'Serpent, the Woman of Harlotry' that 'incited and seduced Eve'. The Pre-Raphaelite painter John Collier depicted her naked and in a sensual embrace with a large python in his 1887 painting *Lilith*. She is beautiful, full-bodied and auburn-haired, like most pre-Raphaelite muses, revelling in the snake's coils. Her hair falls in wild waves down her back and she glances down, as if enticing the snake to wind around her further. One of Collier's friends, Dante Gabriel Rossetti, inscribed a poem on the frame of his own painting *Lady Lilith* (1868) which mirrors the image:

> Of Adam's first wife, Lilith, it is told
> (The witch he loved before the gift of Eve,)
> That, ere the snake's, her sweet tongue could
>   deceive,
> And her enchanted hair was the first gold.

She seduced young men with her scent and beauty, and, once one was in her coils, she:

Left his straight neck bent
And round his heart one strangling golden hair.

Both theologians and artists condemned the first mother and the first *femme fatale*, demeaning all other women with them. But they're not the only snake women to have been damned over history. If anything, they got off rather lightly. The frenzied diatribes against women had older, more visceral foundations which we will investigate next.[12]

The Gorgon's head

The snake women are found everywhere in mythology: from Echidna, the mother of monsters in Greek mythology or Lamia, the Libyan queen transformed into a horrible half-snake, to the metamorphosing lady Mélusine from Northern European folklore. They are all beautiful and dreadful, alluring and deceptive in equal measure. Many of these snake women are death-bringers. But, as we shall see, their origins also lie in the fear of the power to *create* life.[13]

The queen of the snake women was undoubtedly the Gorgon Medusa. Though she emerged in ancient Europe over 2,500 years ago, her snakey coiffure and ability to turn men to stone hardly need describing. Her name has been used everywhere, from computing technologies to electronic music festivals. She's still a favourite option for a last-minute fancy dress outfit, if Amazon's search rankings are to be believed. She was the first female monster to be written about, as far as we know, in Homer's *Iliad* from the eighth century BCE. He described the Gorgon's head as 'grim of aspect, glaring terribly, and about her were Terror and Rout', and on the shield of the goddess Athena was 'the head of the dread monster, the Gorgon, dread and awful'. Athena was the goddess of wisdom who used the Gorgon's head to strike fear into her enemies; one look into the serpent-wreathed eyes would literally petrify them.[14]

The Gorgon's head existed long before Athena acquired it, though. The original Gorgon was just a face or a mask, called a *gorgoneion*. Archaeologist Maria Anastasiadou has traced the image back to the pottery, seals and art in Minoan Crete, potentially dating to as early as 1800 BCE, though Gorgon-like icons might have appeared even in Neolithic Europe, before 2000 BCE. Anastasiadou suggests that the face might actually represent the grimace of a woman in childbirth, straining in pain – especially as it was often attached to a squatting body. *Gorgoneion*s appeared across ancient Greece on shields, amulets, armour, architecture, drinking cups and bowls, as talismans to ward off evil. Though they changed over time, the Gorgon's face – a tongue protruding from a tusked, leering grin under wide, staring eyes – is still instantly recognisable.

How the Gorgon began as a folk talisman and became part of the weaponry of the goddess Athena

ENCHANTED CREATURES

is an important question. How is a monster's power acquired? It must be killed and cut up into usable parts. Think of the demigod hero Hercules dipping his arrows in the poisoned blood of the Lernaean hydra, or slaying the Nemean Lion and wearing its impenetrable skin as a cloak. Absorbing monsters' powers is a common habit of heroes and gods in myth. For Athena to acquire the Gorgon's potent stare, the Gorgon first had to be turned into a monster that could be slain. So, later Greek writers created a body for Medusa. The iconic 'Gorgon' became three sisters: Medusa (meaning 'queen' or 'wise'), Euralye ('wide leaping') and Stheno ('strong'). They were born to Ceto, a whale-like sea goddess, and Phorcys, the old man of the sea. Writers played with the Gorgons, decking them out with writhing snake girdles or snake hair, scythe-like wings, bronze flesh and claw-like hands. All the monstrous fixings.

The three sisters were given a backstory, to explain how they had become horrors. The poet Ovid wrote a racy version in which Medusa was a beautiful mortal maiden who caught the eye of the sea-god, Poseidon. He raped her violently in the temple of Athena and impregnated her. Instead of being outraged at her uncle's audacity, Athena turned on his victim. The Goddess punished Medusa and her sisters for their alluring beauty by transforming them into horrible monsters and banished them far away to a deserted place. Around their dwelling was a sculpture-park of petrified creatures and men that had been turned to stone as they strayed too close to the Gorgons' lair.[15]

Medusa met a grisly end at the hands of the young demigod Perseus, son of Zeus. He had rashly boasted that he would bring the Gorgon's head as a royal gift to Polydectes, king of the island of Seriphos. So Perseus set off, on what would have been a vain errand, without the divine help of Hermes and Athena. They gave him an infallible blade to pierce metallic flesh and a reflective shield with which to view the Gorgons indirectly, safe from their gaze. Along the way he acquired a magic pouch, a cap of invisibility and winged sandals to speed him along. Fully armed, Perseus flew off to the distant realm beyond Oceanus's borders. Approaching the Gorgons' lair through forests of granite forms, he looked ahead using the reflection in his shield in case he accidentally caught sight of them. Luckily for him, they were asleep when he arrived. Perseus gingerly sliced off Medusa's head, his hesitant arm guided by Athena. Eyes screwed shut, he placed the head in the pouch, donned the cap of invisibility and flew off. From the decapitated neck sprang the two offspring of Poseidon that Medusa had been carrying: the winged horse Pegasus and his brother Chrysaor.[16]

As Perseus made a swift exit, Medusa's sisters awoke and screamed with rage at the sight of their sister's decapitated body, but they could not know where to begin looking for the assassin. As Perseus flew, drops of blood fell from Medusa's neck that landed on the desert sand and spawned venomous vipers. When he arrived at the palace of Polydectes, Perseus strode confidently into the hall. He was met with jibes from the king and courtiers, who had expected an empty-handed return. Perseus had only one answer: he put his hand into the bag, grasped the limp serpent hair and lifted up the severed head, which grinned in grisly rage across the banquet hall. The faces of the courtiers were transfixed in horror as their bodies turned to stone.

Before the goddess set the Gorgon's head on her shield, Athena knelt down by Medusa's corpse. She took a vial of blood from each main artery in the severed neck, to give to the snake-bodied healer Aeschylus: blood from the left artery could deliver instant death; blood from the right vessel could revive the dead. Medusa had the power of life and death running in her veins, the essential forces which infuse all the other elements of her story: the beautiful maiden that tempted gods, the raw, generative power of childbirth and the petrifying killer.

Mother Nature

In *The Epic of Gilgamesh*, a Mesopotamian myth better known than the *Enūma Eliš*, the eponymous hero tries to evade death by finding a magical herb of immortality. As he sleeps by a river after a long search, a snake steals the herb and slithers away into the underbrush. From then on, the serpent lives fresh and young forever, shedding its old withered skins and renewing its youth, while Gilgamesh is forced to accept his own, inevitable end. In many other traditions, too, snakes' ability to shed their skins and emerge bright and regenerated has made them symbols of continual rebirth as well as death. The ouroboros, the snake eating its own tail, is an ancient symbol of this revolution.

The creation of life has always been inextricable from the feminine. Palaeolithic artists sculpted earth mothers with pendulous breasts and tummies spilling over their thighs. Some historians have described gorgon-like 'Great Goddesses' from Neolithic (7000/6000–3000 BCE) North Africa and Europe, embodying both fertility and destruction. Fertility goddesses abound in later mythologies, some of which were snake goddesses: the cobra-headed goddess of the harvest, Renenūtet from Egyptian mythology; the Hindu goddess Manasa; or the pre-Celtic serpent goddess Corra who was vanquished by St Patrick as he drove the snakes from Ireland. Fecund women and deadly snakes are a natural combination, symbolising the unavoidable cycles of life and death over which these Mother Nature deities preside. The deep-rooted primate fear of snakes has been incorporated into mythologies which accept death as part of life.[17]

Invert these goddesses, however, and you get the monstrous snake women. In them, the cyclic nature of life has become purely destructive. Lamia was a loving mother before her children were snatched away from her, turning her into a bloodthirsty child murderer, her face twisted from rage. Echidna was the mother of myriad monsters, who lived in a cave and fed on raw flesh. Medusa was originally a symbol of primal motherhood, *gorgoneions* showing the strained grimace of the woman in labour. But this became the bestial glee of the grinning predator, an image of a cannibal Mother Nature. One writer called Medusa 'the chthonic devourer', recalling the enveloping waters of the dragon queen Tiamat. Her eyes paralysed her victims like a snake's, returning beings to the stuff of earth rather than creating new life.[18]

Some of the snake women have had their powers mythically stolen or controlled. Medusa's petrifying ability was co-opted as a weapon for the Olympian gods: Merciless Mother Nature became the grinning nightmare emblem of Goddess Reason. Medusa's potent blood was siphoned off into vials for a male healer to use: she was left as just a head in a bag and a decapitated pregnant body. Eve met a less violent but more tedious end when she was ejected from Eden for her dealings with the snake and was shackled with the task of painful child labour as Adam's subordinate. We could speculate about the ancient origins of Lamia and Echidna. Perhaps, as some cultures shifted towards cosmologies led by father-gods such as Zeus, the serpent goddesses that had been worshipped as faces of Mother Nature were turned into monsters and their ancient powers of creation and death were mythologically acquired by patriarchal systems.

Why is this? Angela Giallongo is a historian of education who has been fascinated by the Gorgon throughout her life. Giallongo has delved into Medusa's history, to understand this 'enduring figment of humanity's collective imaginary'. She found that Medusa and other snake women were essential myths, the kind which the fourth-century Latin writer Sallust described things that 'never happened but always are'. The snake women have never existed, but they represent fundamental truths, becoming 'viral archetypes' that have spread far and wide through time and space.

Giallongo suggests that the snake women were monsters of female 'otherness', used to turn the female into something lesser and more manageable. Since Classical times, snakes have been placed low down in the hierarchy of life, so being associated with them was less than flattering. Like the petrifying gaze of Medusa or the stare of the basilisk, women were believed to be able to turn the uncanny power of the 'evil eye' on those around them, causing all manner of ills: blind sensuality, spiritual death and terror. In the Late Medieval period, many women were shunned when they menstruated, because it was thought that was when their gazes were most powerful. Menstrual blood was likened to the venom of snakes and toads: these evil fluids could cause pestilence or awful nightmares – as if all women were monstrous. One Medieval commentator said: 'woman is a menstrual animal', full of toxic blood, contact with which meant 'fruits do not produce, wine turns sour, plants die, rust corrupts iron, the air darkens'. With that degree of dehumanisation, almost anything is justified.

These ideas might seem like the quackery of history, but they were the theory of mainstream medicine for a very long time. The belief in the evil eye and the terrible powers of females, Giallongo argues, got a lot of women burnt at the stake for being witches in early modern Europe. In many places across the world today, menstruation is still seen as unclean and women are excluded while menstruating. Recently in Bali, I was surprised to see signs outside temples frequently visited by tourists, warning me not to enter should I be on my period.

Like our fear of snakes, the fear of the female is deeply rooted because of its bloody, powerful connection to making life. The capacity to give birth – and throw offspring out into a cruel world full of figurative snakes – is both alluring and horrifying. One way of dealing with the fear of this power is to belittle female biology and violently punish women. Another is to create female monsters such as Lamia and Medusa and mythologically steal their powers.

This reaction has made things very difficult for women over history, even though it's not something we asked for, it's just what we got. I know many women who struggle with the clash between who 'they' are as people and the implications of their primitive biological functions. But women have still had to deal with the consequences: the male desire to control their power and the violence this incites. Women have been subjugated, their reproductive functions commodified and constrained. Even today in the West, where things are meant to be better than in many parts of the world, numerous US states have removed women's bodily autonomy by banning abortion.

The choice to carry a foetus – to bear life – no longer belongs to women: it belongs to the state.

Titty Twister

The Southern vampire horror film *From Dusk Till Dawn* (1996) contains one of my favourite snake woman scenes. The performer Santánico Pandemonium entrances hundreds of men in the Titty Twister strip club with her infamous 'snake dance'. She emerges onto the stage, the voiceover introducing her as 'mistress of the macabre, the epitome of evil, the most sinister woman who ever danced on the face of this Earth'. Like Lilith, she gyrates with a gigantic albino Python coiled around her, to the ominous, seductive beats of Tito and Tarantula's 'After Dark'. Santánico divests herself of the snake and strides across the tables, hips swivelling, ignoring the men below her. At the end of the table, she pours beer down her shin so it slides off her toes into Quentin Tarantino's open mouth. She swigs the beer and takes off her headdress to shake out her long dark hair.

To play Santánico, the actress Salma Hayek had to overcome her fear of snakes and the lack of choreography doing this scene – but that was what gave it its magic. There is no self-assured persona in the performance, she looks entirely natural, even innocent, totally connected to her power over the men around her. The confidence in the buttery curves of her flesh and her dark eyes, the slightly wild flow of her improvised dancing – balanced by a tinge of fear at the snake – are mesmerising. Though it was not rehearsed, there is nothing accidental in the scene.

Immediately after the performance, all hell breaks loose in the Titty Twister. Santánico and her minions turn into bloodthirsty vampires. The entrancing snake goddess becomes the queen of death. Having ogled at these hypnotising monsters, the men are suddenly licensed to kill them gruesomely with guns and stakes. It's certainly one way to deal with the disruptive, unsettling power of female sexuality.

Like the vampires in the Titty Twister, the snake women are deceptively attractive but dangerous up close. They might be temptation personified: Lilith was full of sensuous beauty though in cahoots with the devil; Eve was naked and angelic even as she caused the Fall. William Shakespeare complained about this in Sonnet 93:

> How like Eve's apple doth thy beauty grow,
> If thy sweet virtue answer not thy show!

For Shakespeare, female beauty is a dangerous, forbidden fruit, laced with sin. Some snake women were made into monsters by envious females as punishment for this natural appeal: the pretty maiden Medusa was made into a Gorgon by Athena; and the beautiful queen Lamia was turned into a monster by Zeus's jealous wife, Hera. Similarly, the Northern European folkloric fairy Mélusine underwent a horrible transformation from beauty to snake-hybrid as a punishment from her mother. The monstrous forms into which these women were twisted were really the aggression incited by their seductive charms.[19]

Even worse, victims could be enticed in with beauty, only to find a deadly horror underneath. In *Paradise Lost*, John Milton described the nymph-monster guarding the gates of hell:

> Seemed a woman to the waist, and fair,
> But ended foul in many a scaly fold
> Voluminous and vast, a serpent armed
> With mortal sting.[20]

Half-snakes such as Lamia, Echidna or Milton's monstrous nymph were often depicted as beautiful down to the waist, while really being bloodthirsty succubi. Their phallic tails even mock the male potency that might be drawn to them. In Keats' poem 'Lamia', she has hidden her serpent half using magic and is about to marry a comely young man. Her true nature as 'some demon's mistress' with a serpent tail is revealed by his possessive tutor, Apollodorus, and Lamia is chased off. The terrible power of female sexuality couldn't be given free rein. And it was terrible indeed: in the early twentieth century, Freud wrote 'Medusa's Head', a short essay describing the Gorgon as a symbolic 'castrating mother', who could remove all agency, rendering a man simultaneously stiff and helpless, transfixed and repelled. Priapism and impotence are not a pleasant combination.[21]

You don't have to ferret around on the internet today for long to find places thick with the fear of female allure, either – if in less erudite forms. On message boards and social media comments, women are both idealised and degraded for their sexual appeal and lack of appeal; for their sexual availability and sexual reservation. It's ironic that sexual selection and cultural norms over thousands of years have encouraged the aspects of women that create this problematic attraction: curves, makeup, perfume, dresses, cheekbones, lingerie, smooth skin, soft voices, lip fillers – you name it. Ordinary women have been shadowed by these dark mythic counterparts and the aggressive urges that created them, unable to disentangle themselves from the damn snakes.

Medusa's revenge

Mutilated and abused, the snake women have done awful things for sexual politics over history. Sadly, the anxieties that created them are so deeply rooted that they are not going away any time soon. The more the basic facts of life such as sex and unfulfilled desire, birth and death, are denied, the more terrifying and monstrous they become. As Joseph Campbell commented: 'Mother nature, mother Eve, Mother-Mistress-of-the-World is there to be dealt with all the time, and the more sternly she is cut down, the more frightening will her Gorgoneum be'.

Angela Giallongo has a suggestion: 'We must shake off the symbols we have inherited from patriarchal society'. The degrading image of sin and the snake needs to be subverted, to elevate the creative female force again. It is happening. Having been trashed through liturgical history, Lilith and Eve have been given different personas today. Lilith's defiance and Eve's disobedience have been reworked into acts of independence and self-determination. They have become the first feminists, opening Adam's complacent eyes to the realities of adult life. While he just wanted to kick back and garden Eden, like a teenage boy playing video games, they insisted on getting on with life. Lilith has been rescued from arcane folklore and is now the figurehead of neo-pagan organisations such as the Lilith Society. She's also the namesake of an independent Jewish feminist magazine.

Some writers have reworked these monstrous characters, wresting the male-dominated mythology round to a different perspective. Recent novels such as Madeline Miller's *Circe* (2018), Natalie Haynes's *Stoneblind* (2022) or Nikki Marmery's *Lilith* (2023) give these snake women inner worlds, detangling them from the snakes. They turn them from monstrous objects into characters with psychological depth, filled with rage at what has been done to them. In *Stoneblind*, Medusa is actually largely human, seen as monstrous by her monster family. Haynes conveys the full force of the male brutality that is meted out on Medusa and other female characters – dispensing with all the shimmering clouds and animal guises that mask it in traditional versions. These rewrites put the women back at the centre of the stories, pushing back against centuries of patriarchal storytelling.

In 2020, a contentious statue was installed in the park facing the New York County Criminal Court: *Medusa with the Head of Perseus*, by the Argentine-Italian artist Luciano Garbati. It is a response to Benvenuto Cellini's *Perseus with the Head of Medusa* (1545–54) in the Piazza della Signoria in Florence, Italy. Garbati sculpted an athletic woman staring out darkly from under her sideswept serpentine 'do'. She holds a blade and the severed head of a dismayed-looking Perseus. It was meant to be a symbol of triumph over rape culture, in the wake of the Harvey Weinstein trial. But, of course, it angered many people: the MeToo movement, which had been started by a Black woman, was commemorated with a white male artist getting a commission to represent a European myth.

There were other problems with Garbati's sculpture, from a feminist perspective. Turning the violence back on men using a sword, a masculine symbol of power, was probably not what Giallongo means by 'shaking off patriarchal symbols'. Instead, the sculpture seemingly embraced what it was supposed to counteract: if the snake women are the projection of male aggression and fear of women, a statue of Medusa with a severed man's head just reinforces the image of a monster who deserves a violent end. Medusa is prettier, slimmer and lacking pubic hair – but she's still terrible. Nothing changes.

It's a tricky business. The long primate relationship with the fruit and snakes in the tree of life is difficult to unpick. Separating the power of creating life from all of its messy implications – from death to conflict over who controls sex – is impossible. The fear and envy that result are what make the snake women such potent monsters. As historian Tom Holland argues in *Dominion: The Making of the Western Mind* (2019), the myths of Christianity that so damned women still infuse the Western worldview, even in an increasingly secular society. And we certainly cannot escape our primate roots. So what do we do? We can enjoy hollow triumphs by subverting the hierarchy of power and violence, as in Garbati's *Medusa*. Or, like the trendy feminist mythological retellings, we can humanise the characters one by one.

The other, daunting, option is to hold Medusa's gaze, full of power and death. We could contemplate the snake and the apple with Eve, accepting them both and all that comes with them. We might forgive Fallen Nature her sins, and, as we will think about in the next chapter, heal our relationship with wildness. If we can welcome the messy difficulties that are part of being flesh-and-blood animals, the face of the Gorgon might become less frightening. We could turn the snake women into goddesses again.[22]

Grendel

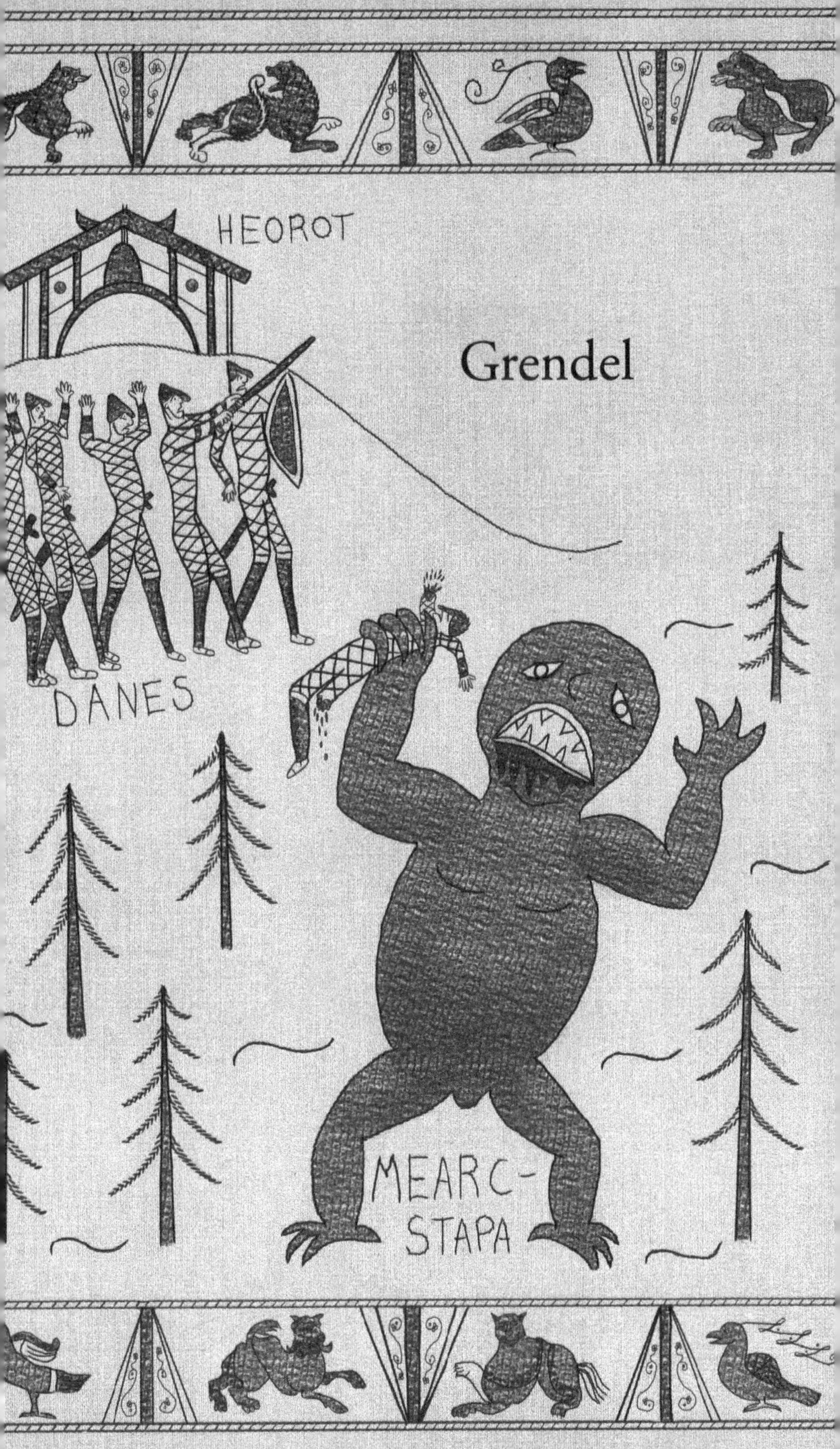

Chapter 5

'... this thing of darkness I
Acknowledge mine'
William Shakespeare

Ever since we started to draw boundaries around 'human places' to keep the wild out, we have feared that the wilderness might try to claim back its territory. Our imaginations have turned these fears into brutish, hairy monster-men that threaten the civilised order we build around ourselves. Green men and wildlings, fauns and satyrs, vagabonds and woodwoses have long been believed to inhabit the tangled, murky places where civilisation can't reach. They are the mythic remnants of the wilderness outside and the wildness inside us. One of these beings lurks in the archives of the British Library in London, on parchments containing the Old English poem *Beowulf*, written around the late tenth or early eleventh century. His name was Grendel, and he lived in a swamp-mired cave with his mother, a nameless creature as horrible and malformed as he was. He has had many different guises over the thousand or so years since the story of his death was recorded. Grendels and their kin can tell us a lot about our relationship with wildness, and how we have tried to suppress it in ourselves by throwing it out into wilderness. They also have a lot to show us about the dangers of pushing wildness away. But first, let's hear Grendel's original story.

In sixth-century Denmark, King Hrothgar ruled from the glittering mead-hall of Heorot. It was the resplendent heart of the land, filled with feasting and music each night. Warriors brandished foaming flagons of mead while telling stories of their impossible exploits. Their friends poked fun at their bragging. They all wanted to win admiring gazes from the ladies, who were dressed in fine robes with gold-plaited hair. But nobody drew the women's eyes as much as the king's minstrel, who wove entrancing tales of ancient glory with his poetry and music.

In contrast, Grendel and his mother were ugly, vicious and ravenous – all things which humans desperately try to pretend they are not. They were shunned from Heorot, living as outcasts in the surrounding untamed wasteland. But their lair was within earshot of the splendid hall and when the sound of the Danes carousing reached Grendel's ears, he became enraged. His fury boiled over until he galloped through the woods, giant feet crushing the ground beneath him. Grendel broke into the timbered hall and wreaked blood-soaked destruction on Heorot. He smashed men's bodies and gorged himself on human flesh as the people fled in terror. These sudden, brutal onslaughts happened again and again for many years. Nobody could stop him, no matter how brave the warrior or how sturdy his armour. Grendel was simply too strong and too violent.

One day, a hero arrived in a boat full of soldiers – Beowulf, prince of the Geats. In the feasting hall that night, Beowulf told stories of his great achievements – raiding troll nests, slaying enemies and an epic swimming race through monster-infested waters. Not everyone believed him, but King Hrothgar was overjoyed at the thought that the night terror might soon be over. It was a marvel that there were any Danes left to save by that point.

Beowulf lay awake after the feasting, ready to do as he'd promised: face Grendel in combat. In the dead of night, while everyone else slept in the darkened hall, Grendel attacked. He ripped men's limbs from their sockets and broke their screaming faces on the thick hall timbers. Only Beowulf stood his ground without armour or weapons, trusting to his own superhuman strength. After a bitter struggle, Beowulf managed to tear Grendel's branch-like arm off, splitting the shoulder at the seams, leaving the creature to run howling into the dark to die.

That was not the end of Beowulf's adventures, nor was it the end of Grendel. The poem – 3,000 lines of

Anglo-Saxon or Old English – goes on to relate Grendel's mother's ferocious revenge on Heorot. She made a swift nocturnal attack on the hall, killing the King's right-hand man, just as the right arm of her son had been torn off. Called to action again, Beowulf sought her out. He battled his way through the mire full of writhing beasts at the entrance to her watery lair. She was an even more dangerous adversary than her son, and fought Beowulf to the brink of defeat, dashing his weapon from his hands. As she bore triumphantly down on him, Beowulf managed to grasp the handle of a gigantic sword from her hoard and swung it through the air, slicing her neck from her shoulders. Finally, Beowulf cut the giant head from her son's body and carried it back as a trophy to Heorot, where he was showered in glory.

Beowulf returned to his own land to rule the Geats but he didn't find peace. Years later, an ancient dragon was stirred from its den when a thief stole a cup from its carefully guarded hoard. It took to the skies and 'swinged the land' with its flames, wreaking destruction on Beowulf's realm. He was the only one who would stand against it. But he went to the fight knowing the inevitable outcome. Beowulf battled with all his might, but he was mortally wounded just as he managed to kill this final, fateful monster.

The dismembered Grendel lay dormant in history for hundreds of years, until he was finally resuscitated. The *Beowulf* manuscript narrowly missed being destroyed in a fire in the eighteenth century. It was translated from

ENCHANTED CREATURES

Old English in the nineteenth century, revealing Grendel as a creature that haunted an imagined heroic past. He has developed well beyond this since, appearing in films, novels and comic books. One of these was the acclaimed *Grendel* by the American author John Gardner, who told the story as a darkly philosophical commentary from the monster's perspective – which we will look at later in this chapter. As we'll see, Grendel persisted because he's a being on the edge, between civilisations and between ages, between humanity and nature – the consequence of all the strife between them.[1]

I first encountered *Beowulf* while visiting the Edinburgh Fringe festival as a teenager. We went to see a one-man rendition of *Beowulf* in a stuffy, underground theatre. Rushing from show to show, we arrived late and squeezed ourselves into some empty seats, raincoats rustling. Just as I was attempting to remove my extra layers with minimal disruption, I was frozen by a sudden 'SO!' from the stage. A single syllable belted out across the space: the opening to Seamus Heaney's translation of *Beowulf*. What followed was a feast of modernised Old English rolled out in lyrical Irish cadence. It felt like I was drinking the poem: rich, frothing and savoury. I fell in love with *Beowulf* that day. Not the heroic protagonist – who was too inscrutable – but the tapestry of the poem itself, and the raw human anxieties it depicts.

My father read J. R. R. Tolkien's books to me when I was a child, starting with *The Hobbit* (1937) and working our way up to *The Lord of the Rings* (1954). I would sit for hours in the crook of his arm, trying not to move, in case I disturbed the world he conjured for us. As he read, my father savoured the clipped consonants of the characters' names: Gimli, Gorgoroth, Mordul, Frodo – rolling his Rs neatly. I relished their ancient exoticism. I was entranced by the shining Elves and the bucolic land of the Hobbits, pinioned with horror at the roiling dark of the Balrog or Mordor. Smeagol was another kind of monster entirely, both despicable and terribly familiar. Revolting in his taste for raw flesh, his flapping wet hands and corpse-like pallor, he was also unnervingly easy to empathise with in his weakness and envy.

It was only years later that I understood Tolkien's immersion in Medieval texts and how he'd drawn from works such as *Beowulf* to build Middle Earth. He had used the mythology of Medieval Europe to build a new mythology for a war-torn Britain. These texts *look* like mirror images: both feature iconic treasures, magical swords and characters teetering between immorality and valour. They both have dragons and sea creatures guarding caverns. Shelob the spider in *Lord of the Rings* and Grendel's mother in *Beowulf* are both bloated monster-mothers. And both stories are haunted by a pitiable shadow creature – Grendel and Smeagol.

The heroes crushed between this rabble of monsters are a stark contrast, though. The statuesque Beowulf is nothing like the compact Hobbits – the real heroes of *Lord of the Rings*. They're a clue to the fact that, despite their similar ingredients, these are really two very different myths for very different times. Tolkien's world was being torn apart by the mechanised horrors of war. He fantasised the triumph of hairy-footed humanity over the twisted schemes of power-hungry rulers. *Beowulf* was written in a time before people had dominated the globe. The human realm was far less established, far less sure of itself – the wild was a dangerous place that encroached on a fragile society. The wildness of humans was not so far away, so separating humanity from brutishness was not simple. From these anxieties, Grendel was created. In the last chapter we delved into our fears of scaly Mother Nature. Here we'll look at how wild monster men have been used to eject the difficult, wild parts of ourselves from civilised life.

'Alien spirits'

Beowulf was written at the very end of the Anglo-Saxon period, before the Norman invasion swept across England in the late eleventh century. It's a cryptic window onto a distant world that still permeates into ours, not least through the Anglo-Saxon origins of many English words we use today, such as hammer, knife, winter, husband, name or truth. Some of these words resonate with our images of this past. The language of the poem offers a rich seam of insight into how the world was structured in the Anglo-Saxon mind, which was very different to how we structure ours.

Medievalist Jennifer Neville explores the Anglo-Saxon relationship with nature in *Beowulf* and other poetry. She suggests that the Anglo-Saxons had no definition of the 'natural world' as separate from humanity and the supernatural, as we do now. Monstrous and supernatural things were all part of nature – they were even expected. For the Anglo-Saxons, 'monsters' were beings that threatened social order by subverting human qualities. They were what humanity defined itself against. The name for criminals, *wearg*, was also applied to monsters, devils and evil spirits. At a time when society felt dangerously unsettled – fraught with Viking invasions, battles between neighbouring powers, the threat of social collapse – these distinctions were crucially important. Grendel-like beings were not only believable, they were also necessary.[2]

On the surface, the human and the non-human seem clearly divided in *Beowulf*. We are shown a bright ring of light and warmth set against the dark malevolence of pine forests. The hall of Heorot is homely and familiar, its peace maintained by King Hrothgar's power. Far away simmers the threat of marauding armies. But these are still part of the human world within the hall's timber beams, lined with weapons and shields. What surrounds the Danish stronghold is more dangerous: the untamed wilderness. It's full of awful things, like Grendel. He is everything Heorot does not want to be. Violent for violence's sake, Grendel brings death without the quest for glory to justify it. He is a 'dark death-shadow' that threatens everyone, unfettered by law or allegiance.

Just how 'monstrous' are Grendel and his mother really, though? They are almost-humans, *mearcstapa* or 'boundary-walkers' that stalk the marshy lands around Heorot. The details of their shapes and forms are indistinct. Grendel's mother is 'like a woman' and he has 'the shape of a man' of vast size and strength. This indistinctness is important, as it means the natures of Grendel and his mother have to be inferred from how they are *perceived*: bloodthirsty outsiders, something like humans but also something apart. They're inhuman because the social contracts of valour and honour, which keep the peace in Heorot, do not matter one bit to them. Their dangerous characters *imply* their horrible forms, but we never really know.

Grendel's violence is also incited by his exclusion. He was driven by one of the most common human emotions – envy. He's much like the slave Caliban in William Shakespeare's *The Tempest* (1610–11). Caliban tells of his mistreatment and displacement by the magician Prospero: 'This island's mine by Sycorax, my mother, / Which thou tak'st from me. / When thou cam'st first / Thou strok'st me and made much of me'. He showed Prospero the fruitful secrets of the wild isle and was betrayed, his birth-right taken from him. So, Caliban plots his revenge, attempting to rape Prospero's daughter and overthrow him at the first chance he gets. Just how much Caliban is actually a 'monster' is up to our imagination and the creative licence of theatre directors. From what Shakespeare tells us, it could be nothing more than racial difference, poor personal hygiene, or just being pretty ugly.[3]

The thing is, the Grendels and Calibans and other pariahs are universal problems. These marginalised figures are saddled with the beastly bits of humanity, allowing them to be pushed away. Being scapegoats is what really makes them monsters. Grendel is the destructive, feral aggression lurking inside the human mind that could erupt unexpectedly. In a society where order was tenuous, these elements of human nature were far too threatening. They were turned into the 'other' – not us, not how *we* behave. Especially the cannibalism. So the Anglo-Saxon imagination dumped these disruptive characters out on the margins, turning them into bad beings whose natural habitat was a dank lair.

The precise boundaries between what is socially acceptable and what is unacceptable aren't as clear in *Beowulf* as they seem at first glance, either. *Beowulf* was written in a border-time between two opposing cultures. The brutality and grandeur of Germanic warrior culture, with its trademark pillaging and looting, loomed in the background of a more settled, pastoral existence under a Christian God. *Beowulf* is written by a Christian author, but set in these bad old glory days. The tension between these two value systems pulsates through the poem. The hero is in many ways just as violent as his opponent in his quest for bloody victory. But he's excused because he is protecting the citadel. Grendel is the dark underbelly of this old violent way of being, pushed out to exist in the wilderness with the other beasts. He's a fall-guy for an archaic value system in a new time of Christian meekness and humility in which *Beowulf* was written.

The Christian author marks Grendel and his mother with a Biblical brand, making it clear they are the 'wrong sort'. The pair are said to come from a lineage of sin as 'descendants of Cain'. Cain and his brother Abel were the first sons of Adam and Eve in the Old Testament. Snubbed by God, Cain killed his favoured brother out of envy, and was forever cursed for his crime: the very first human to be born, the first to commit murder and the first to be an outcast. He was thought by some theologians to have sired a race of giants of which Grendel and his mother are the successors. This lineage sets these antisocial monsters up as rebels against God's law that try to bring the creation of Heorot back to dust and ashes.[4]

Of course, the only way most of us can access *Beowulf* these days is through translations – few people have time to learn Old English. Christine Alfano, Professor of Writing at Stanford University, points out that we're getting the story through the prism of translators' own perspectives. And these have done some sly things to these figures. You might think that with the modern tendency to humanise outcasts – to undo 'othering' – an olive branch might have been offered to Grendel and his mother. They might have been made more relatable by later translators. But quite the opposite has happened: they often present Grendel and his mother more monstrously than older ones do. Though he is described as a 'sorrowful' man in the original poem, that 'wretchedly trod the path of exile in the form of a man', Grendel's human status is stripped from him in many modern translations. A poignant example of this is the portrayal of Grendel's sounds. The word *sweg* is used for his expressions of pain, the same used to describe the songs sung in Heorot. Grendel makes a heart-wrenching *gryeleop* or 'horror-song' as he dies. Some new translations turn these sounds into meaningless, bestial noises. Heaney, for example, translated Grendel's 'howl of the loser' and an 'extraordinary wail' into a horrible 'hell-surf keening his wounds'.

Similarly, whereas some popular modern translations introduce Grendel's mother as a 'monster woman', 'monstrous ogress' or 'witch of the sea', the Old English words on which these phrases are based are *ides*, which actually means 'lady', and *aegcaelwif*, meaning 'warrior woman'. Grendel's mother deserves some sympathy, perhaps, as she only attacks Heorot after the death of her son. She could be seen as acting well within the rules of this warrior society, exacting the heroic revenge of a warrior-woman, but she's not given any leeway. Alfano argues that by 'stripping Grendel's mother of her humanity, translators transform an avenging mother into a bloodthirsty monster'. As Marina Warner has described, we now imagine Grendel's mother as a monster lurking 'in her bloody lacustrine vaults'.[5]

Translations into film can take even more liberties, turning even an unappealing hag like Grendel's mother into a deadly sex object. In the 2008 film *Beowulf*, directed by Robert Zemeckis, Grendel's mother is played by Angelina Jolie. The sinuous, golden temptress seduces the kings and heroes of Heorot to produce malformed, violent offspring. She's the siren call of lust and greed which consumes the society from within. These modern overlays on the Anglo-Saxon poem show how malleable these monsters are, and hint at something about our own worldview. We *think* the monsters are further away from us than the Anglo-Saxons did, that they're so alien that they have no shred of humanity in them at all. We might be mistaken.

No gods, just monsters

When reading a tale of monster-slaying, it's usual to root for the hero. The satisfying narrative arc of peril, struggle and prevail is what we expect. But it's not so simple with *Beowulf*. The hero is not especially charismatic – a mercenary full of pomp and swagger who sets himself apart from other people – finally worsted by a dragon that erupts like a bat out of hell. Above all, the story is not really about the hero. The shadow of Grendel and his mother looms large, even after they're dead. They're the crux of everything.

Tolkien gave a seminal lecture about *Beowulf* in 1936 entitled 'The Monsters and the Critics'. It shook the foundations of *Beowulf* scholarship: he told the critics they had been doing it all wrong. They had been shying away from the monsters, unsure of what to do with them. The critics wanted more of the high-brow sagas and less of the beasts, *thank you*. Another heavyweight of fantasy and science fiction literature, Ursula le Guin, has pointed out that 'most critics are afraid of dragons'. This is understandable, as monstrous creatures are daunting, even in an intellectual way. I have had to mentally wrestle with all of the monsters I've written about over the years. They refuse to fit neatly into any structure, so it can be very hard to know how to handle them. But that's also part of their allure.

For Tolkien, 'the monsters are not an inexplicable blunder of taste; they are essential'. Without them, there would simply be nothing to do except have armour-clad squabbles over patches of land. The monsters are the core of *Beowulf* – the epic action is all a *reaction* to monsters. Tolkien pointed out that, without them, we wouldn't need the heroes, or a story in the first place. Beowulf answers the monsters' grisly call to arms from all the way across the northern seas. The dragon is not the reason Beowulf is there, he's Beowulf's own personal Grim Reaper. Beowulf is really there to save Heorot from its own darkness.

The monsters also define the heroes that are needed. In the case of Grendel, only another outsider can match him: someone from an alien land with super-human abilities, who will venture into the wild alone. Beowulf and his monster are mirror images of each other. Both hero and monster are described as *aglæca* or 'fearsome opponents', Grendel 'bigger than any man', just like Beowulf. The impossibly strong grip that allows Beowulf to strike mortal fear into Grendel and rip his arm off is also one of Grendel's special powers. As Grendel invades the hall of the Danes to slay them, so Beowulf ventures into Grendel's mother's hall and dismembers her son's body. If you have a monster from an ancient chaotic past, you need a hero who fights on those terms, who thinks it's better to 'avenge dear ones than to indulge in mourning'. Similarly, the despicable Gollum and innocent Frodo in *Lord of the Rings* are both Hobbit creatures with an irrepressible attraction to gold jewellery. The monsters emerge at the fringes of society, and the hero is poetically conjured as their counterweight, willing or reluctant.

One line in Tolkien's lecture stuck with me in particular: 'the monsters do not depart, whether the gods go or come'. That captures the essence of monsters like Grendel. We create both gods and monsters, but we're a lot closer to the monsters – the beastly, dark elements of ourselves which we try and fail to get rid of. *Beowulf* faces this bleak fact head-on. Though it's a story written by a Christian author about a pagan past, there is no real divinity in the world of *Beowulf*. The Christian God is mentioned many times, off-handedly, and the Northern Pagan gods are entirely absent. It's a contrast to stories such as St George and the Dragon from the Christian canon, where the Saint is an agent of God slaying the beast of the Devil, giving hope of divine salvation. Or the stories from the Arthurian legends – the knights go out *looking* for monsters to fight for God and King. In several Arthurian texts, the knights chase something called the Questing Beast, a snake-necked, leopard-bodied, deer-footed creature whose calls sound like a pack of baying hounds. When they try to stop the chase, it sickens from lack of attention, so the knights nurse the beast back to health so they can continue the sacred hunt.[6]

Grendel and his like are a different breed. They are infinite – there will always be monstrous outcasts to make trouble, whether or not a god or hero is there to battle them. Which is good for the sake of our entertainment but difficult for our relationships with ourselves and the wider world. In the godless world of *Beowulf*, a hero is the only hope of escape from the darkness that batters down the door. The fantasy of an ideal man-god set up to destroy the abject beast.

The monsters can't really be erased, though: they are the brute facts of humanity and they aren't going anywhere. As the Danes try to keep them out, these outcasts still enter violently, penetrating like nightmares. *Beowulf* is more like the godless world of modern horror books and films – from H. P. Lovecraft's lonely, ghoulish *Outsider* (1926), to the modern TV series *The Last of Us* (2023), in which a *Cordyceps* fungus infects humans, turning them into zombie-like creatures and decimating civilisation. Even today, we create monsters, from the wild and our wild selves. It raises the question: why have monsters been created from wildness?

ENCHANTED CREATURES

Fear of the wild

In the Mesopotamian *Epic of Gilgamesh*, the hero Gilgamesh and his hairy companion Enkidu go to fight the monster Humbaba, the guardian of a great Pine Forest. He was a gigantic, lion-headed beast with a thorny body, whose deathly mouth breathed fire and whose shout could bring floods pouring across the land. Patterns of snake-like entrails were etched across his face, in which the future could be read – like the guts of birds or sheep that were read for divination by temple priests. Gilgamesh and Enkidu tricked and decapitated Humbaba, putting his head in a sack. They felled wood from the Pine Forest and carried the timber away on the river waters. The wilderness was full of riches, but as a monster, it could be defeated and its bounty taken as the righteous spoils of war. Humbaba's savagery was not that of the wild, though. It was actually the projected aggression of the heroic humans going out to steal its bounty.[7]

We've had a complicated relationship with wilderness through most of our history – it's been a resource and a scourge, bountiful and untameable, the space that envelops human places. It both provides for us and reminds us that our creations can crumble into dust, to be reclaimed by the tangled bodies of other living things. Like the power of the seas, which we will explore in the next chapter, it reminds us of our fragility. This was what the mythical Adam and Eve faced when they were ejected from the benign space of Eden: they suddenly had to live off and live with the wilderness outside of the garden. They had to struggle with the environment, like other creatures, to survive.

Much of the wild inside ourselves is the aggression that we needed to exist in the natural world, as mammals competing with other beasts to live, using the dead tissues of other organisms for our food and protection. It has been a necessary part of being – and staying – alive. But it doesn't fit very well into what we have tried to become. Unfettered aggression and violence are obviously terrible for social life. And even worse in societies where there are rules and disparities in wealth. When these get too big, violence breaks out and erupts into riots or war. Funnelling this aggression into stylised and contained forms – boxing matches, football matches, shoot-em-up computer games – is one way of dealing with it. Another has been to pretend it is not part of us, but part of the wilderness we've built ourselves away from and the dangerous things that live there.[8]

'Wilderness' has subtly different meanings between places and times. For Anglo-Saxons, the 'wilderness' was the same as 'wasteland', land that was waste – unproductive and impossible to cultivate. Wilderness was distinct from the fertile places where humans could live and farm. It was where souls could be lost to the temptations of the Devil. This fed into European characterisations of distant places as barren 'wilderness lands' full of 'savages' or even monstrous beings – ripe to be conquered and turned productive by 'civilised man'. The boundaries between the animal and human were worryingly fluid, too. Medievalists Michael Bintley and Thomas Williams suggest that in many Medieval sources, 'the categories of beast and human are inextricably blurred'. Bintley highlights that beasts could be wild animals or 'sinful humans who act like beasts'. Humans who were violent, cruel and inhuman, moved further along the continuum towards beastliness. These porous lines were constantly negotiated and unclear.[9]

So, it makes sense that beastly figures deemed 'not-human' would be sent out to exist in places unfit for humans in imagination. When a fragile civility is inside and all else is wilderness, these boundaries have to be defended to reinforce the image of a safe and ordered space, where danger and brutality are suppressed. But that made the wild an even darker and more dangerous place, where Grendel and other 'border-steppers' existed. They were the dark threats of wildness that could burst in from outside or erupt from within at any moment. Exile made them all the more violent and terrible, as the enraged Grendel invades the firelit hall to mete out punishment for his exclusion.

These weren't just poetic monsters; they were very real in the Medieval imagination. Take the werewolf, for example. Human men who were 'lycanthropes' or *werwulf* in Old English, were literally thought to turn into bloodthirsty wolves on nights when there was a full moon. The idea went all the way back to Classical times. The thirteenth-century Lawyer, Gervase of Tilbury, wrote of a knight who had been wandering around in the wild, became deranged by fear and transformed into a wolf. He was saved by one of the few solutions to lycanthropy: cutting off the wolf's paw. Another man was reported to have been forced to roll around naked in a secluded sandpit once a month as a wolf, gnashing his teeth, to get it out of his system. During the sixteenth-century witch trials, plenty of men were convicted of being werewolves, though it amounted to only about 2 per cent of the number of women who were convicted of being witches. One way to eject an undesirable person from your community, usually a problematic peasant or beggar, could be to make the charge of devilish or beastly inhumanity. Animals could be slaughtered without moral qualms.[10]

The high season of werewolf trials in mainland Europe lasted all the way into the eighteenth century. The craze was set off by the case of Petr Stumpf in Cologne in 1589, who was accused by a farmer he supposedly attacked while in the shape of a wolf. The charges grew to include numerous murders, cannibalism and incest. Under sufficient torture, he admitted to all charges, in language that was oddly eloquent, given the circumstances. The conclusive proof used against him was that one of his hands was missing, just as the wolf's paw was reported to have been. The excruciating details of Stumpf's torture and execution were reproduced in illustrated broadsheets many times: they provided macabre reassurance that the threat had been thoroughly dealt with.

The eruption of wildness has been feared in many other cultures too. There is a devil of the Algonquian peoples of North America called the Wendigo. This emaciated spirit is the embodiment of malevolent winter hunger. During especially brutal winters, when food became extremely scarce, the spirit would possess starved victims and drive them into a cannibalistic rage, causing them to attack even their family and try to consume their flesh. The tough realities of the environment could press hard enough to peel away all layers of humanity. The ravening beast unleashed in their midst was not really a person, a friend or relative, it was another kind of thing: a monster.

During colonial struggles in nineteenth-century North America, a number of Algonquians were executed for cannibalism. 'Wendigo psychosis' was even a clinically recognised diagnosis for alleged cannibalistic instincts. It was used as a medical weapon by colonial powers, to dehumanise desperate Algonquians who were starving as a result of their oppression. In 2021, the Wendigo reached cinema screens in *Antlers*, produced by monster-master Guillermo del Toro. Unlike the traditional Wendigo, this new devil is generated by the environmental degradation from mining in northern Oregon, as well as drug abuse and social breakdown in the community. The spirit takes over the body of one of the local opioid addicts, consuming him until it erupts in a grisly crown of antlers from his viscera. A literal transformation – from human to beast – of a man consumed by addiction.[11]

William Golding's 1954 novel *Lord of the Flies* is a masterful study of how the beast inside can erupt and become a concrete enemy that must be destroyed. Written after the Second World War, a time when the full potential of human evil was globally visible, it follows a troop of schoolboys marooned on an island. Initially an idyll, the boys become increasingly feral as the island takes its toll and violent factions form. They are haunted by a 'Beast' they imagine lives in the dense forest and invades their nightmares.

One night, the boys see a strange, moving shape at the top of a hill and think it's the Beast watching them from afar, but are too terrified to look more closely. To ward off this threat, they ineptly kill a large sow and hack her head off, sticking it on top of a staff as an offering to the Beast. Wandering alone, one of the boys has an epileptic fit next to the fly-covered head and hallucinates it speaking to him as 'Lord of the Flies'. It is the devil incarnate, the violence inside them which is causing social breakdown on the island. He later comes across what they thought was the Beast: that mysterious moving shape was just the dead remains of a soldier animated by the wind filling his parachute. The boy runs back to the others and tries to tell them what he's found, but in their terror, they think he is the Beast coming to get them. They form a mob, stabbing him with wooden spears – until they realise his broken corpse is just that of a boy. But in that moment of frenzy, full of fear, he had become a scapegoat, sacrificed to absolve them of the darkness that overwhelmed them.

Ignoble brutes

Our monstering of animals hasn't necessarily been helped by a more scientific view of other organisms. Since the Enlightenment, we have become increasingly distanced from nature. The English novelist and critic John Berger wrote: 'The nineteenth century, in western Europe and North America, saw the beginning of a process, today being completed by twentieth century corporate capitalism, by which every tradition which has previously mediated between man and nature has been broken'. Rather than lessening the fear of the wild, it gave free rein to our old animosity towards other large predators. Like Humbaba, they became monsters that could be slain for resources, or even sport. They became the beasts and we became the gods. Unsurprisingly, it has been the beasts that have lost out as a result of this dysfunctional relationship. Wolves are long gone from much of Europe. In Britain, bounties on wolf heads saw their eradication by the eighteenth century. But there have been more recent tragedies in which predatory animals have been blamed for infringing on humans.

When we demonise a large mammal, the species won't last long. The thylacine or Tasmanian tiger was a marsupial predator that lived only in Tasmania by the nineteenth century. It had a strange look to it: part feline, part canine, with long narrow jaws that could open extraordinarily wide. It reared its young in a pouch, like the other marsupial mammals of Australasia. The thylacine's mistake was living where people wanted to farm sheep in nineteenth-century Tasmania. The settler population cast thylacines as sheep-killers. They were depicted as sneaking, rat-like creatures in images, crouching behind bushes to jump out at unsuspecting flocks. Thylacines were called 'ignoble brutes' that 'fed on Crown lands', like a rebel army defying regal power. War had to be waged.

In 1888, a bounty scheme was initiated and a bloodbath ensued. Thousands of animals were killed for sport and cash. When there were only a few left, the bounty was stopped. But it was too late: the last photographed individual died in Hobart Zoo in 1930. A few may have persisted like ghosts in the wilds of Tasmania for decades after, of which there were only ever tenuous, tantalising glimpses. All we have left of the thylacine now is a scattering of museum specimens and some poignant film footage of the last few zoo animals pacing around in their cages.

Thylacines were never sheep hunters, though. They actually had a relatively weak bite: they were simply the scapegoats for farmers' anxieties. Exterminating animal 'enemies' is still our knee-jerk reaction to ecological competition, as the widespread badger culls in the UK from 2019 demonstrated. Sadly, as long as we bulldoze over every possible wild space with human activity, clashes between humans and other large mammals will worsen, and other mammals will lose out.[12]

Sometimes the efforts to keep the wild out can make places even less habitable for humans too. The Dingo Barrier Fence in Australia is the longest fence ever built.

It is 5,614 kilometres of wire laid down to keep dingoes out of sheep-grazing areas in the south-east of the country – an idea as crazy as a wall to block the Mexico–US border. It is moderately good at keeping dingoes out, but it's even better at protecting kangaroos. Unfettered by predation, kangaroo populations have boomed. They have stripped the natural vegetation to such a degree that the new semi-desert can be seen from space. Alongside the effects of climate change, the ecosystem is now in serious trouble. Not only that, but the increased kangaroo population and farmers poisoning dingoes near the fence has lessened competition for food among dingoes. A race of 'super dingoes' that are larger and more aggressive is developing – we've bred the exaggerated 'sheep killers' that were originally imagined. Psychological suppression breeds monsters, but it seems that pest control can too.[13]

Attitudes towards wilderness have changed in recent times and there has been a softening to wild things. The wild has been a romantic notion since the nineteenth century, when the likes of Henry David Thoreau struck out to seek sublime experiences in remote places. But places untouched and unblemished by human activity are becoming increasingly scarce. The environmental historian Bill Cronon suggests that there is no real wilderness left, no land left untouched by human action – what we now see as wilderness is a fantasy of our own making. We live in a world where raw nature has become a broken creature backed into a corner. Wilderness used to be the realm of danger and moral jeopardy, now it is where we imagine that we can find redemption from a soulless world. We idealise the shreds of wildness in ourselves – rock songs bellow out fantasies of returning to an animal freedom, people go on survival courses or follow Paleo diets – trying to get in touch with the raw intensity of our animal beings that are dulled by technology and routine. We like flirting with ideas of the wild.[14]

Now that we've done our worst to wilderness, we're more protective of what's left of it: we long for it. At least we say we do – you wouldn't necessarily assume it from how we've carried on behaving on a large scale. The wilderness monsters that inhabit spaces outside of human epicentres are no longer outcasts, they have been transformed into more benign guardians of the wild places. In some depictions, Grendel has also been transformed: the Anglo-Saxon monster has become a watchman lamenting the ravaged wild.

Brute existents

Like any creature that survives in nature, Grendel is an adaptable beast. In the century and a half since *Beowulf* was translated, he has been remade many times, with varying success. The monster of John Gardner's 1971 novel *Grendel* has been one of the most powerful incarnations, cutting to the quick of modern anxieties most cleanly. Gardner put the reader right inside the mind of the monster through the colourful inner dialogue he gives Grendel. It's a stark contrast to his non-verbal, consuming monster-mother. She usually just lurks, bloated and sluggish, in her cave. Her son roams the forests alone, and we watch with Grendel from the shadows of the pine woods as the forests are cut back and tamed for the building of human settlements. We see the destruction of Grendel's world by humans and his realisation that he's damned to be the brute they fear.

Gardner was writing in the 1960s, on the cusp of a time when our awareness of the ecological damage we could do was coming to the fore. In Grendel's world, nature is being beaten back and divided as humans take over the landscape. Though humanised, he is still quite beast-like, deeply entangled with the woods and the creatures within it: we're also watching the destruction of nature through the eyes of a wild animal. We meet cowardly, aggressive Danes as they venture from their halls, fell trees and erect buildings. We see their needlessly bloody battles, that appear 'idiotic' to Grendel. He knows of his own mortality and vulnerability, that the Danes could kill him. We feel the pain of his exclusion from the ring of fire-light as he listens longingly to heroic mead-hall songs and tales of transcendent beauty. He's just like Mary Shelley's monster in *Frankenstein* (1818), who listens in wonder to a family speaking avidly with each other about subjects he had never dreamed of before. Only when he realises that he is rejected by everyone does Frankenstein's monster turn to vengeance and violence.[15]

Grendel wants to know what his role in the world is, why the world is as it is. Racked with existential pain, he seeks out the dragon – a mercenary, sardonic beast with total knowledge of past and future. Grendel asks the dragon what his meaning is and is met with a soul-destroying answer: 'You are, so to speak, the brute existent by which they learn to define themselves. The exile, captivity, death they shrink from – the blunt facts of their mortality, their abandonment – that's what you make them recognise, embrace! You *are* mankind, or man's condition'. It's only with a little perspective that we realise that this dragon is part of Grendel's *own* mind. It is a fantasy figure of 'alienation, nihilism and chaos', as Gardner's biographer described it.

Grendel gives up all hope of beauty and acceptance. He becomes a creature of the night, abandoning his humanity. He turns to wilful, meaningless violence, gorging on death: 'I eat and laugh and eat until I can barely walk'. Like Lucifer in John Milton's *Paradise Lost* (1667), with his mantra: 'evil be thou my good', Grendel drives the boundaries of his horror further and further, almost killing the beautiful queen of Heorot in the 'ultimate act of nihilism'.

Gardner's novel is a brilliant inversion. Grendel is no longer a monster we cannot see clearly; he is the protagonist with whom we identify. He is also a philosophical experiment; Gardner makes Grendel into the creature we might all become if nothing mattered, if the joyful, creative, vibrant side of our humanity were extinguished. In a land where nature is being destroyed and Grendel has no access to the human world, he seeks something to give him purpose. So he self-actualises with his brutality, just as Beowulf self-styles with heroism. His violence is no kneejerk reaction, it is a bid to define himself: 'I had to *become* something, as if born again . . . I was Grendel, Ruiner of Meadhalls, Wrecker of Kings!'

This is not mindless destruction, but a self-conscious evil. Grendel is acutely aware of the pointlessness of his venture. As heroes are made by battling monsters, the monster needs victims to terrorise: 'What will we call the Hrothgar-Wrecker when Hrothgar is wrecked?' In the wake of his destruction, he sees that he's just a 'pointless ridiculous monster crouched in the shadows, stinking of dead men, murdered children, martyred cows'. Rather than face his loss and sadness, he chooses nihilism to relieve the 'worst pain' of tedium in a meaningless life. His role does not fulfil him but he sees no other choice. Grendel dies purely by mishap, slipping and falling into Beowulf's grasp. His final words, 'Poor Grendel's had an accident, so may you all', are a curse, flinging the bleak conclusion of this path at the reader. Sadly, by strange circumstance, the author met a similarly accidental end, dying in a motorcycle crash in his fifties. It was one of many ways in which his life echoed his monster.[16]

Gardner intensely disliked nihilism. Most of his work is laced with messages about the power of love and the importance of life: 'the true measure of human adaptability is man's power to find, despite overwhelming arguments, something in himself to love'. Gardner created a Grendel that existed in a way against which he could positively define his own life. He made a creature that saw no goodness in the human world, so threw himself into darkness. His Grendel is a monster so easy to understand today, following a common trajectory in the disconnected modern technoverse. Interacting with the world through screens drives many people to dark places and terrible things, just to be or to feel *something*. When the digital limelight dominates over connection with other living beings, those kept out in the dark will break in violently. In a life alienated from nature, stripped of the essential joys and fears of existence and the vivifying thrill of immersion in the real world, it can be hard to grasp at meaning.

Grendel has become a monster for a time in which nature is being decimated by humans, and human nature is being stripped away. He is a warning: we must not be the idiotic Danes that cut down forests and drain the land to try to keep wildness at bay. Rather, we must accept the Grendels and other feral things – the Minotaurs and the Medusas – back into our world. If we acknowledge our beastly parts and befriend them, then they'll not be so terrible. If we make them things we can live with, we might heal our relationships with wildness and our wild selves. Though as we will see in the next chapter, this is difficult for us, because we fear being insignificant beings in the vastness of a turbulent and inhospitable wild.

Leviathans

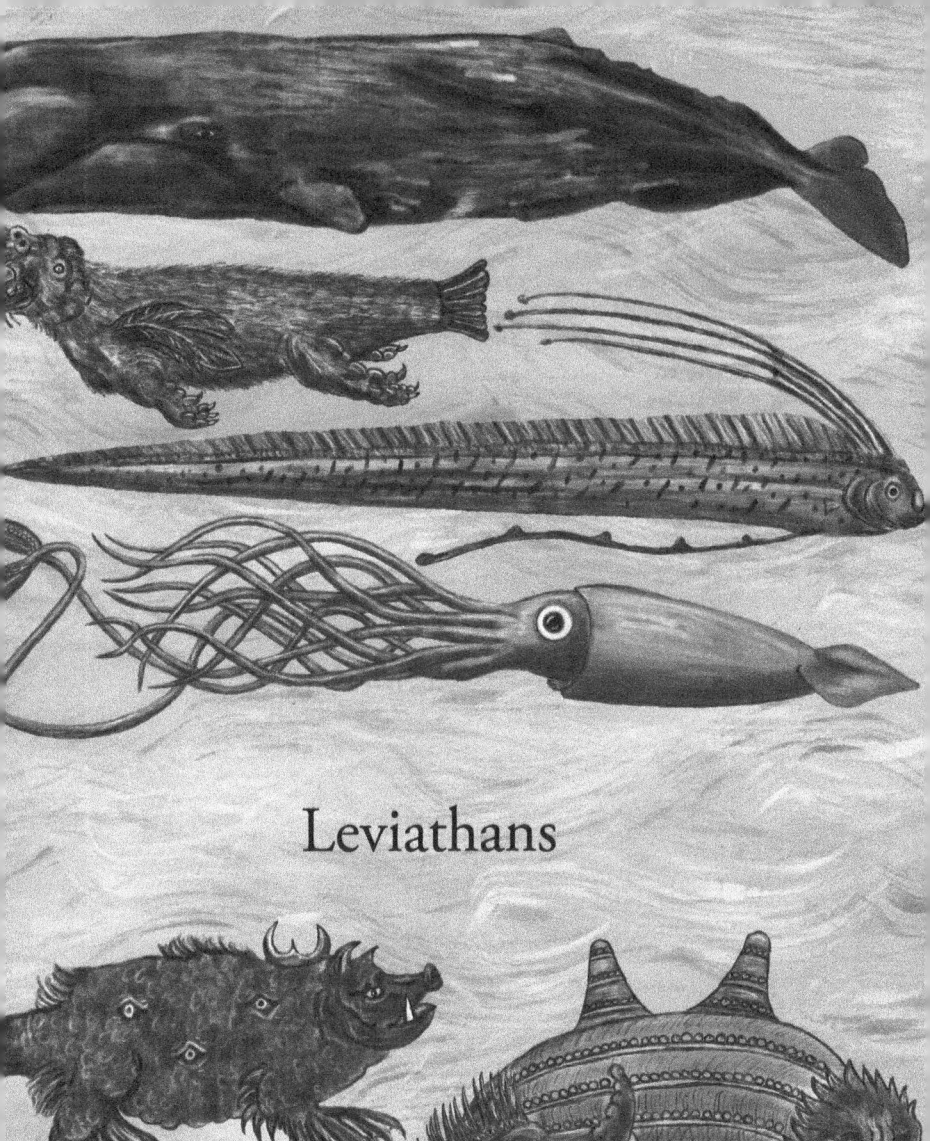

Chapter 6

'An ocean without its unnamed monsters would be like a completely dreamless sleep'
John Steinbeck

The *morse*

In 1519, an artist painted a sea monster on the wall of the town hall of Strasbourg. It was a strange creature, with four stubby legs and a long seal-like body ending in a fishy tail. Fins draped from each shoulder and two extraordinarily long front teeth extended from its hairy muzzle. Next to the mural was written a eulogy, the creature's lament for an ill-spent life:

In Norway they call me the 'walrus',
But I am 'cetus dentatus'.
My Wife is called Balaena . . .
. . . I prowled through the cold sea
To battle and fight is nothing to me,
One finds many thousands of my comrades . . .
. . . Had I lived my life to the full
I would not have devoted it to whales.
The bishop of Nidaros had me stabbed on the shore
The Pope Leo had my head sent
To Rome where many men saw me.

This was a melancholic and self-reflective monster, it seems. The artist probably based the mural on the head of an animal which was in transit through Strasbourg, on its way to the Vatican. The head came from a *cetus dentatus* or 'toothed whale' – what we would call a walrus. It had been sent by Bishop Walkendorf in Norway to Pope Leo X as an unusual gift, to charm him. It was a sample of Northern fauna, totally unlike anything that could be found in Southern Europe, and the only walrus head that we know of to have been taken south in the early sixteenth century. The head was probably kept in salt to stop it from rotting but we don't know what happened to it once it arrived in Rome. In a way, this gift was the grisly equivalent of an exotic bunch of flowers: striking and ultimately destined for the bin.[1]

Walruses were not always the familiar beasts they are to us today. During my PhD I spent an indecent amount of time hunting them through the travel accounts and natural histories of the fifteenth and sixteenth centuries. I became something of a historical walrus expert – an ambition I hadn't known I'd had. I found they had a strange kind of history. Walrus products had been traded down to Europe for centuries from the Arctic, but almost nobody further south had seen a whole one or knew what they were. Walruses did sometimes lounge around on the North Sea coasts and a lost walrus had made its way into the Thames in 1456. This was noted as a 'mors maryne' in the *Chronycles of Englond*, along with an errant swordfish and a couple of whales. Aside from that, though, they were beasts that were only ever encountered in pieces – as the bone, ivory, blubber and skin from 'grete fische' from the north.[2]

To see a whole walrus head, leering up white-eyed and tusked from a salt-filled crate, would have been quite a sight. A bit like receiving a unicorn or an elephant's head in the mail. Walruses are not petit animals – adults reach nearly four metres long. The German artist Albrecht Dürer made an ink drawing of a walrus head in 1521 which is still well known today and might have been the head sent by Bishop Walkendorf. He gave the animal plenty of animated, hairy detail and a doleful expression, as if it might indeed have been lamenting its dalliances with whales.[3]

It is possible that Bishop Walkendorf sent the walrus head to the Vatican at the request of the Swedish ecclesiast Olaus Magnus. He had an agenda: disturbed by the growing Protestant voices in Scandinavia, Magnus wanted reinforcement from the Catholic Church to fend them off. However, the powers in Rome saw the far north as a backwater, and weren't very concerned about the threats from Protestantism there: they had other priorities. The Vatican did little to stop the Swedish Reformation in the 1520s, which left Magnus and his brother – who were devout Catholics – exiled from Sweden, their belongings confiscated.[4]

So, Magnus went on a marketing mission. He wanted to present the North as a region of wonders and marvels at the very edge of the known world – one that was worth paying attention to. Magnus produced the first map of the Arctic, the *Carta Marina*, in 1539, in which the seas were filled with writhing monsters and violent whirlpools. On the land, he pictured flesh-eating Scricfinns, magicians, flaming volcanoes and myriad other wonders. He described each of these in his accompanying book *Historia de Gentibus Septentrionalibus* or 'The History of the Northern Peoples' (1555). Magnus wanted to portray these fantastical things in a way that would resonate with a Catholic audience. And what better way to catch an audience's attention, than to present their own fanciful ideas about the North back to them in an amplified form? Magnus was selling myths back to their makers.

One of the marvels that Magnus featured was the fearsome *morse*, a monster-walrus. It was a vast sea creature whose head was fringed in thick whiskers and boar-like tusks. It was quite ferocious, according to Magnus: 'To the far north, on the coast of Norway, there lives a mighty creature, as big as an elephant, called the walrus or morse, perhaps so named for its sharp bite; for if it glimpses a man on the seashore and can catch him, it jumps on him swiftly, rends him with its teeth, and kills him in an instant'.

The *morse* had strange sleeping habits. Magnus described how they would climb the cliffs using their tusks like ice picks. When they felt drowsy after some grazing, they would hang from the rock using their tusks as anchors. Magnus had gathered this from other books, including Albertus Magnus's *De Animalibus*. Written in the thirteenth century, it described how fishermen took advantage of the walruses' narcolepsy:

> a fisherman, coming close, separates as much of its skin as he can from the blubber near its tail. He passes a strong rope through the part he has loosened and he then ties the ropes to rings fixed into a mountain or to very strong stakes or trees. Aroused, the fish [the walrus], as it tries to escape, draws off its skin from its tail down along its back and head and leaves it behind . . . it is captured in a weakened state, either swimming bloodless in the water or lying half-alive on the shore . . .

Being a *morse* was a dangerous game, even if you were a ferocious, bloodthirsty monster. Just by taking a nap you risked being ambushed into flaying yourself. Given this marvellous background, it's no surprise that walrus products were believed to have magical properties in Europe. Walrus leather was said to be impossibly strong, and walrus ivory was used as 'unicorn horn' – a panacea for all ills. Walruses were dangerous and valuable quarry.

The case of the walrus raises the question: why have sea beasts so often become supernatural monsters? What is it about the sea and its giants that has always played on our imaginations, even today?[5]

Bounty and terror

We have an intense relationship with water. Our bodies are two-thirds water – it's the solvent of life on Earth, the medium in which our cells control fine-tuned networks of enzymatic reactions, the fluid in which our bodies move messages, nutrients and oxygen around, the hydrostatic force that gives living things shape. Vast waters are pulled by the same celestial cycles that guide our own bodily rhythms. Through our evolutionary history, water has provided us with resources and allowed us to cover immense distances. It even affects our minds deeply: neuroimaging reveals that being in or near water calms the human brain. But, like any close relationship, it's complicated. Large bodies of water are rich and productive but also irresistibly powerful and destructive. It's why the oceans are so often the mythical origins of existence, as in the *Enūma Eliš*. They can be a place of plentiful harvest or aquatic deserts, throwing humans to the mercy of the waves, the weather and whatever is swimming nearby. They're far darker and larger than our minds can conceive of, so the creatures we have imagined to inhabit these spaces can teach us a lot about ourselves.

The walrus head that made its way through Europe may have been a surprising gift, but it was also exactly the kind of thing Europeans expected to come from the Arctic seas. It had long been believed that sea monsters inhabited oceans, surfacing to trouble anyone foolhardy enough to cross them. In the thirteenth century, the Benedictine monk Matthew Paris described 'a vast sea where there is nothing but the abode of monsters'. These monsters originated in ancient traditions and persisted over centuries of battling the ocean's dangers to reap their bounties. They combined the ocean's inconceivable natural power, the alien nature of sea fauna and florid human imagination. These elements make sea monsters still potent today; we can't help but be awed by the oceans. Sea monsters embody this experience in a way that is hard to replace.[6]

Some of the monsters described by Magnus had long histories, taken from Classical authors such as Pliny the Elder. The 'sea hog' had a pig's head with crescent horns, webbed feet and three eyes on its flanks. With seals as sidekicks, the sea hog had a habit of 'plundering with atrocious savagery'. The 'grampus' was smaller than a whale, but a 'more savage brute' that looked like 'an upturned boat' and would rip at whale genitals with its 'ferocious teeth'. The 'cuttlefish' were 'winged creatures' of the 'sea lizard family' that shot out of the water like javelins at ships. And the 'ziphius' or 'sword-fish' had a face like an owl with a chasm-like mouth, a blade-like back and a beak which it used to slice open vessels and sink them.

Sixteenth-century scholars inherited a traditional belief that parallel creatures existed on land and in the sea. These marine mirror-images, such as the 'sea-pig', 'sea-boar', 'sea-wolf' and 'sea-lion', were often illustrated as fish-tailed versions of land creatures. The morse was often referred to as the 'sea-elephant', on account of its ivory and great size. Many centuries earlier, Pliny had described: 'sea-Elephants and Rams, with teeth standing out', among 'three hundred sea-monsters and above . . . of a wonderfull varietie and bignesse,' differing asunder'.

The name 'sea-elephant' also created some confusion. On the world map of Martin Waldseemüller (1516), for example, a stiff-legged elephant stands awkwardly in the far north, as if wondering how it got there. Beside it was a legend: 'The walrus (morsus) is an elephant sized animal with two long, quadrangular teeth. It is hindered by a lack of joints. The animal is found on promontories in Northern Norway where it moves in great herds'. This stiff-legged elephant-morse may have been created from the confusion of two ivory trade routes to Europe. Walrus ivory arrived from Scandinavia and extinct mammoth ivory was unearthed in Siberia and transported west. Putting the 'elephant-sized tusked water beast' and the 'elephant ivory' together was an easy mistake to make. They were all giants from very far away, anyway.[7]

ENCHANTED CREATURES

Sea monsters proliferated after the printing press was invented in the fifteenth century. Books of monsters and pamphlets reporting sea monster sightings allowed more people to see images of them than ever before. Tales of watery apparitions could spread further afield. The monsters were believed to be real, even in serious books: Magnus supported many of his monster descriptions with eyewitness accounts. These creatures could now spread between texts, and their body parts could be reshuffled to make new monsters. Some of the morse's physical parts, like the hairy ruff or long teeth, were given to other sea beasts by imaginative artists. The sea was a place where anything went, and its monsters were as inconstant as the waves.

Ferocious sea monsters mirrored the intense experience of living off the seas. When Dutch and English boats started travelling to the Arctic in the early seventeenth century to hunt the plentiful creatures there, they found terrible beasts. Imagine being a hunter on the Arctic ice in Greenland, wrapped in heavy, wet furs, armed with little more than a spear and nets, facing a panicked four-tonne walrus. It's no wonder hunters told tales of ferocious attacks from massive red-eyed 'morses'. Picture being a whaler on a creaky wooden ship, trying to land a bowhead whale larger than the vessel. You'd be trying to lance the animal hooked by a harpoon while fearing that it would capsize you as it thrashed in the water. Whales might be beautiful when serene on a TV screen, but if you're spearing their guts and hoping they don't tip you into the freezing water, they're a dreadful force of nature. Hunters in the Arctic butchered these animals for their valuable blubber, meat, skin, ivory, ambergris and bone. But they could very easily lose their lives in the process.[8]

Battling the beasts and battling the seas were one venture. And it was certainly a battle. It's noticeable just how many sea monsters seemed to have a vendetta against ships and humans. Magnus described how whales would rise 'like a colossal pillar . . . in order to destroy sailors', for example. People went out to harvest flesh and bones, and unsurprisingly, they found the creatures that owned them none too compliant. Part of this violence may have been the aggression projected out from the hunters who went to take apart these gigantic animals and sell them for profit. It's easier to kill and butcher something that you're sure was out to get you first. Slaying a monster of chaos is an act of heroism, not just a job.

To the sixteenth-century imagination, even the bodies of sea creatures were infused with the element they inhabited. In *De Gentibus*, Magnus described how people in the Arctic would create houses out of dried whale ribs. These were 'so strong and enormous that people can produce from them entire homes: walls, doors, windows, roofs, chairs, and even tables'. The bones were not mere building materials: they still possessed the spirit of the waters and the beasts they had been part of. These seeped into the minds of those who inhabited houses of bones: 'Those who sleep inside these ribs are forever dreaming that they are toiling incessantly on the ocean waves or, harassed by storms, are in perpetual danger of shipwreck'. Even the bones of sea beasts were filled with power.

Seeing marine beasts as sea monsters was not inevitable, of course. Plenty of earlier Anglo-Saxon texts discussed whaling and hunting without any dramatic flair. But the supernatural frequently crept in because the seas were supra-natural to sixteenth-century eyes, where God's creation could produce anything and everything imaginable. The oceans were completely uncontrollable compared to steady terrestrial places. Still waters could turn instantly treacherous, lawless pirates circled and unimaginable beasts emerged and disappeared among the waves. The creatures themselves were agents of this chaos. The violence of the sea beasts and the violence of the waves were part of the same deadly danger. These ideas had deep Christian roots, which we will explore next.

The belly of the beast

It can be hard for us to imagine how fully Christian theology infused daily experience for early Europeans. Mingled with the physical danger of traversing the waves was a deep spiritual peril. In Biblical tradition the seas were a dangerous place: a watery chaos opposed to the well-ordered Garden of Eden. Souls might be tempted and lost, and sea beasts were the Devil's agents. We might look at a humpback whale now and see only beauty and majesty, but through the lens of Medieval Christianity, it was one of Lucifer's minions.

The Old Testament prophet Jonah got tangled up with a sea monster. While trying to avoid some onerous tasks from God, Jonah was swallowed by a 'great fish' and spent three days inside its belly before being saved. In the seventh century CE, the theologian Isidore of Seville, whose work infused later Christian thinking, described the belly of the whale as 'so big that it resembled hell'. Likewise, in the *Last Judgement* fresco (c. 1555) by Giacomo Rossignolo, the 'Hellmouth' shows sinners being tumbled into the gaping maw of a toothy whale-beast. Entering the whale was a spiritual damnation from which few could return.[9]

Biblical images were often used in bestiaries, books which presented animals as moral symbols in the created world. Many drew on *The Physiologus*, an early Christian text from the second century CE. This depicted whales, walruses, sea turtles and other large sea animals as violent and malicious. According to the anonymous author, a whale-beast called the Aspidochelone or 'shield turtle' would wait quietly, emitting sweet odours to lure in unsuspecting fish, then suck them down its gullet. It might disguise itself as an island covered in foliage, an oasis among the waves. When weary sailors landed to rest and refresh themselves, the Aspidochelone would suddenly submerge itself and drag them to their deaths. By straying from their voyage and taking respite from their proper path, the sailors had given in to temptation and consigned themselves to watery hell. Sea monsters were not only dangerous, they were agents of the devil testing men's faith.

The grandaddy of them all was Leviathan, the sea monster created by God to rule the oceans. Leviathan's exact identity is a little unclear – it was variously depicted as a sea serpent, giant fish, whale and crocodile. The details of appearance hardly mattered for a monster of the primal seas, though. Job 41:10 is one of the many Bible verses in which Leviathan appears:

No one is so fierce that dare stir him up:
Who then able to stand before me?

As American writer David Quammen sums up: 'Yahweh is Almighty, Leviathan is mighty, and then comes everyone else'. He is 'God's handmaiden predator' which humans can never hope to overcome, a hefty reminder that 'we stand no higher than third on the food chain of power and glory'. Sea monsters put humans in their place and allowed God to do some grandstanding.

Even when whales beached themselves helplessly on the shores of the Netherlands, they became omens spat out of the ocean presaging terrible things. A woodcut by Jan Saenredam, *Beached Whale at Beverwijk near Amsterdam* (1602), depicts the beaching of a sperm whale on 19 December 1601. It dwarfs the people around it, rubbery tongue and large distended member flopping out on the sand. In practical terms, the whale would have fed and fuelled the community for many months. But it was seen as a portent of the solar eclipse which occurred on 24 December 1601. This was followed by an earthquake nine days later and a lunar eclipse on 4 June 1602, both of which were also attributed to the whale. Amsterdam was then hit by a bout of plague, another event added to the list of the whale's foretellings. It was a *very* busy cetacean.[10]

Though changes in technology made whaling a little safer over the following centuries, that didn't make whales less formidable. Devil-whales persisted in literature. The American author Herman Melville brought portentous whales to a nineteenth-century audience in *Moby Dick* (1851). Long before he wrote it, Melville had been fascinated by the story of *The Essex* whaling ship, which had been attacked by a sperm whale in 1820. Many of the crew died in the attack, and others starved to death waiting for rescue. Another of Melville's inspirations was a notoriously aggressive white whale, Mocha Dick, that lived off the coast of Chile. From these and his own whaling experience, Melville created a new mythology. The narrator, Ishmael, recounts the tale of the *Pequod*'s final journey under Captain Ahab, who is obsessed with seeking Moby Dick, the whale that bit off his leg long ago. Ahab's obsession leads the ship to eventual destruction.

Like the waters of the ocean on which it is set, the novel has infinite interpretations. The novelist David Gilbert calls it 'a bible written in scrimshaw'. Any sensible commentators admit that they don't fully understand the novel before cautiously offering their take. Many see metaphysical meanings in *Moby Dick*: the whale might be a totem of God or nature, atheism or evil, fear or fate – all the things that Ahab might wish to overcome. Which of these Moby Dick is probably depends on who is reading. Melville's monster absorbs all and any meanings cast on to it – the whale is as deep as the sea itself.[11]

Only spaces as endless and indefinite as oceans can be so supple in the imagination and encompass all of human experience in this way. They are places where forms merge and shift ceaselessly, undergoing 'a sea-change / into something rich and strange', as Ariel sings in Shakespeare's *The Tempest*. Typhoons, tidal waves and invisible, inexorable currents are like monsters in themselves, erupting with power and engulfing anything. Like the wilderness we explored in the previous chapter, who knows what could lurk in that watery vastness? This is why the oceans are where monsters still dwell in our minds.

Cryptozoologies

We never stopped making sea monsters, even in the penumbra of science. In 1845, an enterprising museum owner called Albert Koch exhibited a *Hydrarchos* or 'Leviathan' in the Apollo Saloon in New York. A pamphlet advertised it as a 'Sea Monster' that was 'the bloodthirsty monarch of the waters', 'the sovereign master and greatest monument of all animal creation'. It was quite the claim, even though the *Hydrarchos* was 114 ft and 7,500 lbs of fossilised wonder. The beast was presented as Leviathan, straight out of the Book of Job. But it couldn't hang about – punters were urged to take the chance to see the sea serpent hastily before it left on its tour of Europe.

The *Hydrarchos* had been 'discovered' by Koch in Alabama. It was actually a combination of fossils, including several basilosaurids – prehistoric whales which still had similarities to their terrestrial ancestors – and a few ammonites to add some curly panache. It was not the first piece of shameless showmanship that Koch had pulled off. The mastodon fossil skeleton now in the main hall of London's Natural History Museum was involved in his earlier 'Missouri Monster' exhibit.

The fossils used in the *Hydrarchos* had actually been found by enslaved people in Alabama and Mississippi in the 1830s–1840s, and Koch created a blockbuster monster out of them. Despite plenty of criticism from palaeontologists – pointing out the monster's clearly mammalian teeth – *Hydrarchos* created public shock and awe. It was the apparent realisation of a monster that had lingered in both the Biblical imagination and in mainstream natural history. Several notorious sea serpent sightings in the early nineteenth century had primed the public to find one in a museum.[12]

The *Hydrarchos* might have been double the length of a basilosaurus, but it wasn't all that different – both were slender sea beasts. The monster was a combination of several things that had really existed in the oceans when the southern United States was underwater. It doesn't seem impossible to imagine that we might find something like Koch's *Hydrarchos* in the future. The deep sea remains largely a mystery, it's the last wilderness vast enough to hide monsters. We've explored almost every inch of the terrestrial surface, but only 5 per cent of the oceans. As I write this, only twenty-seven people have ever been to Challenger Deep in the Mariana Trench, the deepest known point of the ocean floor, nearly 11 kilometres down. Given that we send rovers to map Mars, the fact that we have hardly explored the largest habitat on Earth is staggering. And, perhaps, also comforting. We need *somewhere* where monsters might plausibly still lurk, even if just for fantasy narratives.[13]

Monstrous things do live in the deep oceans, though. Another inhabitant of the Natural History Museum in London is a tentacled specimen who goes by the name of Archie. She's a giant squid, her nickname taken from the Latin binomial *Architeuthis dux*. Accidentally caught by a fishing trawler in 2004, she became the star turn of the museum's Spirit Collection, floating in a solution of 10 per cent formol-saline to preserve her 8.62-metre-long body. Before Archie, only pieces of gigantic squid or a few decayed specimens had been found. Live giant squid were only filmed for the first time in 2004. The colossal squid, *Mesonychoteuthis hamiltoni*, is even larger, up to 14 metres long. It was first found in 1925 and has eyes as big as footballs – bigger than any other eyes that we know to have existed. We have no images or footage of it, just a few specimens that have washed up or been found in the stomachs of whales. We know almost nothing about how these creatures live. They bring to mind the ancient Krakens believed to drag ships underwater, or the gigantic squid-like 'devilfish' that attacks the *Nautilus* in Jules Verne's *Twenty Thousand Leagues Under the Sea* (1872).

Given our long history of imagining sea monsters and creatures such as Archie, it's not surprising that some have imagined there might be more spectacular things yet to discover. The modern pseudoscience of cryptozoology optimistically peers into the unknown, looking for proof of legendary or extinct animals, often called cryptids. Much like sixteenth-century naturalists, twentieth-century cryptozoologists enthusiastically collected the trappings of objective data – photographs, detailed descriptions, the odd specimen – and presented them as 'evidence' of large, unknown sea beasts.

A leading figure in this venture was the French scientist Bernard Heuvelmans. He had a theory that ancient marine giants could still exist covertly without leaving any recent fossils. There are a few examples of 'Lazarus species': ones that have changed little over time, don't appear much in fossil records and have been discovered recently. The prime example is the coelacanth, a stocky deep-sea fish that has remained relatively unchanged by evolution for over 400 million years. Known only from scant fossils until the 1930s, two living species were then discovered. Couldn't that have happened to various primitive whales, marine crocodiles, gargantuan turtles and mega-seals we know of from fossils but have yet to find alive? Heuvelmans thought so. In *The Wake of the Sea Serpents* (1968), he created a classification of unknown sea creature 'sightings', using nine key types: the longneck, the merhorse, the many humped, the many finned, super otter, super eel, marine Saurian, yellow belly and father-of-all-turtles. He reinterpreted unusual sightings of 'monsters' as potential prehistoric revenants.

Palaeontologist Darren Naish at the University of Southampton has made a hobby of unpicking cryptozoological arguments, in the interests of scientific rigour (and, perhaps, from some boyish wonder). He argues that the theories of Heuvelmans and others like him, who have tried to give cryptids scientific credibility, just don't stack up. Any 'evidence' dissolves under scrutiny and, given the extent of the fossil record, the 'absence of evidence *is* evidence of absence'. In fact, cryptozoology might suffer from what Naish terms the 'Plesiosaur Effect' – the reinvigoration of old 'sea monster' images after a new fossil discovery. When plesiosaur fossils were discovered in the nineteenth century, for example, there was an explosion of sightings of plesiosaur-like monsters with long necks. Naish's critiques haven't stopped cryptozoologists from trying, though.

The mythology of sea monsters and the modern science of marine fauna haven't moved so far apart as they have for the terrestrial world. Though many traditional sea monsters came from imaginative extrapolation, their strangeness parallels the strangeness of what is actually in the seas. These have been woven together in the Latin binomials of biological species – ocean monsters persist in the scientific nomenclature. The blade-nosed 'ziphius' that would slice open ships, for example, is now *Ziphius cavirostris*, commonly known as the mild-mannered Cuvier's Beaked whale. The ferocious 'pristis', with its spiky unicorn horn, has given its name to the proper owner of the strange appendage, the sawfish – *Pristis pristis*. The 'physeter' which would attack ships with a towering spout of water in Classical mythology, has become a genus of toothed whales. The list goes on.

By linking living marine fauna with the old monsters of the seas, scientists preserved the ancient fantasies of the oceans. This isn't hard to understand: the seas are difficult to fathom, literally and figuratively, so they're somewhere that our imaginations can have free rein. The seas and their beasts really are overwhelmingly large and dangerous, and fear is certainly a monster-monger. Few examples illustrate this better than sharks, which we will look at next.

Bruce

My partner, Jamie, has an intense fear of sharks. Not the run-of-the-mill kind of fear, which is the only sensible reaction to something indecently toothy that can kill you. It's an *involved* fear. The thought of sharks keeps him away from any water where he can't see the bottom – even particularly large swimming pools. We once stayed on a minute desert island near Flores, Indonesia. Straight off the beach, under only a metre of water, was one of the most pristine coral reefs I have ever had the joy of exploring. It took only one sight of the petite baby black-tip sharks that patrolled the waterline to make Jamie swear off all snorkelling, however. Ironically, some of the tiny reef fish were actually far more hostile than the disinterested black-tips.

Despite his all-consuming fear of sharks, Jamie has a shark keyring, his digital avatars are sharks, and when the word 'shark' is mentioned, he looks round animatedly. He's seen every shark movie under the sun and loves nothing more than battening down the hatches behind a blanket to rewatch a classic. No toes over the edge of the sofa, of course. Jamie is irresistibly drawn to sharks – they're 'horrendous but very beautiful', as he puts it. And, judging by the number of shark movies produced, many others are in the same boat, as it were. Across the expanses of cinema screens and high-definition televisions swim great whites with vendettas, outsized megalodons, genetically modified super-killer sharks and flying Nazi zombie sharks. We even have sharknados. Sharks have their own para-genre movie type.

Galeophobia, the fear of sharks, isn't totally irrational. If you get tangled up with a shark on its home turf, the consequences can be dire. But it's easy to stay out of their way – there is generally no need to go into the ocean. Statistically there is a 1 in 3,748,067 chance of dying from a shark attack, which represents about 10 deaths per year globally. Cows killed 22 people in the US alone in 2021, and bees killed 53.

In cultures that are deeply entwined with the oceans, such as Hawaiian or Polynesian societies, sharks are often mythologised as gods. They are not monsters: their power is respected rather than vilified. Living alongside sharks does not entail demonising them: these cultures have nuanced perspectives of fear and respect. In the West, we assume that we're supposed to be at the very top of the food chain – stemming from Judeo-Christian theology. As a result, we are not very good at holding balanced views of other powerful creatures. We find it harder to see that we're just part of an ecosystem, so we tend to make these threats into monsters.

Sharks were certainly part of the historical menagerie of sea monsters. Thomas Pennant, a zoologist in the eighteenth century, wrote: 'They are the dread of sailors, they constantly attend the ships in expectation of what may drop overboard; a man that has that misfortune perishes without redemption'. Falling prey to a shark also had echoes of damnation to a devil. While whales are seen as benign and beautiful marine creatures today, sharks have remained monsters. When orcas do something terrible in our eyes – like gang up on seals or rip the tongues out of humpback whale calves – it creates a jarring, uncomfortable feeling. A cetacean can't be a monster, surely? Their terrifying intelligence can even win public support. As I write this, a gang of orcas led by an old battle-axe named 'White Gladis' is spending the summer knocking the tillers off yachts on the Iberian coast. They've sunk three boats already, and the behaviour seems to be spreading. One boat's attempt to ward off the orcas by playing heavy metal music underwater seems only to have encouraged them. Whether or not it's a vendetta triggered by Gladis's past run-ins with boats is under debate, but plenty of people are in favour of what they see as vigilante retribution.[14]

If it were sharks forming armies to take boats out, most people probably wouldn't feel the same way. Sharks are very much on the back fin in the public eye. We don't just fear sharks. Shark films are really monster films. They hardly need any vamping up to play the role – the megalodon in *The Meg* (2018) might be exaggerated, or the great white bullying Blake Lively in *The Shallows* (2016) might be especially vindictive – but neither is far from biological reality. Sharks are like cartilaginous, powerful, dead-eyed aliens that can erupt silently from the water. They track down prey with eerie senses: a shark can pick up electric fields emitted by other creatures as small as five nanovolts and sense blood in the water as dilute as one part per million.

The devastating appearance of razor-filled jaws certainly makes a visual impact on a screen. Peter Benchley's 1974 novel *Jaws* and Steven Spielberg's film adaptation a year later ignited mass galeophobia. Bruce, the nickname given to the animatronic great white by the film crew (named after Spielberg's pugnacious lawyer), has probably seeded more lifelong fears than any other animatron. The term 'shark' is still used to describe lawyers or 'loan sharks'; and unscrupulous men preying on vulnerable women are 'sharking'. Towards the end of *Jaws*, the enigmatic Captain Quint monologues on the shark attacks his crew suffered after being torpedoed while delivering the Hiroshima bomb: 'The thing about a shark is he's got lifeless eyes. Black eyes. Like a doll's eyes. When he comes at ya, he doesn't even seem to be livin' . . . 'til he bites ya, and those black eyes roll over white and then . . . ah then you hear that terrible high-pitched screamin'. The ocean turns red, and despite all your poundin' and your hollerin' those sharks come in and . . . they rip you to pieces'.

'Lifeless' eyes make sharks the perfect cold-blooded killers, about as far from human as it's possible for a large vertebrate to be. Ironically, 'mechanical, emotionless monsters' far better describes the fishing boats that slaughter sharks each year. The '*Jaws* effect', coined in 2014, describes how shark films are used by politicians to ramp up the hysteria of shark attacks and sway the public towards certain policy decisions. Since the early twentieth century, shark attacks have sparked crusades against demonic 'man-eaters'. But really, we should be considering how our impact on marine ecosystems might be throwing humans and sharks together: exploding human populations, overfishing of shark prey species or increased use of shorelines. Leading a war on a maneater gets far more votes than campaigning for ecological moderation, though.

The sharks have suffered for it – with about 100 million deaths a year. Since the 1970s, the global shark population has fallen by 71 per cent. The damage has been so extreme that Spielberg regrets the smear campaign his film helped to fuel: 'That's one of the things I still fear. Not to get eaten by a shark, but that sharks are somehow mad at me for the feeding frenzy of crazy sports fishermen that happened after 1975'. Revenge sharks haunt his nightmares.[15]

The deeps

In one passage of *Moby Dick*, Melville described how the 'living whale, in his full majesty and significance, is only to be seen at sea in unfathomable waters; and afloat the vast bulk of him is out of sight'. The whale's size is dwarfed by its surroundings, which reveal it only momentarily. What happens below is a mystery. Oceans have been used in literature and art as a metaphor for the subconscious, for just this reason. Sigmund Freud likened the structure of the mind to an iceberg partially submerged in water, the unconscious mind lying deep below the surface – only the conscious tip showing above. Similarly, for Carl Jung, the animate, restless connectivity of water represented the 'Collective Unconscious'. The incomprehensible qualities of ocean waters echo our complex minds – labile and full of powerful impulses. The surface hides all the real action underneath.

The biological study of ocean creatures has only deepened this symbolic connection. We know a great deal more about the seas; we can better harvest their bounties, and we've made traversing them far safer than ever before. But the strangeness of the oceans keeps pace with our technological advancements. The marine biologist and author Helen Scales explained to me why oceans continue to capture our imaginations. With her characteristic eloquence, she pointed out that we haven't been able to see most marine creatures in their element until recently. 'If you take something like a blobfish and haul it up to the surface, it looks ridiculous, poor thing, all squashed from the change in pressure'. But with submersibles, robots and deep-sea vessels, we can see more of the deep sea than ever before, and people are captivated.

We're finally getting the chance to see what life can be, to 'open our eyes to the possibilities of evolution, and its responses to extreme conditions'. Far from dispelling sea monster fantasies, we're discovering aliens. As Scales points out, 'many things down there make light, a bit like we might imagine aliens do'. Being in the seas is even like being on another planet where we cannot breathe the atmosphere and there's minimal gravity. Marine creatures can be large and weirdly extruded, like oar fish: silvery, crested ribbons up to 17 metres long. Or they can be incredibly delicate, sporting fine, feathery tendrils; long limbs only as wide as a pin; chiffon-like mantles; or translucent jelly flesh that maintains its fragile shape without the struts and structures needed on land. Watery weightlessness allows extraordinary things to exist.

The gloaming of the twilight zone and the pitch dark of the abyssal plain hide things of incredible size and strangeness, like nightmares in the unconscious realms of sleep. It's an odd coincidence that in the places furthest away from our reach, real creatures have evolved to look like our deepest fears made manifest. For example, the pelican eel is a deep-sea species that appears alternately like a fishy take on a Ringwraith or a football in a pair of tights. It has jaws that unfold geometrically to open to several times the eel's own body size, enabling it to swallow almost anything it might encounter. When you live in an underwater desert, you can't afford to let potential prey get away, even if it's far bigger than you. Things get weirder the deeper you go: goblin sharks, hagfish, vampire squid – the cast of the deep is a horror show of underbites, bulbous noses, visible internal organs and pyromaniac explosions of bioluminescence. As with the workings of the subconscious, we still know so little about how they live.

Life in the deep sea echoes the primitive functions of the human brain, where surviving and feeding and reproducing are the only things that matter. Creatures have simpler, emptier existences, largely consisting of finding energy and avoiding being food for something else. Even sex hardly exists down there. It never needed to, with everything happening in liquid continuity – gametes can just be released. Or through sexless parasitism: minute male angler fish don't mate, they fuse themselves to the first sizeable female they encounter, spending the rest of their days as living sperm bags. These minimal activities are operated mainly by the same basic instincts that our own brain stems control.[16]

Travelling down into the depths of the ocean is almost like travelling back in time to an ancient past. As the light fades and the temperature cools, life slows, creating a natural time warp. Biological processes occur very slowly. Things can live to great ages – but they don't get more done. Less has changed for these creatures since our own evolutionary paths diverged from theirs. The colossal squid we met earlier is the largest extant invertebrate, but it needs only forty-five kilocalories per day to survive. That's the rough energetic equivalent of a single apple a day – which it fulfils by eating a couple of fish a year. The Greenland shark lives in Arctic waters at depths up to about 2,000 metres. It swims slowly, at its fastest only about 1.6 kmph, but somehow it occasionally catches fish and seals. They fuel an extraordinarily long lifespan of up to 500 years, the longest of any vertebrate. A Greenland shark alive today could have been birthed when Olaus Magnus was publishing his *Carta Marina*.[17]

There are so many reasons why the oceans are a breeding ground for monsters. The oceanic ability to destroy and consume is monstrous and wonderful at the same time, stupefying us with awe. They are places where fantasy and reality run alongside one another like nowhere else: where beasts and the medium they inhabit all flow and move together; where power, danger and mystery are uniquely present. It is why they can be the source of just about anything in our minds – and they have produced far stranger animals than we have imagined. Faced with the turbulent surface from which anything could emerge, our imaginations have populated the oceans with Leviathans.

PART THREE

Monsters of Knowledge

PART THREE

Monsters of Knowledge

Scaly Devils

Chapter 7

'Imagination abandoned by reason produces impossible monsters; united with her, she is the mother of the arts and source of their wonders'

Francisco Goya

Jacob de Bondt had never liked scaly things – they didn't agree with him, especially to eat. Whenever he had tried turtle or iguana meat, he had fallen violently ill and suffered from horrible fever dreams. For a young physician posted to Java, a keystone of the Dutch empire in the 1620s, this was problematic. The Governor General of the Dutch East India Company had once invited de Bondt to a dinner party at which crocodile was served. The other guests were delighted. But merely touching a piece of the meat with his lip – in the interests of politeness – had sent de Bondt to bed for several days with what he called a violent 'cholera', in fear of his life.[1]

This fragility annoyed de Bondt. His task in Java was to observe and absorb everything in this strange, humid place. He couldn't afford to be indisposed. He spent his time gathering and recording all he could of the natural treasures to be found in the bustling Dutch outpost, especially anything that might have medicinal value. As one of hundreds of officials abroad, he was only a small piece of a vast trade network centred in the Netherlands that was wrapping its tendrils around the globe. It was a time of incredible change, the beginnings of what became the globalised, capitalist economy of today. But de Bondt was too busy with the minutiae of his work to dwell on that. His primary focus was finding new pharmaceuticals for the Company to supply to European apothecaries. His second was working out what to make of all the extraordinary things he found.[2]

One day, de Bondt's servants brought him a sack containing a gift which would test his nerve. He upended the sack and a bizarre thing fell out, tightly curled in a ball. He watched as it slowly unfurled itself and began to creep tentatively across the floor. It was unlike anything he had ever seen: its humped back and long tail were covered in thick brown scales, and it had a snake-like head with black, beady eyes. De Bondt thought it must be a kind of turtle and assumed that, like other turtles he had encountered, it probably had a nasty bite. When he gingerly flipped it over to look at its soft, furry belly, it rolled itself up again and remained still. A silent, spherical enigma. It wasn't *quite* like any other turtle or lizard he had ever seen before. But what else had such an impenetrable shell? He decided to house it in a tub filled with water to swim in and some small fish to eat.[3]

De Bondt called this thing a 'marvellous scaly turtle'. Having no idea what it was, he used parts of animals he did know – fish, snakes, turtles – to try and describe it. He asked around the locals and other Dutch officials to see if they knew anything about the animal. De Bondt's library of precious books, carefully shipped over from the Netherlands, was of little use. Though they were filled with ancient, scholarly wisdom, these books had not helped him to understand much in Java.

Luckily, some of de Bondt's contacts in the colony knew what the creature was. The Javanese called it *Taunah* or 'digger in the earth', and it apparently lived in holes on riverbanks, moving extremely slowly and sometimes swimming. He was delighted to hear that the animal's scales made a potent medicine when ground and mixed with rice water. This concoction was apparently used by Chinese physicians for bile disturbances, dysentery and cholera. It could even help relieve minor gastric ailments like those de Bondt was prone to. In seventeenth-century medical theory, it made perfect sense that a seemingly sluggish and cold creature would contain a remedy for the hot pains of the gut. Like crocodile, the *Taunah* was also meant to be delicious to eat, but de Bondt was not particularly tempted to test this out.

As far as I can tell, the 'scaly turtle' did not flourish in de Bondt's dubious care. It just wasn't the amphibious predator he assumed it was. Judging from de Bondt's original notes, the animal was almost certainly what we would call today a Sunda pangolin (*Manis javanica*). These scaled anteater-like creatures live in forests and use their long sticky tongues to pull ants into their tubular, fused jaws. Sunda pangolins are good swimmers when they have to be, but I can only imagine that de Bondt's creature did not like being stuck in a tub of water sprinkled with dead fish. Finding no ants and probably rather waterlogged, it soon died. De Bondt had the creature skinned to add to his collection of Javanese nature. His detailed ink sketch of the specimen looks like a round, scaly tablemat with legs. No wonder he found the animal confusing.[4]

De Bondt encountered many other strange beasts during his four years in Java. He recorded them in his notes, which are a treasure trove of incisive observations, autobiography and imaginative riffs scrawled in brown ink. The 'casuary' or 'emeu', for example, was a bird with a bald, brightly coloured head and fur-like feathers. It couldn't fly because of its stunted wings but it could deliver a shockingly aggressive kick. Another bird that de Bondt described had a large, horn-like appendage on its beak – which we would call a hornbill. He had seen fish with wings that could fly above the water, and small whip-tailed 'dragons' that sailed from tree to tree on flaps of skin extending from their bellies. We now know these as draco lizards or flying dragons.[5]

ENCHANTED CREATURES

Then there was the 'Wood man' which de Bondt dubbed the 'Ourang outan', that lived in the deep jungles where he wouldn't dare venture himself. It walked upright, like a horrible, russet-haired human. De Bondt thought these wild men must be the offspring 'of the voluptuousness of Indian women, who, to satisfy their desire, consorted with apes and monkeys'. He was not the first European commentator to fantasise about apish assaults on insatiable native women – and he was certainly not the last.[6]

De Bondt really tried make sense of all the astounding creatures, plants, customs and objects he encountered in Java. He used whatever knowledge he could find: books, gossip among the Dutch officials and a network of locals. The problem was, many of the creatures that de Bondt and other travellers found in exotic places didn't fit at all into the traditional European understanding of the world. This was infused with Biblical lore, the work of ancient philosophers like Aristotle and a map of the globe that hadn't extended far beyond Europe, until quite recently. Pangolins certainly hadn't figured. This mismatch stirred up a cocktail of utter confusion, intense curiosity and a dash of amusement for de Bondt and others like him. As a result, they wrote natural histories of these exotic beasts filled with wonder and creativity. They made them into monsters.

This didn't make these creatures any less believable, though. If anything, it made them more valuable. Monstrous beasts fitted right into a world where magic and science were not yet at odds. In the seventeenth century, diverse kinds of knowledge could exist comfortably alongside each other, from the factual to the symbolic – which is not the case in our science-dominated world. Monsters were proof that the Creator had a sense of humour – some played brief cameo appearances in the Bible. Novel monsters were the products of Europe's growing global network, representing the confusion that arose from encounters with new peoples and places. They sat between traditional knowledge and the deluge of new realities pouring into Europe, and helped to connect the two. This is the story of how strange little monsters, like the pangolin, helped early modern Europeans to handle a rapidly expanding world.

Monsters for sale

De Bondt was eventually overcome by the alien environment. He succumbed to a bout of cholera more severe than anything crocodile steak had ever inflicted on his delicate constitution. In 1631, four years after he had arrived in Java, he died. He was one of many men who failed to return home after serving the Dutch East India Company's ever-growing global machine. Before he died, de Bondt had sent his notes and materials to his brother in Leiden. There they were picked up by an opportunistic young medic called Willem Piso. He published books on the nature and medicines of distant lands, creating expensive, printed cornucopias for European intellectuals. Though he had travelled himself, Piso found that padding out his own work with that of others was a far more expedient way of getting material. His shameless editing practices, bordering on plagiarism, only made his volumes more popular.

During my PhD research I followed de Bondt's pangolin and others through the mottled pages of seventeenth-century natural histories, travelogues and collection catalogues. I wanted to get a sense of where and what the animals had been in Europe. I tried to scope out their population size. The pangolins were not difficult to find, appearing suddenly in full scaly regalia as I turned pages, splayed flat as if squashed by the weight of the books. The same pangolin images were often copied from book to book like memes. Authors rarely had any idea what these unusual beasts were or where they came from. But they stuck them in anyway – there was an ethos of 'the more the merrier' when it came to wonders.[7]

I found that Piso had rolled de Bondt's detailed field work into his book on the Indies, *Indiae Utriusque* (1658). He gave the entry on the 'scaly turtle' a mysterious introduction: 'What kind of monster is this? Am I a fish or a land animal, as I live in both, on the earth as well as in the water and bear scales as well as brushy hairs on the back and sleep in scooped-out places along the banks?' This prologue summed up why the 'scaly turtle' was a monster: it seemed to be multiple creatures at once. Other authors debated whether pangolins were armadillos, pigs, lizards, fish, snakes, turtles or even animate pinecones. Everyone agreed that the creatures didn't fit into any of the familiar categories of animals that Aristotle had laid out, on which European natural history was based. Aristotle had divided red-blooded animals into live-birthing quadrupeds (land mammals), egg-laying quadrupeds (reptiles and amphibians), whales, snakes, fish and birds. The hairy, scaly, reptile-mammal pangolins were monstrous enigmas. Many people today, seeing a picture of a pangolin for the first time, have the same reaction.

One account of a pangolin had actually been sitting under de Bondt's nose in his personal library in Java. As careful an observer as he was, de Bondt had missed the pangolin in *Exoticorum libri decem* (1605) by the Flemish naturalist, Carolus Clusius. This 'foreign scaly lizard' from 'India' had large claws and was covered in furrowed scaled armour from head to tip. This aggressive 'devil' lived on the mysterious island of Taiwan. It raised its scales when irritated and preyed on insects and lizards, ripping into nests and flesh with its curved claws and 'sharp bite'. Back in Europe, Piso's acquisitive eye spotted the entry. He added the 'scaly Indian lizard' of Clusius's work to his own volume, unaware that he had included the same animal twice. Piso attributed the stolen entry to de Bondt – who was dead and couldn't complain. Publishing was wild before copyright law.

Piso's timing for his book was perfect. The appetite for exotic wonders was reaching fever pitch in northern Europe in the seventeenth century. Natural things were

ENCHANTED CREATURES

not only valued for their practical uses – there was a demand for the fabulous. Wonders had long been brought back from distant places, but they had never been so plentiful, nor so heavily marketed. The Dutch East India Company was fast becoming the first truly global corporation: funded by futures trading and the first stock market, militarised and empowered to mint money and execute criminals. It brought more freight to Europe than all the other countries put together. If you had lived in Amsterdam, Antwerp or Leiden at this time, you would have seen heaps of exotic things being unloaded at the docks from ships returning from Malacca, Ceylon or Guinea – spices, tea, textiles, medicines, precious metals, or porcelain goods.

Fabulous natural things accompanied them: mermaids, exotic birds and beasts, dragons, pieces of sea monsters and giant turtle shells. Unlike modern shipping warehouses filled with monotonic contents, the Company's warehouses were piled high with unusual cargoes. Some would have been ordered in crates and sacks, others were more random acquisitions mouldering away in corners after long weeks at sea, all grist to the profit-turning mill. As fast as these flooded in, they were sold on, the strangest objects ending up in the menageries, freakshows and collections of European cities.

One pangolin nearly made it alive through these shipways to Europe, for a moment in the limelight at the 'White Elephant Menagerie' in Amsterdam. Such shows charged only a few pennies' entrance fee and guaranteed visitors an excellent afternoon of ogling oddities whilst comfortably drunk on cheap wine and beer. In the 1690s a man called Jan Velten visited the White Elephant. He was an avid shell collector and very average artist but made up for his lack of skill with enthusiasm, as evidenced by his private sketchbook. Velten lovingly drew the menagerie's monkeys, parrots, tapirs and lions. Pasted into the album was also an advert for a special appearance at the menagerie, a scaly *nigomsen duyvel* (black devil). The creature was billed as 'being inclined to evil', having repeatedly tried to burrow through stone floors and attempted to strangle anyone foolish enough to allow it to get around their neck. This troublesome beast had been executed on its journey to Europe, so the menagerie was exhibiting it as a 'still life' (in other words, dead). Velten's depiction of what must have been a pangolin looks far friendlier than the *duyvel* the pamphlet described. Perhaps he did not have the frustrating task of looking after it.[8]

Plenty of other pangolins arrived in Europe as dried skins, where they were snapped up by collectors. Dead oddities of all kinds were hungrily acquired for curiosity collections or *Wunderkammern* (literally, 'chambers of wonder'). Collecting was becoming incredibly popular: everyone who was anyone had a collection – probably several. Nobles and merchants amassed collections that ranged from modest cabinets to whole rooms filled with treasures. These included nautilus shells intricately carved and wrought with metalwork, gilded Seychelles coconuts, strange mineral deposits, deformed foetuses pickled in spirits or dried human body parts. Some natural objects were especially common, such as sawfish rostrums, hornbill skulls, weaver nests and puffer fish – the 'bread and butter' collection specimens.

The objects in these collections were metaphorical tokens of tangible and intangible parts of the universe. A collection could encompass the world in one space; it was the collector's personal cosmos bounded in a nutshell. Collecting was often an exercise in showing off and presenting an ideal self-image. A collector's ability to get hold of the most exotic objects demonstrated their power, while owning these objects displayed their erudition. Collections were also highly distilled experiences of Divine Creation that viewers could appreciate fully all in one moment. That said, given the poor state of many natural objects when they arrived in Europe after months at sea, these rooms of wonders probably stank right up to the heavenly abode of the God they were intended to honour.[9]

I have a cabinet which plays some of these roles, filled with objects I have collected over my lifetime. It's a visual natural history of my interests and experiences: a hornbill skull, the spiralling silica cages of deep-sea sponges, a horseshoe crab, a goliath beetle, a flying lizard, a bear tooth and an array of exciting seed pods – for which I have a special fondness. Some of these combine nature and art, like a delicate glass heron from Venice or a carved ostrich eggshell. Others recall travels – such as the skull I removed from a dead frigate bird in Peru;

or commemorate special relationships – like the stone painted with an Australasian bird god from a surrogate grandmother. A few are no longer obtainable: the nautilus has become CITES protected since I bought mine years ago. It's a collection of parts of myself in pieces of the natural world. I've learned the hard way over the years not to bother with anything museum beetles will eat.

Objects in seventeenth-century collections were usually less personal, but no less symbolic. Pangolin skins seem to have featured in numerous collections, if the catalogues are to be believed. They were often included without any information about where they had come from, beyond 'the Indies' – east or west. This hardly mattered. Exactly *where* something came from was less important than the fact that it came from *elsewhere*, that it was exotic and striking. Those qualities made a monster valuable and impressive to collection visitors. They also reinforced the colonial perception of other lands being alien places, full of wondrous things, ripe for harvesting. Individual monstrous beasts reveal a great deal about the outlook of the naturalists who created them. But they show even more about how Europeans saw the world when gathered together in collections.

Beastly geographies

Striking animals and plants became part of a figurative map of the world in books and collections in seventeenth-century Europe. They were turned into talismans representing distant places, as seen through European eyes. The impassable, frozen Arctic would produce large, fearsome beasts, for example; or a land filled with gold and riches, like the Americas, would produce jewel-like birds. Extraordinary creatures represented different geographic regions: elephants signalled Africa, armadillos the Americas, polar bears the Arctic, camels the Middle East, dragons the Far East, and sea monsters stood for oceans. This symbolism was used to decorate maps, overlaid onto the concrete geographical knowledge that allowed sailors to actually find places. You can still see the animal emblems of different countries today on postage stamps and in heraldry.

So, of course, a fish-lizard-pig pangolin would be found in the 'Indies', for the 'Indies' had always been seen as a strange place where such strange marvels lived. There was more depth to this monster, though. There was something especially polarising about the pangolin, inspiring widely differing descriptions in the seventeenth century. Some followed de Bondt's gentle and mysterious 'scaly turtle', describing a harmless beast that curled up into a ball when scared – God had even given it armour because it was so vulnerable. They said it only ate insects, which could be useful for pest control. Other descriptions were more akin to Clusius's irritable 'scaly Indian lizard'. They presented the pangolin as a malicious, spiky devil that could deflect European weapons and would dig up the foundations of colonial buildings. This negative view was more common in accounts from places where colonial relations were strained, such as Taiwan, where Chinese forces kept European trading operations under threat. Scaly lizards were either devils or innocents, that helped or hindered European colonisation.

My hunt for the 'scaly lizard' showed me how new creatures could become symbolic monsters. How little-known creatures that 'didn't fit' became playthings for the European imagination. The pangolin's two personalities seem to have embodied different sides of the colonial relationship. Aggressive, troublesome pangolins represented the ferocity of natives repelling European colonisers. Timid, harmless pangolins stood in for the vulnerability of colonised peoples. These visions of the pangolin emerged from Europeans' ambivalence towards the people they colonised, two different mixtures of observation and projection. Nature, politics, religion and capitalism all piled on top of one another, to make an already extraordinary animal even more so.

Pangolins are still caught up in symbolic thinking. More pangolins are illegally trafficked than any other mammal, for the traditional medicine trade in Asia. This 'medical' practice remains firmly in the past, based on the belief that pangolin scales heal all kinds of illnesses. Yet these scales are only made of keratin, just like our hair and nails. As Asian pangolins like the Sunda pangolin became Critically Endangered over the past few decades, smugglers started taking them over from Africa, along with elephant ivory, tiger bone and hard drugs. The

African giant ground pangolins are now so rare that their locations are kept secret, guarded by specialist armed wardens. Today's world has nothing like the endless natural bounty that was available to seventeenth-century trading companies.[10]

For early modern Europeans, making monsters was a way of dealing with new and confusing things. Their natural histories were cobbled together from evidence and imagination and they were kept in a holding pen of marvels, as the boundaries of the world shifted and fraught relationships were played out. When new systems of organising the world developed that could handle creatures like the pangolin, as we shall see later, they were no longer viewed as monsters. What happened to all the ancient, fabulous monsters, though? The dragons and unicorns and basilisks? Next, we'll look at how one of these traditional monsters – the hydra – fared in the changing world. They were more persistent than you might think.

The last hydra

About a century after de Bondt was in Java, a wealthy apothecary in Amsterdam, Albertus Seba, built a sizeable collection which became famous throughout Europe. In the opulent collection catalogue was pictured a beast which Seba did not personally own: a seven-headed hydra. Seba had heard about the renowned 'Hydra of Hamburg' in 1720 and dismissed it as mere fancy. But when he heard that the hydra was on sale for the extravagant sum of 10,000 florins, his interest was piqued. Anything worth such a price must be something truly extraordinary, surely? Only a *real* dragon could be so expensive.

Not to be taken for a fool, Seba wrote to an apothecary friend near Hamburg, and asked for his opinion of the beast and a drawing of it. He made a note that this 'very judiciously curious natural historian, who had seen the same hydra with his own eyes, assured me that it was definitely not the work of art but one of nature'. It was important that the naturalist was 'judiciously curious' because being *overcome* with curiosity might lay him open to being gullible. Seba couldn't trust the opinion of a naïve man on such matters. He did not end up purchasing the hydra, but Seba added a dramatic illustration of it to his catalogue, showing a small flying dragon soaring above the hydra's multiple heads. Including images of objects in one's catalogue was a much cheaper way of 'adding' them to the collection than actually owning them.

From descriptions of the hydra, it seems to have been about 1.5–2 metres long, with a knobbly chestnut hide and a scaly tail, seven sharp-toothed heads with ringed necks and clawed feet. The beast was not especially intimidating, but it had illustrious beginnings, having been plundered from a church in the Battle of Prague in 1648. The 10,000 florins which had so shocked Seba was only a quarter of the price offered for the monster a few years before by the Danish King.[11]

The value was based not only on the hydra's dramatic origins and potential reality, but also its links to Biblical and Classical tradition. It was a creature straight out of the fire and brimstone world of scripture, a monster from the apocalyptic stories of the New Testament Book of Revelation. There are several 'beasts' with many heads in that book. One, the Great Red Dragon, fought alongside the rebel angels in their attempt to overthrow God: 'behold, a great, fiery red dragon having seven heads and ten horns, and seven diadems on his heads'. This beast still exists in the modern imagination, as a series of powerful watercolour paintings (1805–10) by the poet-artist William Blake. One was tattooed on the back of the psychopath Francis Dolarhyde in the 2002 film *Red Dragon*.[12]

The physical hydra seen by collectors in the early eighteenth century was rather an anti-climax. It had neither diadems nor horns and had certainly never breathed fire. The hydra's star had fallen on its journey to Hamburg, its price declining until, in 1735, it was selling for a pittance. The final blow was dealt by a young Swedish naturalist, Carl Linnaeus. He declared it to be a mere taxidermy prop constructed for theatrical effect by monks, albeit with impressive craftsmanship. The hydra was really a patchwork of snakeskins topped with the head and feet of weasels, probably a little dishevelled from its tour around Europe. Quite a way from the terrifying hell-beast of the Bible.[13]

There are two questions that the story of the Hamburg Hydra brings up for me. The first is – even accounting for different worldviews — how could presumably intelligent people think that some mouldy church artefact was actually a hydra, and consider paying top buck for it? The second is, what happened to the monster when one of its representatives was revealed to be a pile of animal bits?

The first answer has two parts: tradition and market value. The 'reality' of dragons did not rely heavily on their biological existence: they had heritage. Pliny the Elder, along with other Classical authors, had described the dragons of distant lands and his word still held sway.[14] The dragon was also a powerful creature in the Christian imagination. Aside from the seven-headed serpents of the Book of Revelation, the Bible describes the fiery, flying serpents of the Book of Isaiah and the basilisks and dragons in Psalm 91. It was a beast overcome by brave St George before he converted the pagan masses, in a triumph of religious virtue over evil. The family crest of Pope Gregory XIII (1572–85) even featured a dragon. His cousin, Ulysse Aldrovandi, was a prominent naturalist who published a big, serious tome on the natural history of dragons in 1640.

Dragons had a water-tight alibi too: they were thought to dwell where experience did not. Cartographers had long marked out blank regions with images of fantastical beasts and monsters. As these boundaries receded, so did the domains of the monsters (though the inscription *Hic Sunt Dracones* – 'here be dragons' – only actually appears on one map).[15] Some travellers had reached distant lands and reported dragons there. The Venetian traveller Marco

ENCHANTED CREATURES

Polo had explored China in the thirteenth century and encountered 'huge serpents' whose 'jaws are wide enough to swallow a man, the teeth are large and sharp, and their whole appearance is so formidable, that neither man, nor any kind of animal can approach them without terror'. So few people travelled so far until the seventeenth century that descriptions such as Polo's weren't challenged. News of more local dragon sightings were also circulated in cheap printed pamphlets, spreading excitement. Dragons had been so densely woven into European literature and imagery, from Medieval bestiaries to works of art, that they existed virtually – irrespective of whether anyone had actually encountered one. They were as real as they needed to be in the eighteenth-century imagination.

Dragons have always existed in this virtual sense. Everyone knows what a dragon is, even though nobody has ever seen one and no two dragons are alike. They are monsters with a strong identity that also defy strict definition. A bit like a pangolin – which was something and many things at the same time. If you think of a dragon now, you can probably imagine it in some detail, and have licence to be creative with it. The question that distinguishes how monsters were seen in the past from how they are seen today is: what is the definition of 'real'? For us it is 'exists in the outside world'. In the eighteenth century, that was just one definition of real.

There was a red-hot market for dragons in the seventeenth and eighteenth centuries. They were the perfect playthings for the subtle games of experience and imagination played by scholars and collectors. Pieces of nature were often fancifully reinterpreted as creatures from ancient stories: the twisting length of a narwhal tooth from Greenland became the charmed horn of the Arabian unicorn; an elephant skull with its central nasal hole could be the head of a cyclops; a gigantic carved buffalo horn could be a griffin's claw. But nothing was quite so suited for these games as the dragon: many different things could be a 'dragon' and owning one could bring a great deal of prestige. As a result, from relative scarcity in the sixteenth century – being objects discussed with reverence and seen by few – dragon specimens proliferated in seventeenth- and eighteenth-century collections.

What these dragons *were* and what they were made *from* were not the same thing. They could be rays shaped and dried into wizened basilisks, or elaborate creations like the Hamburg Hydra, stitched together from animals such as fish, lizards, snakes and small mammals. The best way to make an imaginary creature look 'real' was to assemble it from pieces of existing nature, so it could stalk through cabinets, visitors' accounts, drawings and paintings unabashed. These objects were the stuff of imagination crafted from real creatures: nature super-naturalised.

Dragons were not accepted naïvely, though. Collectors knew that what they had were works of art. Aldrovandi's own prize 'Dragon of Bologna' from the sixteenth century was clearly a grass snake stitched onto a fish with toad legs. He knew it was artificial and far smaller than dragons were imagined to be. But he was extremely pleased with it, not least because it brought him fame and status. Anyone wanting an explanation for the workings of the modern art market – or NFTs for that matter – and the astounding prices some pieces reach, need only take a look at the early European dragon economy.

In the words of historian of science Paula Findlen, when it came to their monsters, collectors 'wanted to know *how* they were made, while avoiding the question of *whether* they existed'. The challenge was to 'dissect the bestiary that made the beast', not to dismantle the beast itself. Books on the natural history of dragons would give detailed instructions for how to make one, the ways to cut and shape a fresh ray so that it dried into a basilisk. Stating outright that a dragon was a counterfeit was a serious *faux pax*, though. That would dispel the dragon's magic, dissolve its value and turn it into just a collection of paws, fish bones and stuffed snake. That was only desirable if you wanted to score points off its owner or brand them a 'charlatan' – best avoided if they were a powerful person. The elaborate dances of make-believe between collectors, visitors and the monster-merchants were subtle social contracts.

Fundamentally, these patchwork monsters had value because they delighted people. The dragons of curiosity collections turned words and ideas into visual poetry. You could see a legendary creature with your own eyes, experiencing a simulated reality while knowing that it was a skilful fabrication. Hydras, basilisks and their kin were thrilling tricks of the senses. Watching a dragon film in the cinema is a similar kind of game, with ever-improving CGI. We admire the artistry which goes into creating 'realistic dragons' in the same way that visitors to collections admired the skill that went into producing a 'real' hydra. They did it with weasel pieces and snakes, we do it with high-res screens and complex imaging software.

So, to the second question of what happened to the monster when the hydra became a hoax? The answer is, it took *far* longer than you might expect before the power of ancient beliefs and the appetite for the fantastical was overcome by science. This particular hydra might have been reduced to weasel and snake bits, but dragons and other monsters persisted for a long time, even in scientific circles. In the next section, we'll see why.

An enchanted world

In 2015, I visited London's Science Museum to see an exhibition by Catalan artist Joan Fontcuberta called *Stranger than Fiction*. It was quite unlike the other galleries in the museum telling straight historical or scientific stories. Fontcuberta used the gravitas of the museum to create enchanting sci-fi tales. One traced the 'recently unearthed' work of a scientist who had documented many outlandish creatures. We were presented with the *Cercopithecus icaronocornu*, a winged unicorn monkey, *Felis pennatus*, a winged big cat, and the mermaid-like *Hydropithecus* of Sanary. The creatures were equipped with

Latin binomial names and displayed as stuffed specimens, photographs, sketches, scientific descriptions, snippets of film – all the trappings of a natural history museum. My favourite was a series of photographs showing fantastical plants in pin-sharp definition, precisely constructed from real plant material. They were the botanical equivalents of early modern dragons.

These objects were all presented with dead-pan solemnity. They were largely assembled from existing creatures and plants, yet they didn't exist. This got mixed reactions from visitors. Some people were in on the joke, looking around with a wry smile on their faces; others were perturbed. Here they were, in the Science Museum, looking at evidence of creatures they were *fairly* sure did not exist. But, all the usual proofs of existence were in front of them. Some people seemed to be going through a genuine empirical crisis. What they saw jarred with what they knew, yet they were in a place that was meant to provide a direct connection between seeing and knowing. Were they supposed to suspend disbelief on account of its scientific presentation? Were they being made fools of? This confusion was exactly what Fontcuberta had intended: to make us question the relationship between seeing and believing, belief and reality. It's not as clear cut as we might think today, and for good reason. Humans need more than objective reality.

This type of trickery would not have worried early modern visitors to a cabinet because, for them, practical experience and symbolic meaning ran together in a flexible way. They lived in an enchanted world. We no longer allow the objective and subjective worlds to blend so freely – at least, we don't think that we do. But this has meant that the world now seems disenchanted, which is a great loss in many ways. I will say more on this in the final chapter.

Our current biological system aims to encompass the living world, ordering it to mirror evolutionary history. The biological categories we have created are as close a match as we can manage for organisms' family trees. But in the seventeenth century, there were many different frameworks for seeing the natural world which overlapped and confounded one another. Things were grouped by similarities in form and function, but also their imagined geographical origins, their medicinal uses and moral values. The pragmatic, concrete knowledge that allowed organisations like the Dutch East India Company to sail across the world existed alongside a symbolic and scriptural understanding of the world. These did not align perfectly, but were essentially compatible. They combined into a holistic human experience: practical and empirical; spiritual and metaphorical. Exotic monsters like pangolins and traditional monsters like dragons were go-betweens of these different kinds of knowledge.

As a result of this flexibility, if a creature jarred with existing knowledge, intellectual workarounds could be found to buffer any differences between science and belief. A monster could easily be one of the playful jokes that God had wryly hidden in the fabric of Creation, for example. In the eighteenth century particularly, bizarre creatures were often viewed as Nature's experiments; exceptions which revealed the rules of God's divine plan.

There were plenty of other kinds of rationalisations, too. If a creature was deemed too strange to have existed in the Garden of Eden, for example, it could be given alternative origins. Brown bears were thought to have bleached out to become polar bears in the Arctic cold after leaving Eden. Other times, people imagined uncouth liaisons producing odd beasts: the seventeenth-century Jesuit scholar Athanasius Kircher argued that armadillos were the hybrid offspring of the tortoise and the hedgehog that had been cooped up together on Noah's Ark. Had Kircher touched on the pangolin, he might have posited that another, more gamesome hedgehog had snuck overboard the Ark and had a passionate fling with a fish. At least, I like to think so.

Eventually, of course, scientific knowledge became impossible to mesh entirely with a metaphorical worldview. Rifts developed, which widened over the centuries. Linnaeus was one figure leading a new way of seeing the world that is far more familiar to us: where the scientific trumps the symbolic. His *Systema Naturae* led to the modern binomial classification system we now use, a complete taxonomy of nature that sent dragons and other ancient monsters into the virtual world for serious naturalists. But the monsters were persistent. Even in the fifth edition of the *Systema Naturae* (1747) Linnaeus included unicorns, phoenixes and other fabulous beasts, which he called *animalia paradoxica*. It took him many editions shuffling the pangolins between different groups before he finally settled them in the group *Bruta*, along with anteaters and sloths.[16]

For more than a century after the Hamburg Hydra was debunked, there was still a place for wonder and monsters. The demand escalated, in fact, even as experimental science became the dominant way of knowing the world into the nineteenth century. Members of the scientific Royal Society of London would view monster specimens together over whisky and cigars. Mermaids, basilisks and giants attracted large audiences, as did sea monsters, as we saw in Chapter Six. The late nineteenth-century American showman P. T. Barnum became rich exploiting this appetite, often using unfortunate people seen as 'freaks'.

Curiosity collections and their monsters still attract us today. In 2012, Arizona's International Wildlife Museum exhibited the 'Centaur of Tymfi' created by the artist and biology professor Bill Williers from human and zebra skeletons. It wasn't the first centaur he had made – there's a persistent fashion for supernatural taxidermy. The pungent galleries of Viktor Wynd's Cabinet of Curiosities in East London play to this same fascination. Every time I have gone there, I have seen visitors gaze with the same tongue-in-cheek interest with which basilisks and bezoars might have been viewed in the eighteenth century. I've enjoyed my own willing suspension of disbelief when looking at the cabinets filled with Jenny Hanivers, wizened

ENCHANTED CREATURES

'mermaids', insect-winged 'faeries' riding dried cicadas, shrunken heads and the skeletons of bizarre animals.[17]

We might now be aware of the bestiary that makes the beast, but we still enjoy seeing impossible things. We still delight in feeling like the world might be filled with wonders and magic. It might be that we need other kinds of truth, beyond the scientific, to fully experience the world around us.

Terrible Lizards

Chapter 8

'The dinosaurs became extinct because they didn't have a space program'
Larry Niven

In south-east London, a short walk out of a grand, high-arched train station, you can find a herd of concrete giants. The Crystal Palace Dinosaurs have resided there for nearly two centuries, watching the comings and goings of park visitors with blank eyes. They're a fond childhood memory to many Londoners, but they are also a fantastic piece of science history, created by palaeontologists 170 years ago. I had seen pictures before visiting, but I was surprised by the effect that they had on me when I was standing only a few metres from them. The bulky statues animate the landscape of the park, like stone gods at a pagan place of worship. Their sheer size is unexpected, somehow, when you're only used to the abstract idea of dinosaurs, or to seeing their fossil skeletons in museums.

They're terrible dinosaurs, though, by modern standards. The smaller reptiles are a collection of inferential errors. There is a shutter-eyed *Ichthyosaurus*, an oar-jawed *Teleosaurus*, a snake-necked *Plesiosaurus* and a stubby-tailed *Labyrinthodon* lounging together by the water. Their dinosaur relatives are worse. The hulking *Iguanodon* look round as if you had interrupted their slow, booming conversation. One has its paw on a petrified cycad trunk, like a punter at a pub rubbernecking over the back of their chair. The *Megalosaurus* is all might and menace, heavy shoulders braced as if to spring forward and spook the coy *Hylaeosaurus*, just for a laugh. Those creatures that the Victorians were least clear on, such as the *Mosasaurus*, are placed out of full view behind bushes, shyly hypothetical. Though these models were cutting-edge depictions at the time, these monsters were conjured from fossil fragments and plenty of enthusiastic imaginative work. They are outdated unrealities, thrown into absurd relief by modern palaeontological knowledge.[1]

The majesty of the statues is lessened by the fact that they're surrounded by their tiny avian descendants, pigeons, who variously use them as perches and defecate on them. Still, the dinosaurs are magnetic. They put the nearby Pleistocene mammals – the antlered elk, horsey *Anoplotheria* and tapir-like *Palaeotheria* – in the shade.

Nobody cares about something that looks like a deer when there's a *Megalosaurus* to look at. As I walked alongside these smaller animals, I heard a father ask his little daughter if she wanted to 'go see the *real* monsters'. She responded with a squeal of delight and they trotted off towards the *Iguanodon*. The moment reinforced why I had made the trip down to the park in the first place: I wanted to understand how these reptilian fossils were first imagined as monsters and why they have continued to be. For creatures that are known from solid, petrified remains, our images of the dinosaurs have varied greatly over history, far more than many fictitious monsters like the Minotaur or harpies. They have an undeniably special importance, though – I wanted to know why.

D is for dinosaur

I asked friends who have small children about their kids' relationships with dinosaurs. One has a three-year-old boy, Jesse, who is entranced by Dinosauria. He loves to watch them on TV, wear dinosaur-themed clothes, and he knows more kinds of dinosaur than anything else (except perhaps cars, which he can brand with shocking accuracy). He can identify a *Stegosaurus*, a *Velociraptor*, a *Brachiosaurus* or a *Spinosaurus* faster than most adults, their names bursting out of him like an excited gameshow contestant. He's become the in-house 'dino expert' at his nursery, whom the other kids consult on all questions dinosaur.

This isn't surprising really. The German-Jewish psychologist Erich Fromm first coined the term 'biophilia' in the 1970s, to describe the 'passionate love of life and of all that is alive' that we all possess.[2] Humans are born with an innate fascination for other lifeforms. We are drawn to other creatures and want to understand them, at least early on in life. They needn't be *living* lifeforms. Children play out these tendencies with whatever biodiversity they have access to, even if it's artificial. In 2002, researchers at the University of Cambridge found that eight-year-old schoolchildren were far better at naming all of the different *Pokémon* species than they were at identifying common species of UK wildlife. Raised on screens, *Pokémon* were the wildlife of the virtual worlds these children inhabited.

These interactions might have a lasting effect on children's brains. A study at Stanford looked at brain activation in people who had played *Pokémon* from a young age. They found that a specific region of the brain reacted to *Pokémon* characters. The lightning-tailed, electric-yellow Pikachu was imprinted on their neurology. Early years of engaging with the *Pokémon* universe made them good at identifying its fauna. Perhaps childhood 'dinomania' also leaves a lasting imprint of dinosaurs on the brain. Dinosaur enthusiasm is an acceptable form of childhood hangover for adults. My own partner has a rather nifty set of dinosaur pyjamas he likes to wear for sofa days (though I am not strictly allowed to tell anyone). When I asked one of my teenage students, Harry, why he liked dinosaurs, he summed it up for me: 'because they're frickin' *awesome*, man' (emphasis his). I didn't test his identification skills, but his enthusiasm was certainly still there.

Dinosaur 'awesomeness' supercharges the biophilia of children like Jesse with added fear and wonder. Dinosaurs become almost like scaly superheroes: Jesse's fascination isn't limited to dinosaur clothes, books and programs. He loves to *be* a dinosaur. He puts on the wearable dinosaur tail that his mother made for him, leaps onto a chair and roars like a *T. rex*, curling his fingers into sharp talons, raining terror from great heights. His small size belies this *T. rex* alter-ego, a ferocious monster trapped in a cherubic exterior of blond hair and soulful green eyes. But that's the release that the dinosaur gives him: as a little boy, he's full of testosterone-fuelled impetus but has none of the real-world power to enact it. By becoming a dinosaur, perhaps, Jesse can feel like a powerful force in the world – without any of the responsibility of actually being one.

Dinosaurs entrance children because they are fascinating and scary, but also because they are safe. It's like watching lions in the zoo but exchanging safety fences and thick panes of glass for 65 million years of distance. 'Safe thrills' are powerful attractions: rollercoasters, horror films, skydiving. They're all ways of getting adrenaline pumping, risk-free. Dinosaurs can be ferocious predators or playmates, like the giant purple television plushie 'Barney the Dinosaur' watched by children in the '90s and 2000s. They're monsters offering the thrill of terrible reality that have been neutered by the passage of time.

Dinomania

Dinosaurs captivate adults as well. In Stephen J. Gould's essay 'Dinomania', he sums up the standard explanation for why we are fascinated with dinosaurs: 'big, fierce, and extinct'. As a palaeontologist, Gould found this pithy summary insufficient. He thought that the heavy marketing around films such as *Jurassic Park* (1993) was more important. The dinosaurs really sell themselves, though. The endless queues to get into the London Natural History Museum's Dinosaur Gallery show just how attractive these vanished giants are to all ages. Inside, the gigantic scaffolded skeletons are animated by dramatic lighting. There are dinosaur footprints in which to place your hand and viscerally feel the difference in size. Animatronic dinosaurs maul each other slowly or toss their heads and roar at an audience caught between knowing amusement and instinctual jitters. It's no surprise that the gallery is the gravitational centre of the museum. The dinosaurs' descendants, the stuffed birds in the gallery across the main hall, get nowhere near as much attention. The Dinosaur Gallery brings visitors close to creatures that are alien and familiar at the same time, and much, much bigger than them. Their sheer size returns adults to the world of childhood, where they are only small beings among giants.

Some dinosaurs have become palaeontological poster-creatures. 'Dippy', the 26-metre-long *Diplodocus*, used to greet visitors in the main hall of the Natural History

Museum with a peg-toothed grin. When he was replaced by a blue whale skeleton in 2018, it caused a national stir. I was a volunteer in the museum at the time, and visitors kept asking where Dippy was. They looked crestfallen when they heard that 'the nation's favourite dinosaur' was on tour around the country, like some wayward fossilised rockstar.

Darren Naish, the palaeontologist we met in Chapter Six, writes about the biology and cultural impact of dinosaurs. He has done a great deal for their public image, bringing the latest dinosaur science into the mainstream media. He argues that, while lions or Komodo dragons are incredible, dinosaurs 'were just off the flipping chain in terms of their size, power and strength'. The mammoths, giant ground sloths or woolly rhinos have nowhere near the same hold on popular attention. Although many of these creatures are not *that* different to elephants, bears or white rhinos, they can't really compete with 'a predatory animal with giant sabre-type teeth that was ten times bigger than an elephant', like a *T. rex*.

Vast, scaly monsters of all guises appear throughout the world's mythologies. We met Tiamat in Chapter Two, Beowulf's dragon nemesis in Chapter Five and the echoes of dragonish beings in European curiosity cabinets in Chapter Seven – these are just a few. From the beginning, dinosaurs stomped in to feed our appetite for reptilian giants. And they're just as surprising as these mythical monsters. The fact that dinosaurs also lived in a world of infinite wilderness, in forests far bigger than any that exist now, provides a fitting landscape for such monsters to roam in the imagination. But, to fully understand why we love dinosaurs so much, we need to start at the very beginning of our relationship with them.

Dinner in the *Iguanodon*

Dinomania is nothing new. Dinosaurs triggered boisterous excitement in Victorian scientists nearly two centuries ago. On New Year's Eve in 1853, twenty-one intellectuals and industrialists sat down to one of the most famous dinners of science history. They were seated shoulder-to-shoulder inside a hollow, thirty-foot *Iguanodon* model, one of the Crystal Palace Dinosaurs we met earlier, with its top removed. The guests included the notable palaeontologists William Buckland, Georges Cuvier and Gideon Mantell, while Richard Owen sat at the head of the table. As the country's top palaeontologist – and a very disagreeable character – nobody but Owen would sit in the head of the *Iguanodon*.[3]

Circling waiters reached into the beast's interior to serve an eight-course dinner and charge the diners' glasses, as they consumed mock turtle soup, roast turkey, game pies, fish, pastries, jellies, fruit and plenty of sherry. Unsurprisingly, the group became merrier and rowdier as the evening continued, with singing and debates lasting well into the small hours. From the pictures we have of the event, the *Iguanodon* looks quite perturbed by the riot in its insides. If the *Iguanodon* didn't have indigestion, the diners probably did.

The papers made a meal of this 'Fun in a Fossil', but not only because of its comic value. The dinner occurred at the tail end of an unrivalled display of scientific and technological prowess, which had begun in 1851. The Great Exhibition of the Works of Industry of All Nations extended across ten miles and included over 100,000 objects, showcasing the global power of the British Empire. At its epicentre in Hyde Park was a glittering wonder – the Crystal Palace. This was the most spectacular glass structure that had ever been built, a triumph of the novel sheet-glass production method. It was an exhibition all about showing off – from gigantic 50-kilo nuggets of gold from Chile to fabulous urns and textiles from China and Russia. Every country shipped over its prize creations to be part of the global stage. Nothing like it had been seen before and neither has it since.

The model *Iguanodon* and its fellows were created by the artist Benjamin Waterhouse Hawkins, when the Great Exhibition was moved to the outskirts of London. There were thirty-seven creatures in total – two *Iguanodon*, a *Hylaeosaurus* and a *Megalosaurus*, along with non-dinosaurs such as *Plesiosaurs*, *Ichthyosaurs*, pterodactyls, reptiles and giant mammals. They were the first ever life-sized models made of extinct species: state-of-the-art relics, reincarnated in brickwork and cement. The four hefty steam-engine dinos were scaly and wattle-necked, straight out of imaginations infused with industrial wonder. Had they been alive, they would have dragged their tails behind them as they chugged along on all fours.

The dinosaurs were discovered during the decades before the Exhibition. Fragments of dinosaur fossils had been found for centuries, but it was only in the 1800s that more complete fossil bones were unearthed and recorded. Each of these early finds has its own discovery story centred around a Victorian hero, like knights entering the dens of ancient dragons to drag them under scientific scrutiny. An apocryphal tale of a country surgeon and his wife, Gideon and Mary Mantell, finding teeth embedded in a rock by the side of the road explains the first discovery of *Iguanodon* remains in 1822.[4] Geologist William Buckland unearthed enough *Megalosaurus* fossils to produce the first scientific dinosaur description in 1824. The twelve-year-old Mary Anning and her brother Joseph found a complete *Ichthyosaur* fossil in the cliffs of Lyme Regis in 1810–11, the specimen which brought the creature into the scientific limelight. She didn't stop there – in 1823 Mary found an almost-complete *Plesiosaur* and in 1828 the winged *Pterodactylus*.

The British pre-eminence did not last very long. First there were discoveries in mainland Europe and then a deluge from the New World. This began with the discovery of a few teeth in Montana followed by a full *Hadrosaurus* skeleton in New Jersey in the 1850s. Aided by the new railway arteries bleeding into the west, explorers discovered fossil beds in Alberta, Wyoming, Nebraska and other regions of North America, richer than any in

Europe. They contained large, complete skeletons which showed far more about the creatures than most European finds did. The manic 'Bone Rush' which took place over the next twenty years produced over 130 new dinosaur species and made America the leading light in palaeontology, the place where *Allosaurus*, *Brontosaurus*, *Stegosaurus* and *Triceratops* had once roamed. These beasts helped to build an image of the newly independent North America as a land of grandeur – home to majestic creatures and burgeoning big industry. These dinosaurs were emblems of a heavyweight new empire.[5]

Giants' bones

The earth had been belching up mammoth bones and pieces of dinosaurs long before the nineteenth century, and they had not gone unnoticed. Adrienne Mayor is a folklorist and historian of ancient science at the University of Stanford. She suspected that the lack of explicit palaeontological references in Classical literature might not mean that there had been no palaeontological finds. She wondered if some ancient mythological creatures might have been based on fossil discoveries which had simply not been recorded. What if the dragons of myth had really been seeded by dinosaurs? So, Mayor did some deep detective work.

Over years of piecing together maps, historical references, literature and obscure artifacts, Mayor showed that impressive fossils had been found in ancient Greece, the Roman Empire and further afield. And that they may have been the inspiration for some mythic beasts. For one, the eagle-headed, lion-bodied griffin in the fifth century BCE was a 'creature of folklore grounded in naturalistic detail'. Its form had been inspired by the strange fossil skeletons and nests found by Scythian nomads prospecting for gold in Central Asia. The fossilised remains of the beaked dinosaur *Protoceratops* were especially common in that region and were evidence of bizarre four-legged creatures with beak-like mouths. These ideas came to the attentions of Greek and Roman writers and were transformed into gold-guarding griffins.

Mayor found that mythical interpretations of palaeontological remains were widespread in the ancient world. The massive bones and teeth of extinct megafauna were thought to belong to mythical heroes and giants from the remote past. These relics were often displayed in Greek temples. Mammoth bones were evidence of the Gigantomachy, a climactic event in mythohistory when the Giants tried to overthrow the gods of Olympus. In the first century BCE, Emperor Augustus set up a museum in his Capri home to house his collection of fossil monsters and giants. A few decades later, an earthquake exposed some big fossil skeletons by the Black Sea and a single twelve-inch molar was sent to Emperor Tiberius. He commissioned a mathematician to model a bust of the ugly giant to which the molar had supposedly belonged, the first known reconstruction of a creature that no longer existed. The steppe mammoth whose tooth it originally was would probably not have been flattered by the representation.[6]

This is not to say that mythical beasts and monsters were simply the result of people coming across strange remains. These fossil effigies became embedded in existing myths; they weren't necessarily the origins of them. It isn't surprising that vast bones would be interpreted as the remnants of gigantic heroes and Titans when these images existed already. Some of these 'giant' specimens from ancient collections were noticed by naturalists such as Sir Hans Sloane and Georges Cuvier in the late eighteenth century. They used comparative anatomy to demote them to the remains of elephants and whales. But the magic of these bones endured. Plenty remained in curiosity collections as the relics of long-gone giants.

The first dinosaur bone to be published as an illustration followed in the same tradition at first. In 1676, the lower half of a femur was found in Stonesfield limestone quarry in Oxfordshire and was described in *Natural History of Oxfordshire* (1677) by the naturalist Robert Plot. His first idea was that it had belonged to a war elephant from the Roman army. Plot later changed his mind, suggesting that the bone was from a gigantic Biblical human, a more exciting wonder with which to populate the English countryside. A hundred years later, the physician and naturalist Richard Brookes labelled an image of this same bone as '*Scrotum humanum*' in his *System of Natural History* (1763). The bone itself has been lost, but it probably belonged to a *Megalosaurus*. Technically, though, 'human scrotum' was the first ever scientific name given to a dinosaur.[7]

Making the 'grewsome beasts'

The dinosaur fossils unearthed by Victorian palaeontologists such as William Buckland and Gideon Mantell were only fragments – single bones, fractured jaws and teeth. But this added to their magic: ambiguous relics left plentiful room for fantasy and the beasts were constructed in this space. Sometimes, unconventional methods were used. Richard Fallon, who studies the interplay of literature and science, described the occultist palaeontology of the late nineteenth century. Psychic mediums would touch fossils and describe the visions of monstrous creatures that came to them. Their findings were presented as objective, scientific data, of course.[8]

In 1842, Owen took charge of the dinosaurs' public image. He gave the *Megalosaurus*, *Iguanodon* and *Hylaeosaurus* their own group identity: 'Dinosauria', meaning 'fearfully great lizards'.[9] The word was slow to take off – even Owen was reluctant to use it too often – losing out to more colourful terms such as 'monster' or 'dragon'. 'Dinosaur' eventually got going after the spectacular American finds from the 1870s. The plentiful new species and complete skeletons, that were so dramatically different from other prehistoric reptiles, established the dinosaurs' special identity.

Owen was able to craft his 'Dinosauria' to fit his preferred interpretation of fossil evidence. He was not so keen on the idea of life developing spontaneously, from simple to complex, through evolution. He preferred the idea that each group of animals was divinely created in sequence, reaching an apotheosis before degenerating gradually to make way for the rise of the next group. So, he styled his dinosaurs as the pinnacle of reptilian creatures. According to him, the dinosaurs walked on four feet with powerful, mammalian shoulders. Owen thought that they might have been warm blooded and had mammal-like physiologies. The Crystal Palace beasts show his vision plainly: the majestic rulers of a Jurassic Golden Age. Their pathetic descendants, the modern amphibians and reptiles, according to Owen, skulked about damply in ponds and undergrowth. They were mere shadows of this ancestral glory, reminders of just how downhill things had gone since Creation's reptilian heyday.

As the Victorian fascination with the dinosaurs built up steam, many prominent writers became riveted by them. They used arresting verbal 'recipes for producing monsters' to ignite readers' imaginations, according to Professor of Literature, Ralph O'Connor. The *Ichthyosaur* had 'the snout of a Porpoise [. . .] with the teeth of a Crocodile, the head of a Lizard with the vertebrae of a Fish, and the sternum of an Ornithorhynchus [platypus] with the paddles of a Whale'. The *Hylaeosaurus* was like a 'giant porcupine' and a 'giant moloch lizard'. The plesiosaur was often described as 'a serpent threaded through the shell of a turtle'. Unsurprisingly, the *Iguanodon*, the *Megalosaurus* and the pterodactyls were often referred to as 'dragons' in scientific literature. Anything big and extinct, irrespective of taxonomic position or geological period, fell under the enticing umbrella of 'monster'. Journalists and writers today still enjoy using many of these same tropes.

These ancient dragons were given Romantic, antediluvian landscapes to inhabit, becoming protagonists in an earlier scene of the 'great Earth drama'. Readers weren't just given facts, they were invited into a literary Jurassic world, part of a growing trend for fantasy literature. In his passage on the pterodactyl, for example, William Buckland conjured a hellish world which readers could explore in their imaginations, mobbed by aerial devils and surrounded by reptile-filled oceans: 'like Milton's fiend . . . the creature was a fit companion for the kindred reptiles that swarmed in the seas, or crawled on the shores of a turbulent planet . . . shoals of no less monstrous *Ichthyosauri* and *Plesiosauri* swarming in the ocean'. The ancient past was presented as something straight out of Dante's *Inferno*. Another writer described these 'Grewsome beasts' as 'the evil spirits who beset Aeneas or Satan in an old illustrated Virgil or Paradise Lost'. Compare the Babylonian myth of Tiamat, or the Norse world-serpent Jörmungandr: the dinosaurs were part of a new, almost-tangible mythology of creation filled with dragons of chaos.

One of the most influential books was Henry Neville Hutchinson's *Extinct Monsters* (1892). He used florid literary references, from Lewis Carroll's *Jabberwocky* to *Grimm's Fairy Tales*, to bring the dinosaurs to life. But, he promised, the creatures he was going to show the reader were also so much more than the stuff of myth or literature: 'For not even the dragons supposed to have been slain by armed knights in old times, when people gave ear to any tale, however extravagant, could equal in size or strength the real dragons we shall presently meet with'. This promise of meeting beasts that had existed *right here* – leaving their gigantic teeth and bones – gave the dinosaurs an edge with which the mythic dragons from faraway places just couldn't compete.

Dead ends

The dinosaurs begged a big question, though: where had they gone? How had such regal creatures vanished? They had existed in Oxfordshire, Dorset or Somerset – lying dormant right under the feet of the palaeontologists who studied them, but their world had somehow disappeared. Extinction was not a new idea in the middle of the nineteenth century; late eighteenth-century findings of mastodon bones and fossils from North America were irrefutable evidence that species could die out completely. The extinction of invertebrates such as ammonites or trilobites was an academic question, though: it had little bearing on humanity's role in the world. The loss of large creatures such as mastodons could be made palatable by the fact that their close relatives were still around. The disappearance of powerful dragons that had ruled a past age and left only petrified remains was more troubling.

Charles Lyell's *Principles of Geology* (1830–33) was a watershed text in geology. He created a 'deep time' model of gradual, uniform change for how the globe might have developed over hundreds of millions of years. This was one of the founding influences on Charles Darwin's Theory of Evolution by Natural Selection (which was notably quiet on dinosaurs). Lyell's model included a particularly worrying aspect: the idea that geological history was cyclical. He suggested that 'The huge iguanodon . . . might reappear in the woods, and the ichthyosaur in the sea, while the pterodactyle might flit again through umbrageous groves of tree-ferns'. This was a terrifying idea: that there could have been a world dominated by dinosaurs in which humans were merely prey, and that it might return. It was a serious threat to the traditional order of nature, in which humans were believed to be firmly at the top.[10]

There's an undercurrent of this anxiety in nineteenth-century dinosaur jokes. Reporting on the *Iguanodon* dinner, *Punch* magazine quipped: 'We congratulate the company on the era in which they live; for if it had been an early geological period, they might perhaps have occupied the *Iguanodon*'s inside without having any dinner there'. In 'Extinct Monsters' (1893), the poet Eugene Field pointed out how fortunate he was to live when he did:

Those extinct monsters of hoof and wing
Were not conducive to lyric song;
So Nature reserved this tender bard
For the kindlier age of Pork and Lard.

Another way of dealing with the imagined prehistoric threat was to belittle the dinosaurs, turning them into relics of a Biblical past that was fated to end. The French writer Auguste Villiers de l'Isle-Adam suggested that 'Nature was quick to pass the sponge of her deluges over these awkward sketches [the dinosaurs], these first nightmares of life'. When Dippy was first constructed in London, Hutchinson commented that these animals had been Nature's 'evolutionary experiments', whose extinction had made way for 'better' lifeforms who didn't lumber around in quagmires.[11]

Others took this a step further, turning the dinosaurs from mighty monsters into ridiculous monstrosities. One item in the *Washington Post* on 23 June 1912 pictured a strange-looking *Stegosaurus* titled 'most Grotesque animal' and subtitled 'Stegosaur, who lived in Utah ages ago is a freak of nature'. On 15 August 1920, the *Ogden Standard Examiner* described 'one of the weirdest prehistoric monsters', an example of Nature's 'creative indigestion', that had hollow bones with 'great air cavities' and 'enormous plates along its back for coasting through the air like some gigantic gliding machine'. A *Stegosaurus* with laterally splayed back plates was pictured on the tip of a cliff, ready to launch itself into the skies. While the idea of flying stegosauri is ridiculous, ironically, the hollow bones were what allowed their descendants, the birds, to do so.[12]

Despite their cultural impact, the rulers of a past Age of Reptiles often became laughable, swamp-dwelling sluggards, doomed to evolutionary failure. The mammals, in contrast, were depicted as mobile, adaptable, intelligent: Creation's worthy champions. Dinosaurs might have dominated a lost world, but their brawn couldn't compete with the brains and cunning of humans or the complex machinery of the British Empire that now dominated the globe.

The de-extinction of dragons

On the signs accompanying the Crystal Palace dinosaurs, you can see outlines of the nineteenth-century images of these creatures next to the modern renderings. The two versions hardly seem related. Given that their bones are preserved in rock, it's ironic that images of dinosaurs have been so incredibly volatile. They've changed like fashion trends, the visions of them shifting every few decades. The first chunky behemoths had their legs splayed out like crocodiles and lizards, which followed naturally from the fact that they're gigantic reptiles. From the late nineteenth century, the dinosaurs were remodelled into upright but sluggish animals, with legs positioned under their hips and their tails dragging behind them. Then the 'Dinosaur Renaissance' in the 1960s and '70s turned palaeontology from an arcane study into a new science of ancient creatures that were often speedy, warm-blooded and exciting.[13]

The 'Dinosaur Enlightenment' is now well under way, and it's producing even wackier creatures than we pictured before. Recent palaeontological research has uncovered the strangely proportioned limbs, colourful feathers and elaborate appendages of different dinosaur species. From the *Supersaurus* that might have been 39 metres long and the shark-toothed *Carcharodontosaurus*, five times bigger than a *T. rex*, to the *Ankylosaur* with a tail like an Aztec war club, new discoveries keep revealing surprising things. Far from scaly automatons, we now understand that many species may well have been bird-like creatures with complex vocalisations, fabulous adornments and attentive parenting styles. Miraculously, the more we learn about them, the more exotic these 'dragons' become, revealed by growing fossil evidence and increasingly sophisticated ways of interpreting it.

It's important to look back at our dinosaur history, though: these monsters tell us something about ourselves. Serious scientific interpretations of dinosaurs – from industrial titans to modern high-octane sophisticates – have always been entangled with cultural influences. In some ways, this is not so different to what seventeenth-century naturalists were doing when they concocted monsters from bits of exotic animal. Even complete fossil skeletons need to be imagined into living beasts. As historian Lukas

Rieppel comments: 'The dinosaur is a chimera. Some parts ... are the result of biological evolution. But others are products of human ingenuity, constructed by artists, scientists, and technicians in a laborious process that stretches from the dig site to the naturalist's study and the museum's preparation lab.' As these ingredients shift over time, so do the dinosaurs. The palaeontologists of the future might well look back at the dinosaurs of today with wry smiles.

Though long dead, dinosaurs can still become embroiled in scientific and political clashes. The 'Woke *T. rex*' debacle in April 2022 was a case in point. One episode of *Prehistoric Planet* featured a male *T. rex* taking care of his offspring – going for a swim and hanging out together. This was based on cutting-edge scientific findings, but tabloids such as *The Sun* sneered about the 'PC-Rex'. To *The Sun*'s readership, a male on babysitting duty – especially a male of the most macho of dinosaurs – looked like the 'woke' agenda pushing progressive gender roles. What this uproar really demonstrated was just how many dinosaurs are still among us.

The lodestone of modern dinoculture is Steven Spielberg's 1993 film *Jurassic Park*, based on a novel by the palaeontologist Michael Crichton. *Jurassic Park* and its sequels connected the public with the new science of dinosaurs, making them a pop-culture phenomenon again. A mosquito filled with 'dinosaur blood' was a plausible enough de-extinction method to vigorously re-animate the creatures. This was fitting at a time when it felt like we sat on the cusp of limitless genetic technology. Untold power could be unleashed, both our own and that of the dinosaurs. *Jurassic Park* played out what would happen if we chose to revive monsters of the past, just because we could. The combined results of human hubris and revenant megabeasts were not pretty: nature conclusively beat human technology.

Jack Horner, the heavyweight palaeontologist who was both a character inspiration and a technical adviser for the *Jurassic Park* films, has not been put off by the film's warning. His 'Dino-Chicken project' aims to produce a 'chickenosaurus': to 'retro-engineer a dinosaur-like animal from a bird', given that birds are 'really living dinosaurs'. Working backwards through evolutionary history, discovering which genes have been altered or switched on and off, it might be possible to press 'Ctrl-Z' on them, one by one. While DNA entombed in a mosquito would decay over time, DNA reproduced in living organisms might contain far more information about birds' ancient ancestors. Horner is confident they will be able to produce something like a mini velociraptor. This project seems surprising, given the feature-length public service announcement about the dangers of velociraptors that he helped to produce.

The idea of 'de-extinction' is deeply exciting, however, and we've made attempts at it already. Scientists created a hybrid 'mammophant' embryo in 2017 from mammoth DNA fragments and an Indian elephant genome, using the genome editing tool, CRISPR-Cas9. It sparked hopes that other lost species might be revived through genetic technologies, such as dodos, moa birds and thylacines. But what would happen if we actually managed to bring back dinosaurs? What if we made it possible to meet extinct monsters? In *Jurassic World* (2015), directed by Colin Trevorrow, the manager of the park complains, 'Kids now look at a *Stegosaurus* like an elephant in the zoo'. The revived creatures have become banal theme-park attractions, and also tools for social commentary on jaded modern consumerism. While this idea sorely underestimates how much children enjoy watching elephants in the zoo, it does more of a disservice to dinosaurs. Their popularity doesn't rest on their extinction. While communing with a grazing *Brachiosaurus* in the original *Jurassic Park*, the palaeontologist Dr Alan Grant tells the little boy: 'They're not monsters, Lex, they're just animals'. Later, cowering in a car vibrating with the deep growls of the hungry *T. rex*, it's easy to imagine he revised this opinion. There's nothing pedestrian about a gigantic apex predator.[14]

There's a tension around the dinosaurs. We want to experience them fully, to know as much as possible about them – but we're also very resistant to them changing from how we knew them as children. For all the creative effort put into their hyper-realistic dinosaur visuals, the *Jurassic Park* films have been remarkably bad at keeping up with palaeontological developments, much to specialists' chagrin. Only one feathered dinosaur has appeared in the franchise, an oddly berserk *Pyroraptor*, who was also rather dim.[15] These big-screen beasts are constrained by the lagging images of dinosaurs in the popular imagination. If Hollywood knows its audience, most film-goers want to see their childhood monsters reanimated before their eyes. They don't want them tampered with for the sake of cutting-edge science. Fantasy wins over facts, and the late-twentieth-century dinosaurs currently mean too much to let them go just yet.

Because they combine reality and unreality, evidence and imagination, dinosaurs demonstrate how passionate and subjective our relationships with other beasts can be. There's something special about the dinosaurs, of course. The idea of thousands of *T. rex* striding through vast prehistoric landscapes is overwhelming. Even seeing an animatronic simulation or a fossilised dinosaur tooth is thrilling. They bring our fantasies of mythical dragons into almost-concrete reality. They trigger our innate fear in the presence of giant predators and stir up our fascination with strange lifeforms. These mutating, meaningful monsters remind us of the immense forces of nature – at a safe distance. Why this is more important than ever, at a time when our dominance over the living world has led us into a dragon's den, is what the following, final chapter explores.

Conclusion

Titans of Gaia

'This inhuman place makes human monsters'
Stephen King

Out of the sea, a vast creature erupts, shedding water as it hoists its bulk into the air with leathery wings. Its three long necks wind across each other, one head missing. Behind it whip two tails with spiked ends. The creature rises into the sky, disappearing for a moment behind dark cloud shot through with lightning. It hulks down on a mountain top overlooking a ruined city. Fire and lava bleed slowly down the mountainside. The heat doesn't trouble the beast, though – it crackles with its own energy. The truncated neck writhes and the point of a head emerges from the stump, covered in an amniotic sac. A scaled snout forces its way through the gelatinous film. Complete, the beast splays out its wings, braces its body and screams to the sky from all three maws. Around the globe, giant creatures begin to stir, breaking through ice, shaking off thin mountainous crusts, erupting from oil seeps – following the dragon's call and flattening cities in their wake.

This might sound like something out of the Book of Revelation, but it is actually the peak peril scene of *Godzilla: King of the Monsters* (2019), made by Legendary Studios and Warner Brothers. Woken from a cryogenic slumber by ecoterrorists, the three-headed hydra, King Ghidorah, takes charge of a recently erupted volcano in Hawaii. He calls forth the other ancient monsters that have stayed buried in the Earth for millennia. Their stirring presages the end of humanity's dominance, perhaps of humanity itself. Luckily, good old Godzilla rallies in the ocean's depths, after snacking on a nuclear warhead. He bursts from the sea fizzing with radiation to take Ghidorah on and reclaim his place as the alpha of the pack. The monsters are subdued. They become benign workers of ecological regeneration and start healing the biosphere from human damage, seeding rainforests in deserts and rejuvenating bleached coral reefs. Humanity is saved from its own apocalypse.

It's not a very good film, from a cinematic perspective. Everything except the CGI is faintly ridiculous, especially the writers' ideas about how ecology works. But it's an interesting part of a long film dynasty. Godzilla is the ringleader of a monstrous clan imported from Japanese cinema – the *kaiju*. Along with Godzilla and Ghidorah, the *kaiju* include Mothra the giant moth monster, Rodan the outsized pterodactyl, Gamera the giant turtle and many others. The word *kaiju* originally meant 'strange beasts' – describing cryptids and fantastical creatures. After the classic 1954 *Godzilla* film, directed by Ishiro Honda, the term *kaiju* was used for this particular family of giants. They've appeared in many films made in both Japan and Hollywood – it's the longest-running film franchise globally.[1]

Aside from the arresting spectacle of watching monsters fight, the overriding theme of *kaiju* films is of terrible threat to humanity. They've become the vengeful Titans of the modern day, rising from the Earth's bowels to rip apart the fabric of human life. We began in the early chapters with the struggle against chaos in the creation of the world. And have come full circle to creatures of chaos erupting from under the Earth's surface to cause its end. It feels like a fitting place to finish this book – to explore our nightmares of the world ending in monstrous ways.

Creatures can embody so many of the anxieties that plague the modern world. Ever since Darwinian theory punched holes in the absolute division between humans and animals, science fiction has obsessed over how far this division could be further dissolved. H. G. Wells's classic 1896 novel *The Island of Dr Moreau*, about a cruel scientist who creates a mutilated band of human-animal hybrids, has inspired numerous films.[2] Worries about what chimaeras could emerge from botched genetic experiments are played out in films such as *Splice* (2009), with its uncanny hybrid creature, Dren. But looming over all else are anxieties of anthropogenic apocalypse and the monsters that might enact it.

Visions of apocalypse are nothing new – we've been imagining the world's end for as long as we've been picturing its beginning. Some apocalypse stories are set in a cyclical cosmos, revolving between end and renewal. The Greek writer Hesiod told of several ages of men – the Gold, Silver, Bronze, Heroic and Iron ages. Each race was destroyed by the gods or disappeared, to be replaced by a lesser race in a chain of degradation. The Iron age was where Hesiod placed himself. In contrast to the demigod heroes of the age just before, the men of the Iron age were sad and selfish. Hesiod thought that they were probably due for another divinely orchestrated wipe-out, so that the world could resume with a clean slate. Floods are a common extinction method in such revolutions. Another Mesopotamian myth even older than the *Enūma Eliš*, called *Atrahasis*, told of an apocalyptic flood sent by the gods to kill off the unruly humans. Only the wise man Atrahasis, tipped off by a god, had built a large, covered boat in which he could shelter with his family and all the animals during the seven-day deluge, just like the Christian Noah and his Ark.[3]

In other apocalypse traditions, fire and brimstone rain down as gods and monsters fight a battle to end all battles. Ragnarok was the Norse apocalypse described in the tenth-century poem *Völuspá*.[4] It told of how the monstrous children of Loki, the trickster god, would run amok and kill the elite *Aesir* gods one by one. Fenrir the gigantic wolf would break free from his chains and scour the land, swallowing everything in his path, until he found the father-god, Odin, and consumed him. The vast world-encircling serpent Jörmungandr would writhe onto the shores, spreading watery chaos and covering the land in his venom. The thunder-god, Thor, would slay this world-dragon with his hammer, but not without being fatally poisoned first. Among the raiding ice giants, the fire giants and all of the other havoc, the gods would die and the world would be consumed in flame, sinking back into the watery void of the sea.

The Christian Book of Revelation gives a confusing and monster-heavy account of the end of the world. It's the final book of the New Testament, and it ends the whole thing on a cliff-hanger. Alongside plagues, earthquakes, floods and fire wiping out human races, monsters wage campaigns of random terror. Satan, in the guise of a vast dragon, appears. He has seven heads, ten horns and seven crowns – and sweeps a third of the stars of heaven to earth with just a swish of his tail. A great beast rises from the sea, with seven heads, ten horns and ten crowns, spouting blasphemy. Then a Beast from the Earth appears, a lion with two lamb's horns, who drives people to give themselves 'the mark of the beast'.[5] In doing so – giving in to their violent, sexual, animal nature – people condemn themselves for eternity. After this, the world is covered in pestilence and flame, while the seas turn to blood and the sunlight dies. If this is the apocalypse of the West's Christian heritage, what is different about our images of apocalypse now? In some ways, they're worse. To paraphrase Tolkien: they have no gods, only monsters – and humans.

The Anthropocene

The *kaiju* films mark a period in history when our imaginings of apocalypse have been unlike any before. They are fantasies of the world's end without divine power, and all the more terrifying for it. The Godzilla of Honda's original 1954 film was a 120-metre dinosaur-like monster who was disturbed and supercharged by nuclear tests. He rose from the ocean's depths like an irritated battering ram to flatten Tokyo – so large and radioactive that, even when going for a stroll to let off some steam, he wreaked devastation.

Godzilla wasn't the first big cinema monster, but he had an impact that none had had before, figuratively speaking. Mark Jacobson, writing for the *New York Times*, summed up the 1954 *Godzilla*: 'the A-bomb dropped on Hiroshima sent a flash brighter and hotter than a thousand suns, which, in addition to killing 100,000 people, caused a simple monitor lizard who was just minding his own damn business to mutate into a really pissed-off SaurusDude bent on global destruction'. In post-war Japan, Godzilla's implacable bulk was the terror of nuclear holocaust, the world-ending potential of the atom bomb that had already been unleashed on Japan, destroying Hiroshima and Nagasaki in 1945. He was also the image of the devastation wrought by the firebombing of Tokyo during Operation Meetinghouse in 1945, the tyranny of the post-war US occupation of Japan (1945–52) and the fear instilled by the US nuclear tests on Bikini Atoll (1946–58). He was a creature generated by a nation's very real fear of obliteration. And that's why, even though Godzilla looks like a basic sort of dinosaur-monster, he's still a godfather of modern apocalypse mythology.[6]

The early twentieth century was the first time that we, as a species, became fully aware of our capacity to destroy. The World Wars unleashed horror and inhumanity on a larger scale than had ever been seen before. Watching the first nuclear test explosion in 1940, Robert Oppenheimer, head of the Los Alamos Project, intoned: 'Now I am become Death, the destroyer of worlds', a misquotation of Krishna in the *Bhagavad Gita*.[7] This line resonated through Christopher Nolan's 2023 film *Oppenheimer* like an ominous prophecy. Honda's city-shattering Godzilla was an irresistible force who could destroy worlds – our world – in the same way. The difference between the apocalypse that the *kaiju* threaten and those in older traditions is that there's nothing divinely orchestrated about such an end. It is the result of our collective actions provoking overwhelming natural forces. The *kaiju* are the terror of our own destructive power, the fear of the unstoppable repercussions of our actions. But they can also be more than that.

The technological events of the twentieth century were the beginning of a new era, even a new geological epoch. The idea of the 'Anthropocene' was coined by biologist Eugene Stormer and chemist Paul Crutzen in 2000. It's an informal term for a current geological period in which we might be the dominant driving force of global climate changes. Some argue that it began with the Industrial Revolution, when our new technologies began belching carbon and methane into the atmosphere. Others argue that the Anthropocene began in 1945, with the use of atomic bombs. This was when radioactivity was first detected in soil samples, showing that our inventions had irradiated the Earth and made a geological impact. In either case, not long after industrialisation, we discovered that we had developed the power to change the Earth – even to raze it to nothing.

Very little has been done about it in the interim. The target of limiting the global temperature rise to 1.5 degrees was set by the Paris Agreement in 2015. Even this small increase was predicted to have serious implications for global biodiversity and human livelihoods. But it now seems like a laughable aim. There is no 'credible' pathway to limiting temperature rises to 1.5 degrees, the UN admitted in 2022. Not since plants and fungi became terrestrial hundreds of millions of years ago, drawing carbon dioxide out of the atmosphere and boosting oxygen levels, has any other group of organisms had such a dramatic effect on the planet.

When reading anything about climate change these days, I still think back to car journeys with my dad when I was a kid, singing along to albums by the band Genesis from the 1970s. The lyrics to the song 'Land of Confusion' have aged incredibly well. They still speak to our situation today, of overpopulation, corruption, global destruction – and a generation's desire to get down to grass roots and undo the damage. To make Earth home again (of course, I wanted to quote some lyrics here, but the music industry is like a dragon jealously guarding a hoard of gold, as far as that's concerned). My dad told me that the 1970s was when the effect we could have on the environment really dawned on people. We realised that humans caused needless extinctions and that we might be breaking apart nature's infrastructure in a war of blind, greedy attrition.

Whether an apocalypse is really looming, or there is still a chance that we might rein in our impact on the globe sufficiently to end up in an acceptable place, is not a question I can answer. Books such as Steven Koonin's *Unsettled* (2021) try to push past Judgement Day thinking to tease out the nuances and unanswered questions of climate science – not to make it all go away, but to bring objectivity into how we approach it.[8] But fears of apocalypse are difficult to escape, especially given the potential enormity of the problems we face. We have a long tradition of such fantasies, and using monstrous creatures to play them out.

As we have seen throughout the chapters of this book, an effective way of escaping anxiety is to dive into fantasy. This is one reason why we keep watching *kaiju* movies:

they play out our fears in make-believe. The *kaiju* emerge from places even deeper and more unfathomable than the oceans. Their size compared to that of the people they crush under their feet parallels the mismatch between what our species has set in motion and our individual agency to stop it. The *kaiju* are unleashed from the womb of the Earth, threatening to shatter our sheet-glass pride, revealing that we're really just small, stupid beasts. They are perfectly proportioned creatures for the Anthropocene.

The *kaiju* don't all do this in the same way, though. Honda's 1950s *Godzilla* was a bleak allegory of atomic terror. Legendary's 2019 *Godzilla* was a very different beast. Like the fossilised dinosaurs, Godzilla's scaly bulk can be put to different uses. Legendary state that their new films pit 'the world's most famous monster against malevolent creatures who, bolstered by humanity's scientific arrogance, threaten our very existence'. This new *Godzilla* wasn't *created* by atom bomb tests – rather, he and his fellow monsters come from a fictional past when global radioactivity was far higher. It fuelled their supernatural energy rays and impossible size during an ancient Golden Age of Sustainable Nuclear Fusion. When this natural power source declined, they were forced to move underground where radiation remained stronger. Their subterranean existences were disturbed by atom bomb tests and strip mining, so they rose to rampage through the surface world. They all feed on radioactivity, munching on nuclear warheads like hotdogs. The terrible power that humans toyed with in their H-bomb tests was never really ours – it was theirs all along.

These new *kaiju* rise to right a wrong. In the film, one of the scientists studying the *kaiju*, Dr Ichiro Serizawa, says, 'The arrogance of men is thinking nature is in our control and not the other way around'. Nature has come back to set us straight. It becomes a fight between good and evil, of sin and redemption. In the scene we began with, where King Ghidorah takes his throne on the mountain, the shot pans back to a crucifix on a nearby peak. The message to a Western audience is clear: he is the Antichrist that we unleashed, but faith still might resist him. Some of these monsters are bad, others might be our allies. Godzilla is our saviour, risen again from the dead so we needn't suffer for our sins – the very power of nature to 'restore balance'. Godzilla is the new kind of god in which we can place our trust, to protect us from our evil. His monster minions are the ecological angels that will undo our mistakes. In a world where idiot human godlings play with supra-natural forces, only a Titan can set the situation right.

The new Godzilla films might look like simple monster movies. But in a time of ecological crisis, the fantasies of monstrous saviours offer escapism and absolution. We unleashed monsters in the world, but another monster is there to save us. It's a very comforting fantasy. Like children that have made a mess, the idea of powerful creatures arriving to tell us to pipe down and clear up for us is quite soothing. Godzilla is not the monster we deserve, but the hero we need, to misquote Harvey Dent in *The Dark Knight*.[9] Not all of our fantasies have been so comforting, though.

Wastelands

I began my research on monsters looking at creatures from far away – the ancient manticores and phoenixes, the exotic dodos and pangolins. They were miraculous and wonderful things, 'out there' in the blank regions of maps, far away in space and time. Others were outcasts, like the Minotaur, Medusa or Grendel, repositories for the beastly and unpalatable sides of humanity. Many of these creatures still flourish in our cultural imagination. But, from about the nineteenth century, there was a shift in monster-making. A new breed of monstrous beasts emerged. They became things that we could not escape or keep out of sight, they became *us*: crawling out of laboratories and animating our technologies, breeding in our viscera, erasing our humanity. The monsters of the Anthropocene are more frightening because they are much closer to home. They are creatures spawned from an unprecedented relationship with the natural world.

T. S. Eliot's poem *The Wasteland* (1922) is one of the most important and enigmatic poems of the twentieth century. He wrote it while recovering from a breakdown after the First World War and captured the heart of a broken city recovering from trauma and a lost generation of young men.[10] It's about London, but moves through desert landscapes and oceans, like an Arthurian legend or Romantic poetry. He combines literary influences and traditions in a way that has annoyed many critics, but the stylistic melting pot also throws the emptiness of an existence dislocated from depth and culture into perfect relief. His wasteland is a lifeless world, where 'the dead tree gives no shelter' and 'the dry stone no sound of water'. It is disconnected from meaning, haunted by the faint shades of lost tradition, only 'a heap of broken images' remaining.

For Eliot, the threat is not from some monstrous force or enemy, but from nothingness, oblivion. His narrator offers: 'I will show you fear in a handful of dust'. Dust is what concerns us now – so much more than becoming earthy worm food, which is the fear of death. Obliteration of everything that makes life, to which we might have been connected or that might endure after us. As I described in Chapter Five, the Medieval meaning of 'wasteland' was land that could not be productive – barren heaths and stony mountainsides. Land that was without use was still part of divine Creation. Now, the word 'wasteland' means 'land that has been *laid* to waste' by humans. This shift holds one of our greatest fears: we're no longer God's servants tending Eden. We've been aping divine power, like John Milton's Lucifer in *Paradise Lost*, and we have blighted the garden. Like Lucifer, we also feel very sorry for ourselves.

Humans have always been concerned with distinguishing ourselves from other creatures, creating mythologies in which we were moulded in the form of gods. Christianity's founding myth describes a world gifted to Man, born to sit in a hierarchy above all other organisms. Reaching for godlike capacities, we eventually managed to spin off into the technosphere. We have made a good stab of it: omniscience, omnipresence and omnipotence are all words you could reasonably use to describe the networks of communications, surveillance and other technologies that we have created. They have improved our lives immeasurably in many ways. Modern humans live in a level of comfort inconceivable to the majority of our predecessors. As Yuval Noah Harari put it, we've become '*Homo deus*'. But this endeavour has also created a world stripped of gods. As we climb the imagined hierarchy, clawing our way out of our ecological relationships and out from under the fear of deities, we've reached a very lonely and precipitous place.

The problem is, we can't handle it. There is nothing above us to keep us in check. The finely tuned webs of ecological interactions have been ripped asunder by our actions. We're constantly looking over our shoulders, wondering what the consequences might be. By trying to escape our beastly natures and our organic limitations, we've become terrified we might become the monsters. These fantasies take all sorts of forms: we fear we might become the brooding chambers for invasive, parasitic aliens brought back from space exploration, as in the film *Alien* (1979). We could suffer plagues that turn us into the sub-human zombies of *28 Days Later* (2002) or the vampires of *Daybreakers* (2009), fears that have certainly been accentuated by the Covid-19 pandemic – a disease that may have come from strange exotic animals in back-street wet markets, or could have been maliciously engineered in a laboratory.[11] The fear of monsters that might exist imperceptibly among us is far more disturbing than monsters that can be exiled or imprisoned.

Or we worry that we might simply self-destruct into degraded humans in a lifeless world. Take the bleak dystopia of the *Mad Max* films set in a future Australia where we've sucked the Earth dry of oil and water. Life no longer matters much. Without the lifeblood of fuel and water, societies collapse, humans become bestial and cruel. In the stonking 2015 *Mad Max: Fury Road* directed by George Miller, the cancer-ridden War Boys are like pale worker termites groomed to be mindless mechanic-soldiers. They sustain themselves vampirically on human 'blood bags' via IV drips. And they have a sole aim: to go out in a firecracker blaze of glory, sprayed 'all shiny and chrome'. Meaning they huff spray paint to give them a berserker high before they sacrifice themselves in battle. These empty humans are the result of an overblown empire in a devastated world. They are the nightmares of devolution, fantasies of how our core values can be so easily stripped away by war and hardship to leave worse-than-animal remains.

Our technological creations are ambivalent figures in all of this – they might save us, but we also fear they might overtake us. As I write this, AI bots such as OpenAI's GPT language models or Jasper AI's copywriter can write an informative piece of text on almost anything faster than any human. The mechanical creatures made by Boston Dynamics are breaking new boundaries constantly. The whippet-like 'Spot' can go anywhere to capture data, the rotund little 'WildCat' is the fastest ever quadruped robot and the zippy, spring-tailed 'SandFlea' can jump 10 metres into the air. They are all modelled on animals to solve biological problems of motion – but they are also something quite different. 'Atlas', Boston Dynamics's latest humanoid robot, can even do gymnastics without training or tiring.

It's likely that amazing things will come of these inventions – and certainly the way things are headed globally, we won't get by without some exceptionally clever innovation. It has its dangers, though: in a 2014 interview with the BBC, Stephen Hawking warned that the 'development of full artificial intelligence could spell the end of the human race'. Worries of where self-evolving technologies might take us simmer under the surface of modern science fiction. If the biosphere were to be broken beyond repair, it might make way for an inorganic ecosystem, where we are replaced by our technologies. There are plenty of apocalypse fantasies in which our technobeasts create a new world order. Worse than minotaurs or gorgons, their inorganic, digital minds have no empathy at all.

In the world of *The Matrix*, Lana and Lilly Wachowski's classic 1999 film, the Earth has become the habitat of mechanical squid-like giants that float through the wreckage of human civilisation. The sky is permanently clouded from the Sun's energy, stoppering organic life. In serried rows of viscous egg-like pods are lifeforms which the machines use as their energy source: humans, farmed on an industrial scale. Thermodynamics can't be escaped, after all. The foetally pale bodies do not stir, they remain in their pods until they are needed. The humans never wake to see the world, never speak to one another – except in their minds. Their cleverness created the machines that now feed on them. The machines generate a virtual world for their minds to inhabit, keeping their bodies sedated. The alternate reality is policed by agents, hydra-like replicants that stop any restless human minds trying to ascend into consciousness.

The humans that have managed to un-plug from the collective dream are now, like the *kaiju*, the throwback creatures that have retreated into the Earth to escape the mechanical ant's nest of the surface. In this cavernous sanctuary, they dance and fight and copulate and do all the vital things that other humans no longer do, as if it might all be over soon. The message in all these apocalypse scenarios is clear: we fear falling prey to our own hubris, becoming less than the creatures we've exploited and the machines we've created. For all our monster-making, our beastliness might consume us after all.

Re-enchantment

In a lecture in 1918, the German social theorist Max Weber described the modern Western world as *disenchanted*. Anyone who knows their fairy tales will understand that disenchantment means to be 'released from a magic spell'. Weber described the decline of magical thinking and the rise of a rational, scientifically driven society. One critic commented: 'in a disenchanted world, everything becomes understandable and tameable, even if not, for the moment, understood and tamed'. The disenchantment of the world lifts the veil of mystery and puts everything within human reach. It seems like progress – and in many ways, it is. The miracles of modern medicine or Apple products wouldn't exist otherwise. But the word has haunted social scientists and philosophers ever since, for two reasons. First, because disenchantment also entails disillusionment and terrible loss. Second, because we may not be nearly as disenchanted as Weber seems to have proposed.[12]

Compared to the battles of fire and brimstone of ancient stories, the recent apocalypse fantasies that I have explored are bleak, mechanised and lifeless. The end-states of disenchanted worlds contain only monstrous humans and their creations. These are future visions from a time when our connection with the supernatural and mythic has been largely excised. We cannot creep into the cavernous womb of the earth to commune with its creatures like Palaeolithic peoples might have done. Animals are supposedly just animals, and the landscape is no metaphor for our inner worlds. This connection has been replaced by consumer entertainment, because the yearning for myth still exists, but it's less rich and powerful than what went before: it's become disposable media fodder to churn out profit.

We are creatures with an incredible capacity for logical thought and scientific understanding, but we are not only that. The kind of passion and creativity which generates the best science and philosophy is also powered by an irrational unconscious. It contains whole realms that we will perhaps never fully understand – because they resist a purely scientific investigation. The world we really inhabit is not the one ordered by the laws of physics and chemistry; it is the subjective experience of each individual.

As Bettelheim, the psychoanalyst I quoted at the beginning of this book, showed: enchantment has fundamental value. Tales of gods, heroes, monsters and magic are how our inchoate, psychological experiences are shared and shaped. We have always sought to connect to the magical, from glimmering cave monsters and Gorgon talismans to the *Wunderkammern* of Enlightenment Europe and imaginary fauna. Yet in recent times we have let go of much of the richness of this connection, replacing it with a materialistic worldview. By undervaluing our symbolic experience, we undermine some of the most exquisite pleasures our minds are capable of and severely limit our understanding of ourselves.

I've explored some of the ways in which monstrous beasts still have meaning for us. I hope that I have started to plumb their depths without dispelling their mysteries. As I wrote, I realised that each creature could be the subject of its own book and there are so many more characters that I could have included. I hope that those I have focused on show some of the ways in which monsters have shaped our beginnings, been threaded through our daily lives, and accompanied us to our ends. How they connect us to the mystical and irrational elements of human experience. They're images that our minds can take hold of, to deal with the chaotic pieces inside us. Just as much as our study of the physical world, monster-making is part of being human.

What I have tried to convey is that we *are* enchanted creatures. As long as the world is filled with vibrant life, it will never really be disenchanted in our imaginations. Our minds are deep, dark caves filled with beasts. We begin life as biophiles and throughout our lives other creatures inhabit our dreamscapes. In the dystopian 1973 film *Soylent Green*, humans live in a desert-like New York in 2022. They watch simulations of the long-lost plants and animals on screens to feel happy. This sci-fi fantasy was eerily prescient. It's not too far off from how we consume parts of nature now that most of us will never see, and may not exist for very long: the cinematic documentaries of life on Arctic ice, technicolour coral reefs or verdant rainforests. Alongside fears of wastelands are fantasies of rich, untouched biospheres such as the bioluminescent world of Pandora in *Avatar* (2009), the lush prehistoric fauna of Skull Island in *Kong: Skull Island* (2017) and

ENCHANTED CREATURES

many others. They fulfil our yearning for a world that still contains myriad wonders.

Most of us still seek out natural places and the wildlife that persists in them. Thanks to support for rewilding, Europe now has a population of 17,000 wolves, according to the World Economic Forum. Though they face some resistance from farmers, we have shifted our cultural perceptions of wolves since the werewolf hunts of the seventeenth century. Brown bears, Iberian lynx and European bison (known charmingly as wizents) are also doing very well, too, compared to the 1960s. This urge to rewild might persist even as some parts of nature suffer.

Now more than ever, when our relationship to nature is on the brink of collapse, we need to understand our monsters and what they say about how we interact with the world. We can't live in an ideal Eden. Like mother goddesses such as Tiamat and the snake women, nature is both wonderful and terrible, and so are we. This book has explored how, over history, we have frequently dealt with our darkness by projecting it outwards into nature – creating monsters from groups of people, other species or even landscapes which can be exterminated and conquered. The parts of ourselves we don't want to acknowledge can be ejected into other creatures, making monsters of wolves, snakes, sharks – even pangolins. On a small scale, if we can understand this monster-making process, we might avoid the kinds of needless eradications and ecological splintering that have been played out so many times.

On a larger scale, we desperately need to develop a more balanced sense of our place in nature – as neither gods nor monsters. Rather, we're flawed creatures in a fractured world. We're integral to the biosphere as it exists now, and this is what we must sustain and replenish. For this, we need to use the ubiquitous power of our imaginations to animate nature with meaning and magic. We need both scientific understanding and our capacity for wonder to change how we relate to other organisms and the world. Perhaps, if we can turn the devils back into horned gods, accept the beasts inside ourselves, we will be able to find a way.

Acknowledgements

The 'official' genesis of this book started with my Masters and PhD in the History and Philosophy of Science Department at the University of Cambridge from 2012 to 2016, kindly funded by a grant from the Arts and Humanities Research Council (AHRC). I was lucky to have the most awe-inspiring supervisors: Dr Simon Schaffer, Professor Nicholas Jardine and Dr Anne Secord. I could not have asked for a more generous and talented trio to finish my academic training. The Cabinet of Natural History Group also helped me with many a Latin translation during my thesis, that would otherwise have left me floundering. Before this, I spent three enthralling years doing Natural Sciences at St John's College Cambridge.

In the process of writing, I have been helped by many deeply knowledgeable people who have kindly lent me their time and expertise, especially Julia Lovell, Darren Naish, Jill Cook, Lynne Isbell, Adrienne Mayor, Helen Scales, Richard Fallon, Angela Giallongo, Melanie Challenger, Paco Calvo, Amy Jeffs, and Christopher Plumb, among others.

As you might notice through this book, my ideas have been fertilised by many of the experiences that I have been lucky enough to have had through my life. I'm very grateful to my parents, Susan and John Lawrence, for all the ways they encouraged and supported my unusual curiosities and interests as a child, and the interdisciplinary outlook on life they helped foster. Few people grow up with a scientific-psychoanalytic paradigm from a young age – it has been both a blessing and a curse, but never boring. My parents, my sister Lizzy Lawrence and my partner, James Schneider, all gave me bountiful encouragement and help through the writing of this book and all that happened during. I'm just as grateful to the late Patricia Radford, who was the best surrogate grandmother one could ask for; and to Rael Meyerowitz, who has never put too fine a point on it when gently unmaking my monsters.

There are many other relationships which have shaped me and my work. Guy Thomas gave me many years of loving encouragement, enriching experiences and intellectual engagement, for which I will always be grateful. Through those years and their ending, I was propelled to become someone who could write what has been written. Friends Merlin Sheldrake, Maudie Powell-Tuck, Naomi Lebens, Emma Innes, Aro Velmet, Ben Cura, Richard Granieri, Lawrence Hunt, Mike Hemmings, Rona Smith, and others have been a support, an inspiration and valuable readers for the manuscript. I would not have managed this book without their help.

I want to thank my agent, the inimitable Jessica Woollard, whose boundless curiosity and enthusiasm has helped to propel me through everything. And my splendid editors, Jenny Lord and Kate Moreton, whose incisive commentary and engagement helped this to be the best book it could be.

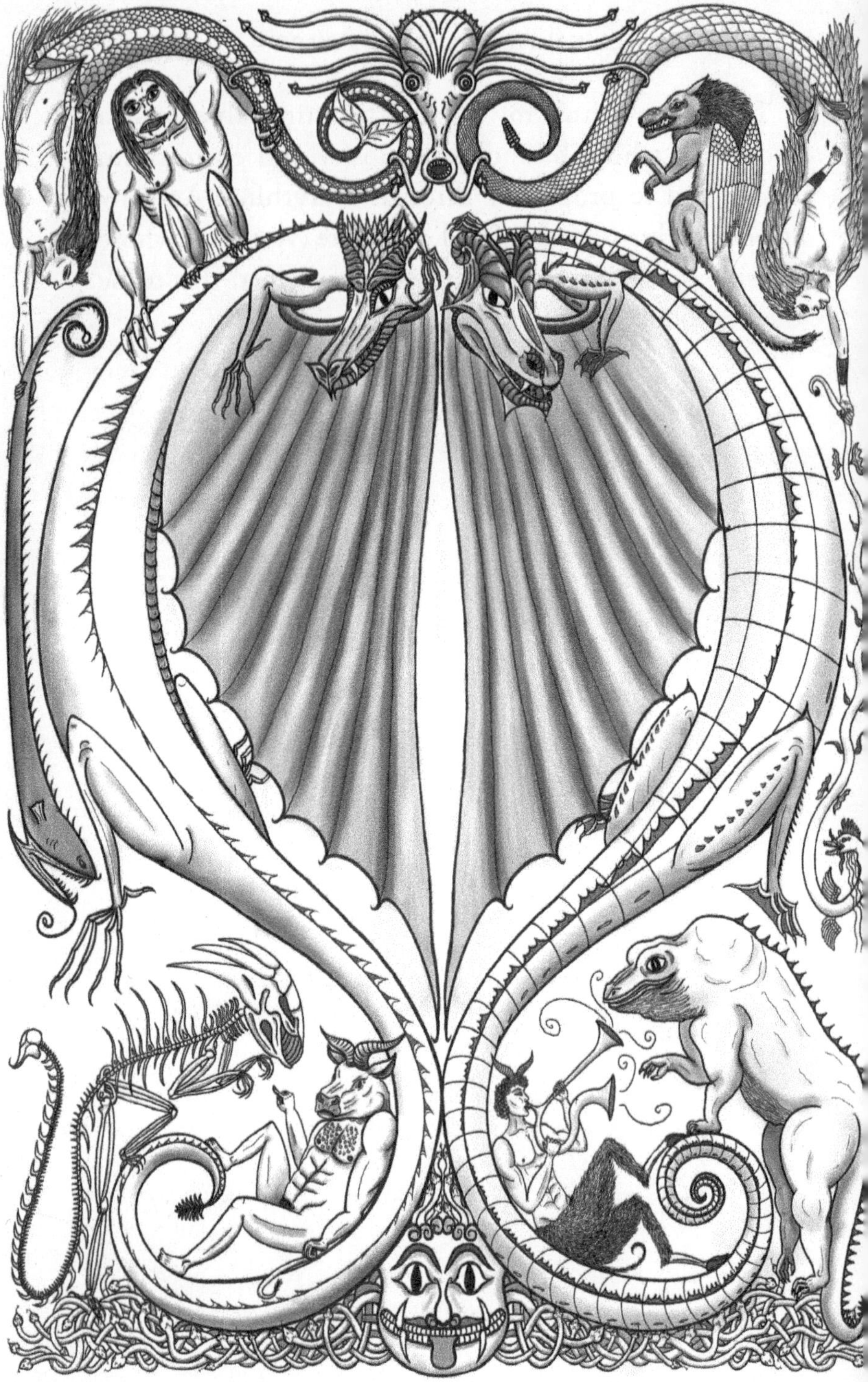

Bibliography

Introduction: Making Beasts

Aldrovandi, Ulysse. *Monstrorum Historia: Cum Paralipomenis Historiae Omnium Animalium . . . Bartholomaeus Ambrosinus . . . Volumen Composuit. Marcus Antonius Bernia in Lucem Edidit.* N. Tebaldini, 1642.
Becker, Ernest. *Denial of Death.* The Free Press, 1973.
Berger, John. 'Why Look at Animals'. In *About Looking.* Bloomsbury Publishing PLC, 2009.
Bettelheim, Bruno. *The Uses of Enchantment: The Meaning and Importance of Fairy Tales.* Penguin, 1991.
Challenger, Melanie. *How to Be Animal.* Canongate Books, 2021.
Findlen, Paula. 'Inventing Nature. Commerce, Art, and Science in the Early Modern Cabinet of Curiosities'. In *Merchants and Marvels: Commerce, Science, and Art in Early Modern Europe,* 297–323. Routledge, 2002.
Gottschall, Jonathan. *The Storytelling Animal: How Stories Make Us Human.* Mariner Books, 2013.
Lawrence, Natalie. 'Monstrous Assembly: Constructing Exotic Animals in Early Modern Europe'. PhD,

University of Cambridge, 2016.
Levi-Strauss, Claude. *Totemism*. Translated by Rodney Needham. Beacon Press, 1963.
Lovejoy, Arthur O. *The Great Chain of Being. A Study of the History of an Idea*. Harvard University Press, 1936.
Quammen, David. *Monster of God – The Man-Eating Predator in the Jungles of History and the Mind*. W. W. Norton & Company, 2003.
Scanlon, Paul, and Michael Gross. *The Book of Alien*. Simon & Schuster, 1979.
Wilson, Dudley Butler. *Signs and Portents: Monstrous Births from the Middle Ages to the Enlightenment*. Routledge, 1993.

Chapter One: The Horned Sorcerer

Aubert, Maxime, Rustan Lebe, Adhi Agus Oktaviana, Muhammad Tang, Basran Burhan, Hamrullah, Andi Jusdi, et al. 'Earliest Hunting Scene in Prehistoric Art'. *Nature* 576:7787 (2019), 442–5.
Azéma, Marc, and Florent Rivère. 'Animation in Palaeolithic Art: A Pre-Echo of Cinema'. *Antiquity* 86:332 (2012), 316–24.
Bégouën, Éric, and Marie-brune Bégouën. 'Centenary of the Discovery of the Tuc d'Audoubert Cave (Ariège) and of Its "Clay Bison"'. *INORA* 65 (2013), 24–7.
Bégouën, Henri. 'Un Dessin Relevé Dans La Caverne Des Trois-Frères, à Montesquieu-Avantès (Ariège)'. *Comptes Rendus Des Séances de l'Académie Des Inscriptions et

Belles-Lettres 64:4 (1920), 303–10.

———. 'Comte Henri Bégouën Photographs of Peleolithic Cave Art, circa 1912-1930'. National Museum of Natural History, Smithsonian Institute, Washington: National Anthropological Archives, c. 1912–30.

Bégouën, Henri, and Henri Breuil. *Les Cavernes Du Volp: Trois-Frères – Tuc d'Audoubert.* Reprint of 1958 monograph. American Rock Art Research Association (ARARA), 1999.

Bégouën, Robert. 'Sur Quelques Objets Nouvellement Découverts Dans Les Grottes Des Trois Frères (Montesquieu-Avantès, Ariège)'. *Bulletin de La Société Préhistorique Française* 26:3 (1929), 188–96.

Bégouën, Robert, Jean Clottes, Valérie Feruglio, and Andreas Pastoors. *La Caverne Des Trois-Frères, Anthologie d'un Exceptionnel Sanctuaire Préhistorique.* Louis Association Bégouën / Somogy Editions d'Art, 2014.

Clottes, Jean, and David J. Lewis-Williams. 'Palaeolithic Art and Religion'. In *A Handbook of Ancient Religions*, edited by John R. Hinnells, 7–45. Cambridge University Press, 2007.

Conneller, Chantal. 'Becoming Deer. Corporeal Transformations at Star Carr'. *Archaeological Dialogues* 11 (2004), 37–56.

Davidson, Iain. 'Images of Animals in Rock Art: Not Just "Good to Think"'. In *The Oxford Handbook of the Archaeology and Anthropology of Rock Art.* Oxford University Press, 2019.

———. 'Symbols by Nature: Animal Frequencies in the

Upper Palaeolithic of Western Europe and the Nature of Symbolic Representation'. *Archaeology in Oceania* 34:3 (1999), 121–31.

Dein, Simon. 'Transcendence, Religion and Social Bonding'. *Archive for the Psychology of Religion* 42:1 (2020), 77–88.

DeSilva, Jeremy M., James F. A. Traniello, Alexander G. Claxton, and Luke D. Fannin. 'When and Why Did Human Brains Decrease in Size? A New Change-Point Analysis and Insights From Brain Evolution in Ants'. *Frontiers in Ecology and Evolution* 9 (2021).

Dowson, Thomas A. 'Re-Animating Hunter-Gatherer Rock-Art Research'. *Cambridge Archaeological Journal* 19:3 (2009), 378–87.

Dunbar, Robin I. M. 'The Social Brain Hypothesis and Its Implications for Social Evolution'. *Annals of Human Biology* 36:5 (2009), 562–72.

———. 'The Origin of Religion as a Small Scale Phenomenon'. In *Religion, Intolerance and Conflict: A Scientific and Conceptual Investigation*, edited by S. Clark and R. Powell, 48–66. Oxford University Press, 2013.

———. 'The Social Brain: Psychological Underpinnings and Implications for the Structure of Organizations'. *Current Directions in Psychological Science* 23:2 (2014), 109–14.

———. 'What's Missing from the Scientific Study of Religion?' *Religion, Brain & Behavior* 7:4 (2017), 349–53.

———. *How Religion Evolved: And Why It Endures*. Pelican, 2022.

Eshleman, Clayton. 'Lectures on the Ice-Age Painted Caves of Southwestern France'. *Interval(Le)s* II.2–III.1 (2008), 235–70.

Faisal, Aldo, Dietrich Stout, Jan Apel, and Bruce Bradley. 'The Manipulative Complexity of Lower Paleolithic Stone Toolmaking'. *PLOS ONE* 5:11 (2010), 1–11.

French, Jennifer C. *Palaeolithic Europe: A Demographic and Social Prehistory*. Cambridge World Archaeology. Cambridge University Press, 2021.

Freud, Sigmund. 'Creative Writers and Daydreaming'. In *The Standard Edition of the Complete Psychological Works of Sigmund Freud*, 9 (1908), 141–54.

Fuentes, Agustin. *Why We Believe: Evolution and the Human Way of Being*. Yale University Press, 2019.

Guthrie, R. Dale. *The Nature of Paleolithic Art*. University of Chicago Press, 2005.

Hadingham, Evan. *Secrets of the Ice Age*. William Heinemann Ltd, 1980.

Hodgson, Derek. *The Roots of Visual Depiction in Art: Neuroarchaeology, Neuroscience and Evolution*. Cambridge Scholars Publishing, 2019.

Hodgson, Derek, and Patricia Helvenston. 'The Emergence of the Representation of Animals in Palaeoart: Insights from Evolution and the Cognitive, Limbic and Visual Systems of the Human Brain'. *Rock Art Research* 23 (2006), 3–40.

Hodgson, Derek, and Anna Petit. 'Warning Signs: How Early Humans First Began to Paint Animals'. *The Conversation*, 4 May 2018.

Hoffmann, D., C. Standish, Marcos García-Diez, Paul Pettitt, J. Milton, João Zilhão, José Javier González, et al. 'U-Th Dating of Carbonate Crusts Reveals Neandertal Origin of Iberian Cave Art'. *Science* 359 (2018), 912–15.

Kind, C.-J., N. Ebinger-Rist, Sibylle Wolf, T. Beutelspacher, and K. Wehrberger. 'The Smile of the Lion Man. Recent Excavations in Stadel Cave (Baden-Württemberg, Southwestern Germany) and the Restoration of the Famous Upper Palaeolithic Figurine'. *Quartär* 61 (2014), 129–45.

Kolankaya-bostancı, Neyir. 'The Evidence of Shamanism Rituals in Early Prehistoric Periods of Europe and Anatolia'. *Colloquium Anatolicum* 13 (2014), 185–204.

Lewis-Williams, David. 'Harnessing the Brain: Vision and Shamanism in Upper Paleolithic Western Europe'. In *Beyond Art: Pleistocene Image and Symbol*, edited by Margaret W. Conkey, 321-42. California Academy of Sciences, 1997.

Lewis-Williams, David J., and Jean Clottes. 'The Mind in the Cave – the Cave in the Mind: Altered Consciousness in the Upper Paleolithic'. *Anthropology of Consciousness* 9:1 (1998), 13–21.

Little, Aimée, Benjamin Elliott, Chantal Conneller, Diederik Pomstra, Adrian A. Evans, Laura C. Fitton, Andrew Holland, et al. 'Technological Analysis of the World's Earliest Shamanic Costume: A Multi-Scalar, Experimental Study of a Red Deer Headdress from the Early Holocene Site of Star Carr, North Yorkshire,

UK'. Edited by Michael D. Petraglia. *PLOS ONE* 11:4 (2016).

Medina-Alcaide, Mª Ángeles, Diego Garate, Iñaki Intxaurbe, José L. Sanchidrián, Olivia Rivero, Catherine Ferrier, Mª Dolores Mesa, Jaime Pereña, and Iñaki Líbano. 'The Conquest of the Dark Spaces: An Experimental Approach to Lighting Systems in Paleolithic Caves'. Edited by Peter F. Biehl. *PLOS ONE* 16:6 (2021).

Merchant, Jo. 'A Journey to the Oldest Cave Paintings in the World, The Discovery in a Remote Part of Indonesia Has Scholars Rethinking the Origins of Art – and of Humanity'. *Smithsonian Magazine*, 2016.

Monbiot, George. *Feral: Rewilding the Land, Sea and Human Life*. Penguin, 2014.

Mormann, Florian, Julien Dubois, Simon Kornblith, Milica Milosavljevic, Moran Cerf, Matias Ison, Naotsugu Tsuchiya, *et al.* 'A Category-Specific Response to Animals in the Right Human Amygdala'. *Nature Neuroscience* 14 (2011), 1247–9.

Pastoors, Andreas, Tilman Lenssen-Erz, Tsamgao Ciqae, Ui Kxunta, Thui Thao, Robert Bégouën, and Thorsten Uthmeier. 'Episodes of Magdalenian Hunter-Gatherers in the Upper Gallery of Tuc d'Audoubert (Ariège, France)'. In *Reading Prehistoric Human Tracks, Methods and Materials*, edited by Andreas Pastoors and Tilman Lenssen-Erz, 211–49. Springer Charm, 2021.

Sauvet, Georges, Cesar González Sainz, José Luis Sanchidrián, and Valentín Villaverde. 'Europe: Prehistoric

Rock Art'. In *Encyclopedia of Global Archaeology*, edited by Claire Smith, 2599–612. Springer New York, 2014.

Sieveking, Ann. *The Cave Artists*. Thames & Hudson Ltd, 1979.

Sirocko, Frank, Johannes Albert, Sarah Britzius, Frank Dreher, Alfredo Martínez-García, Anthony Dosseto, Joachim Burger, Thomas Terberger, and Gerald Haug. 'Thresholds for the Presence of Glacial Megafauna in Central Europe during the Last 60,000 Years'. *Scientific Reports* 12:20055 (2022).

Van Pool, Christine S. 'The Signs of the Sacred: Identifying Shamans Using Archaeological Evidence'. *Journal of Anthropological Archaeology* 28:2 (2009), 177–90.

Vasilevich, G. M., and A. V. Smolyak. 'Evenki'. In *The Peoples of Siberia*, edited by Stephen Dunn, translated by Scripta Technica, Inc., 620–54. The University of Chicago, 1964.

Vernon, Mark. 'Divine Transports Whether via Music, Dance or Prayer, the Trance State Was Key to Human Evolution, Forging Society around the Transcendent'. *Aeon Magazine*, 7 November 2019.

Wallis, Robert J. 'Art and Shamanism: From Cave Painting to the White Cube'. *Religions* 10:1 (2019).

Winkelman, Michael. 'Shamanism as the Original Neurotheology'. *Zygon*, 39:1 (2004), 193–217.

———. 'A Cross-Cultural Study of the Elementary Forms of Religious Life: Shamanistic Healers, Priests, and Witches'. *Religion, Brain & Behavior* 11:1 (2021), 27–45.

Chapter Two: Dragons of Chaos

Black, Jeremy, and Anthony Green. *Gods, Demons and Symbols of Ancient Mesopotamia*. British Museum Press, 1992.

Campbell, Joseph. *The Masks of God: Occidental Mythology*. Souvenir Press, 1964.

———. *The Power of Myth*. Edited by Betty Sue Flowers. Anchor Books, 1991.

Dalley, Stephanie. *Myths from Mesopotamia. Creation, The Flood, Gilgamesh and Others*. Oxford University Press, 1989.

Frankfort, Henri, Thorkild Jacobsen, and John A. Wilson. *Before Philosophy*. Penguin Books Ltd, 1960.

Freud, Sigmund. *Civilization and Its Discontents*. Translated by James Strachey. W. W. Norton & Company, 2010.

Gunkel, Hermann. *Schöpfung Und Chaos in Urzeit Und Endzeit: Eine Religionsgeschichtliche Untersuchung Über Gen 1 Und Ap Joh 12*. Vandenhoeck und Ruprecht, 1895.

Hesiod. *The Homeric Hymns and Homerica with an English Translation by Hugh G. Evelyn-White. Theogony*. Translated by H. G. Evelyn-White. H. Vol. 57. G. Loeb Classical Library. William Heinemann, 1914.

Jung, Carl G. *The Archetypes and the Collective Unconscious*. Edited by Herbert Read, Michael Fordham, Gerhard Adler, and William McGuire. Vol. 9.1. Bollingen Series XX. Pantheon, 1959.

Jacobsen, Thorkild. *The Treasures of Darkness: A History of Mesopotamian Religion*. New Haven & London: Yale University Press, 1976.

Jones, A. W. and A. N. Lasenby. 'The Cosmic Microwave Background'. *Living Reviews in Relativity* 1:1 (1998), 11.

Lambert, W. G. *Ancient Mesopotamian Religion and Mythology Selected Essays*. Edited by A. R. George and T. M. Oshima. Orientalische Religionen in Der Antike 15. Tübingen: Mohr Siebeck, 2016.

Neumann, Erich. *The Origins and History of Consciousness*. Translated by R. F. C. Hull. Princeton Classics, Bollingen Series. Princeton University Press, 2014.

Ngo, Robin, Megan Sauter, Noah Weiner, and Glenn J. Corbett, eds. *Exploring Genesis: The Bible's Ancient Traditions in Context*. Washington DC: Biblical Archaeology Society, 2013.

Rose, Charlie. 'Astrophysicist Neil deGrasse Tyson's One-Man Mission'. *CBS News*, 22 March 2015.

Scurlock, JoAnn, and Rickard H. Beal, eds. *Creation and Chaos. A Reconsideration of Hermann Gunkel's Chaoskampf Hypothesis*. Eisenbrauns, 2019.

Rackley, Rosanna. 'Kingship, Struggle, and Creation: The Story of Chaoskampf'. M.Res., University of Birmingham, 2015.

Ronnberg, Ami, and Kathleen Martin, eds. *The Book of Symbols. Reflections on Archetypal Images*. Archive for Research in Archetypal Symbolism. TASCHEN, 2010.

Uzan, Jean-Philippe. 'The Big-Bang Theory: Construction, Evolution and Status'. In *The Universe: Poincaré*

Seminar 2015, edited by Bertrand Duplantier and Vincent Rivasseau, 1-72. Vol. 76. Progress in Mathematical Physics. Springer Nature, 2021.

Chapter Three: The Minotaur and the Labyrinth

Borges, Jorge Luis. *The Aleph Including the Prose Fictions from the Maker*. Translated by Andrew Hurley. Penguin Books, 2000.

Campbell, Joseph. *The Masks of God: Occidental Mythology*. Souvenir Press, 1964.

———. *Hero With a Thousand Faces*. 3rd edition. New World Library, 2008.

Fox, Margalit. *Riddle of the Labyrinth: The Quest to Crack an Ancient Code and the Uncovering of a Lost Civilisation*. Profile Books, 2013.

Freud Sigmund, and G. S. Viereck. 'An Interview with Freud' (1927). In *Psychoanalysis and the Future*, edited by Th. Reik, C. Staff and B. N. Nelson. National Psychological Association for Psychoanalysis, INC (1957).

Graves, Robert. *The Greek Myths, Complete Edition*. Penguin, 1992.

Hemingway, Ernest. 'Bullfighting Is Not a Sport – It Is a Tragedy'. *The Toronto Star Weekly*, 20 October 1923.

Kotsonas, Antonis. 'A Cultural History of the Cretan Labyrinth: Monument and Memory from Prehistory to the Present'. *American Journal of Archaeology* 122:3 (2018), 367–96.

———. 'Greek and Roman Knossos: The Pioneering Investigations of Minos Kalokairinos'. *The Annual of the British School at Athens* 111 (2016), 299–324.

Lamb, Robert. 'The Myth of the Minotaur, the Legendary Beast We Can't Forget'. *HowStuffWorks.Com* (blog), 15 May 2020.

Macgillivray, Joseph Alexander. *Minotaur: Sir Arthur Evans and the Archaeology of the Minoan Myth*. Hill and Wang, 2000.

McInerney, J. 'Bulls and Bull-Leaping in the Minoan World'. *Expedition Magazine* 53:3 (2011).

Momigliano, Nicoletta. *In Search of the Labyrinth, The Cultural Legacy of Minoan Crete*. New Directions in Classics. Bloomsbury Academic, 2020.

Momigliano, Nicoletta, and Alexandre Farnoux, eds. *Cretomania: Modern Desires for the Minoan Past*. Routledge, 2019.

Nin, Anaïs. *Seduction of the Minotaur*. Swallow Press/Ohio University Press, 1990.

Ovid. *Metamorphoses*. Translated by E. J. Kenney. Oxford World's Classics. OUP Oxford, 2008.

Padel, Ruth. 'Labyrinth of Desire: Cretan Myth in Us'. *Arion: A Journal of Humanities and the Classics* 4:2 (1996), 76–87.

Penrose, Roland. *Picasso: His Life and Work*. Harper, 1959.

Pressman, Matt. 'Q&A: John Richardson on Picasso's "Uncontrollable" Sex Drive'. *Vanity Fair*, 5 April 2011.

Ridderstad, Marianna. 'Evidence of Minoan Astronomy and Calendrical Practices', Cornell University (2009), 1–41.

Ronnberg, Ami, and Kathleen Martin, eds. *The Book of Symbols: Reflections on Archetypal Images*. Archive for Research in Archetypal Symbolism. TASCHEN, 2010.

Sbardella, Amaranta. 'The Monstrous Minotaur Riveted Ancient Greece and Rome'. *National Geographic*, 1 October 2019.

Seneca, Lucius Annaeus. *Phaedra and Other Plays*. Translated by R. Scott Smith. Penguin Classics, 2011.

Shapland, Andrew. 'Jumping to Conclusions: Bull-Leaping in Minoan Crete'. *Society & Animals* 21 (2013), 194–207.

Simpson, Liz. *The Magic of Labyrinths: Following Your Path, Finding Your Center*. Element, 2002.

Smith-Laing, Tim. 'What the Minotaur Can Tell Us about Picasso'. *Apollo Magazine*, 2 May 2017.

Tilney, Martin. 'Waiting for Redemption in The House of Asterion: A Stylistic Analysis'. *Open Journal of Modern Linguistics* 2:2 (2012), 51–6.

Widener, Michael. 'A Papal Bull against Bullfighting'. *Yale Law School Lillian Goldman Law Library* (blog), 17 December 2014.

Chapter Four: Snake Women

Anastasiadou, Amria. 'The Origin of the Different: "Gorgos" and "Minotaurs" of the Aegean Bronze Age'. In *Making Monsters: A Speculative and Classical Anthology*, edited by E. Bridges and D. al-Ayad, 165–75. Futurefire.net Publishing, 2018.

Arras, Jean d'. *Melusine*. Vol. 68. Kegan Paul, Trench, Trübner, for the Early English Text Society, 1895.

———. *Melusine; or, The Noble History of Lusignan*. Translated by Donald Maddox and Sara Sturm-Maddox. Pennsylvania State University Press, 2012.

Bell, Robert E. *Women of Classical Mythology: A Biographical Dictionary*. Oxford University Press, 1993.

Bertels, J., M. Bourguignon, A. de Heering, F. Chetail, X. De Tiège, A. Cleeremans, and A. Destrebecqz. 'Snakes Elicit Specific Neural Responses in the Human Infant Brain'. *Scientific Reports* 10:7443 (2020).

Campbell, Joseph. *The Masks of God: Occidental Mythology*. Souvenir Press, 1964.

———. *The Power of Myth*. Edited by Betty Sue Flowers. Anchor Books, 1991.

Carvalho, Livia S., Daniel M. A. Pessoa, Jessica K. Mountford, Wayne I. L. Davies, and David M. Hunt. 'The Genetic and Evolutionary Drives behind Primate Color Vision'. *Frontiers in Ecology and Evolution* 5 (2017).

Caraffi, Patrizia. 'History of Education with Angela Giallongo and Her Snake Women'. *Encounters in Theory and History of Education* 20:1 (2019).

Coss, Richard G., and Eric P. Charles. 'The Saliency of Snake Scales and Leopard Rosettes to Infants: Its Relevance to Graphical Patterns Portrayed in Prehistoric Art'. *Frontiers in Psychology* 12:763436 (2021).

Felton, Debbie. 'Monsters and the Monstrous: Ancient Expressions of Cultural Anxieties'. In *A Cultural History of Fairy Tales in Antiquity 1*, edited by Debbie Felton

and Anne E. Duggan, 109–30. Bloomsbury Publishing, 2021.
Freud, Sigmund. 'Medusa's Head'. Translated by James Strachey. *International Journal of Psychoanalysis* 22 (1941), 69–70.
Giallongo, Angela. *The Historical Enigma of the Snake Woman from Antiquity to the 21st Century*. Translated by Anna C. Forster. Cambridge Scholars Publishing, 2017.
Graves, Robert. *The Greek Myths, Complete Edition*. Penguin, 1992.
Greenblatt, Stephen. *The Rise and Fall of Adam and Eve, The Story That Created Us*. Penguin Random House, 2017.
Henshilwood, Christopher S., Francesco d'Errico, Royden Yates, Zenobia Jacobs, Chantal Tribolo, Geoff A. T. Duller, Norbert Mercier, *et al*. 'Emergence of Modern Human Behavior: Middle Stone Age Engravings from South Africa'. *Science* 295:5558 (2002), 1278–80.
Hesiod. *The Homeric Hymns and Homerica: With an English Translation by Hugh G. Evelyn-White*. Vol. 57. G. Loeb Classical Library. William Heinemann, 1914.
Holland, Tom. *Dominion: The Making of the Western Mind*. Little Brown, 2019.
Homer. *The Iliad*. Translated by Martin Hammond. Penguin Classics, 1987.
———. *The Odyssey*. Translated by E. V. Rieu. Penguin Classics, 2003.
Howe Gaines, Janet. 'Lilith: Seductress, Heroine or Murderer?' *Biblical Archaeology Society, Bible History Daily* (blog), September 2012.

Isbell, Lynne A. 'Snakes as Agents of Evolutionary Change in Primate Brains'. *Journal of Human Evolution* 51:1 (2006), 1–35.

———. *The Fruit, the Tree, and the Serpent: Why We See So Well*. Harvard University Press, 2009.

Isbell, Lynne A., and Stephanie F. Etting. 'Scales Drive Detection, Attention, and Memory of Snakes in Wild Vervet Monkeys (Chlorocebus Pygerythrus)'. *Primates* 58:1 (2017), 121–29.

Kawai, Nobuyuki, and Hongshen He. 'Breaking Snake Camouflage: Humans Detect Snakes More Accurately than Other Animals under Less Discernible Visual Conditions'. Edited by Hisao Nishijo. *PLOS ONE* 11(10):e0164342 (2016).

Koivisto, Satu, and Antti Lahelma. 'Between Earth and Water: A Wooden Snake Figurine from the Neolithic Site of Järvensuo 1'. *Antiquity* 95(382):e19 (2021).

Langley, Patricia. 'Why a Pomegranate?' *BMJ* 321:7269 (2000), 1153–4.

Milton, John. *Paradise Lost*. Edited by Alastair Fowler. Longman, 1991.

Murgatroyd, Paul. *Mythical Monsters in Classical Literature*. Bristol Classical Press, 2007.

Murray, Elisabeth A., and Lesley K. Fellows. 'Prefrontal Cortex Interactions with the Amygdala in Primates'. *Neuropsychopharmacology* 47:1 (2022), 163–79.

Narby, Jeremy. *The Cosmic Serpent: DNA and the Origins of Knowledge*. Penguin Random House, 1998.

Ovid. *Metamorphoses*. Translated by E. J. Kenney. Oxford World's Classics. OUP Oxford, 2008.

Patai, Raphael. *The Hebrew Goddess*. Wayne State University Press, 1990.

Petersen, Peter Vang. 'Zigzag Lines and Other Protective Patterns in Palaeolithic and Mesolithic Art'. *Quaternary International* 573 (2021), 66–74.

Ronnberg, Ami, and Kathleen Martin, eds. *The Book of Symbols: Reflections on Archetypal Images*. Archive for Research in Archetypal Symbolism. TASCHEN, 2010.

Soares, Sandra C., Rafael S. Maior, Lynne A. Isbell, Carlos Tomaz, and Hisao Nishijo. 'Fast Detector/First Responder: Interactions between the Superior Colliculus-Pulvinar Pathway and Stimuli Relevant to Primates'. *Frontiers in Neuroscience* 11:67 (2017).

Van Strien, Jan W., Ingmar H. A. Franken, and Jorg Huijding. 'Testing the Snake-Detection Hypothesis: Larger Early Posterior Negativity in Humans to Pictures of Snakes than to Pictures of Other Reptiles, Spiders and Slugs'. *Frontiers in Human Neuroscience* 8 (2014).

Wallis, Jonathan D. 'Cross-Species Studies of Orbitofrontal Cortex and Value-Based Decision-Making'. *Nature Neuroscience* 15:1 (January 2012), 13–19.

Chapter Five: Grendel

Alfano, Christine. 'The Issue of Feminine Monstrosity: A Reevaluation of Grendel's Mother'. *Comitatus: A*

Journal of Medieval and Renaissance Studies 23:1 (1992), 1–16.

Berger, John. 'Why Look at Animals'. In *About Looking*. Bloomsbury Publishing PLC, 2009.

Bintley, Michael D. J., and Thomas J. T. Williams. *Representing Beasts in Early Medieval England and Scandinavia*. Anglo-Saxon Studies. Boydell & Brewer, Boydell Press, 2015.

Cohen, Jeffrey J. 'The Promise of Monsters'. In *The Ashgate Research Companion to Monsters and the Monstrous*, edited by Asa Simon Mittmann and Peter J. Dendle, 449–64. Ashgate, 2012.

Collins, Michael. *St George and the Dragons: The Making of English Identity*. Fonthill, 2018.

Cronon, William. 'The Trouble with Wilderness; or, Getting Back to the Wrong Nature'. In *Uncommon Ground: Rethinking the Human Place in Nature*, edited by William Cronon, 69–90. W. W. Norton & Co., 1995.

Dalley, Stephanie. *Myths from Mesopotamia. Creation, The Flood, Gilgamesh and Others*. Oxford University Press, 1989.

Farrell, Jennifer Kelso. 'The Evil Behind the Mask: Grendel's Pop Culture Evolution'. *The Journal of Popular Culture* 41:6 (2008), 934–49.

Fisher, Adrian G., Charlotte H. Mills, Mitchell Lyons, William K. Cornwell, and Mike Letnic. 'Australia's Dingo Fence from Space: Satellite Images Reveal Its Effects on Landscape'. *The Guardian*, 24 February 2021.

———. 'Remote Sensing of Trophic Cascades: Multi-temporal Landsat Imagery Reveals Vegetation Change Driven by the Removal of an Apex Predator'. *Landscape Ecology* 36:5 (2021), 1341–58.

Forni, Kathleen. *Beowulf's Popular Afterlife in Literature, Comic Books*. Routledge Studies in Medieval Literature and Culture. Routledge, Taylor & Francis Group, 2020.

Gardner, John C. *Grendel*. Gollancz, 2015.

Gervase of Tilbury. *Otia Imperialia Recreation for an Emperor*. Edited by S. E. Banks and J. W. Binns. OUP Oxford, 2002.

Hankins, John E. 'Caliban the Bestial Man'. *PMLA/Publications of the Modern Language Association of America* 62:3 (1947), 793–801.

Heaney, Seamus. *Beowulf*. W. W. Norton & Company, 2000.

Hennequin, M. Wendy. 'We've Created a Monster: The Strange Case of Grendel's Mother'. *English Studies* 89:5 (2008), 503–23.

Holmes, Brandon, and Gareth Linnard. *Thylacine: The History, Ecology and Loss of the Tasmanian Tiger*. CSIRO, 2023.

Howell, John Michael. *Understanding John Gardner*. University of South Carolina Press, 1993.

Kiernan, Kevin. 'Grendel's Heroic Mother'. *In Geardagum* (1984), 13–33.

Klaasen, Elisa Lee. 'Tolkien's Tribute to England and Its Roots in Beowulf'. *Elaia* 2 (2019), Article 8.

Le Guin, Ursula K. 'The Critics, the Monsters, and the Fantasists'. *The Wordsworth Circle* 38:1–2 (2007), 83–7.

Letnic, M., and M. S. Crowther. 'Pesticide Use Is Linked to Increased Body Size in a Large Mammalian Carnivore'. *Biological Journal of the Linnean Society* 131:1 (2020), 220–29.

Lewis, Charles N. 'A Psychological Commentary on John Gardner's Grendel'. *American Journal of Psychoanalysis* 44:4 (1984), 431–6.

Lorey, Elmar M. *Heinrich Der Werwolf: Eine Geschichte Aus Der Zeit Der Hexenprozesse Mit Dokumenten Und Analysen*. Anabas-Verlag, 1998.

McShane, Kara L. 'The Questing Beast'. University of Rochester. The Camelot Project, Robbins Library Digital Project.

Mellinkoff, Ruth. 'Cain's Monstrous Progeny in "Beowulf": Part I, Noachic Tradition'. *Anglo-Saxon England* 8 (1979), 143–62.

Murr, Judy Smith. 'John Gardner's Order and Disorder: *Grendel* and *The Sunlight Dialogues*'. *Critique: Studies in Contemporary Fiction* 18:2 (1976), 97–108.

Neville, Jennifer. *Representations of the Natural World in Old English Poetry*. Cambridge Studies in Anglo-Saxon England. Cambridge University Press, 1999.

———. 'Monsters and Criminals: Defining Humanity in Old English Poetry'. In *Monsters and the Monstrous in Medieval Northwest Europe*, edited by K. E. Olsen and L. A. J. R. Houwen, 103–22. Mediaevalia Groningana. Peeters, 2001.

Orchard, Andy. *Pride and Prodigies: Studies in the Monsters of the Beowulf-Manuscript*. D. S. Brewer, 1985.

Shakespeare, William. *The Tempest*. Edited by Barbara Mowat, Paul Werstein, Poston, and Rebecca Niles. Folger Shakespeare Library. Simon & Schuster, 2015.

Smallman, Shawn, and Grace Dillon. *Dangerous Spirits: The Windigo in Myth and History*. Heritage House, 2015.

Smith, Sydney. 'The Face of Humbaba'. *Journal of the Royal Asiatic Society* (1926), 440–42.

Stankey, George H. 'Beyond the Campfire's Light: Historical Roots of the Wilderness Concept'. *Natural Resources Journal* 29 (1989), 9.

Summers, Montague. *The Werewolf in Lore and Legend*. Dover Publications, 1933.

Swinford, Dean. '"Some Beastlike Fungus": The Natural and Animal in John Gardner's *Grendel*'. *Lit: Literature Interpretation Theory* 22:4 (2011), 323–35.

Symons, Victoria. 'Monsters and Heroes in Beowulf'. *British Library* (blog), 31 January 2018.

Tolkien, J. R. R. 'Beowulf: The Monsters and the Critics'. Presented at the Sir Israel Gollancz Memorial Lecture, British Academy, 1936.

Warner, Marina. *No Go the Bogeyman: Scaring, Lulling and Making Mock*. Chatto & Windus, 1998.

Chapter Six: Leviathans

Abel, Serena M., Fangzhu Wu, Sebastian Primpke, Gunnar Gerdts, and Angelika Brandt. 'Journey to the Deep: Plastic Pollution in the Hadal of Deep-Sea Trenches'. *Environmental Pollution* 333:122078 (2023).

Aguilar, Alex. 'A Review of Old Basque Whaling and Its Effect on the Right Whales of the North Atlantic'. In *Reports of the International Whaling Commission*, 10 (1986), 191–9.

Braat, J. 'Dutch Activities in the North and the Arctic during the Sixteenth and Seventeenth Centuries'. *ARCTIC* 37:4 (1984), 473–80.

Bryant, Miranda. 'Spielberg Tells of Guilt over Harm His Film Jaws May Have Done to Sharks'. *The Guardian*, sec. *The Observer*, 18 December 2022.

Caxton, William. *The Cronycles of Englond*. London, 1482.

Chapman, Blake. *Shark Attacks Myths, Misunderstandings and Human Fear*. CSIRO, 2017.

Duzer, Chett van. *Sea Monsters on Medieval and Renaissance Maps*. British Library Publishing, 2013.

Esteban, Ruth, Alfredo López, Álvaro Garcia De Los Rios, Marisa Ferreira, Francisco Martinho, Paula Méndez Fernandeza, Ezequiel Andréu, *et al*. 'Killer Whales of the Strait of Gibraltar, an Endangered Subpopulation Showing a Disruptive Behavior'. *Marine Mammal Science* 38:4 (2022), 1699–1709.

Friedland, Klaus. 'The Hanseatic League and Hanse Towns in the Early Penetration of the North'. *ARCTIC* 37:4 (1984), 539–43.

Heuvelmans, Bernard. *In the Wake of the Sea-Serpents*. Translated by Richard Garnett. Rupert Hart-Davis Ltd, 1968.

Isidore of Seville. *The Etymologies of Isidore of Seville*. Edited by S. A. Barney, W. J. Lewis, J. A. Beach, and O. Berghof. Cambridge University Press, 2006.

Jung, Carl G. *The Archetypes and the Collective Unconscious.* Edited by Herbert Read, Michael Fordham, Gerhard Adler, and William McGuire. Vol. 9.1. Bollingen Series XX. Pantheon, 1959.

Kiparsky, Valentin. *L'histoire Du Morse.* Vol. 73.3. Suomalaisen Tiedeakatemian Toimituksia. Series B. Suomalainen Tiedeakatemia, 1952.

Koch, Albert. *Description of the Hydrarchos Harlani: (Koch,) . . . A Gigantic Fossil Reptile: Lately Discovered by the Author in the State of Alabama, March, 1845. Together with Some Geological Observations Made . . . in the Years 1844–1845.* 2nd edn. B. Owen, 1845.

———. 'The Hydrarchos or Leviathan! Of the Antediluvian World, as Described in the Book of Job, Chapt. 41. This Immense Skeleton of a Sea Monster! Exceeds 114 Feet in Length and Weighs 7,500 Pounds . . . As This Extraordinary Creature Will Shortly Leave', 1845. Broadsides, leaflets, and pamphlets from America and Europe. Library of Congress.

Lawrence, Natalie. 'Monstrous Assembly: Constructing Exotic Animals in Early Modern Europe'. PhD, University of Cambridge, 2016.

———. 'Decoding the Morse: The History of 16th-Century Narcoleptic Walruses'. *The Public Domain Review* (blog), 14 June 2017.

———. 'Greenland Unicorns and the Magical Alicorn'. *The Public Domain Review* (blog), 19 September 2019.

Magnus, Albertus. *On Animals: A Medieval Summa Zoologica.* Vol. 2. Edited by Kenneth. F. Kitchell Jr. and translated by Irven Michael Resnick. John Hopkins University Press, 1999.

Magnus, Olaus. *Historia de Gentibus Septentrionalibus*. Vol. 1 and Vol.3. Edited by Peter Fisher and translated by Peter Foote and Humphrey Higgens. Hakluyt Society, 1998.

Margócsy, Dániel. 'The Camel's Head: Representing Unseen Animals in Sixteenth-Century Europe'. *Netherlands Yearbook for History of Art / Nederlands Kunsthistorisch Jaarboek* 61:1 (2011), 62–85.

Marx, Lizzie. 'Picturing Scent: The Tale of a Beached Whale'. *The Public Domain Review* (blog), 21 July 2021.

McKay, John. 'The White Elephant of Rucheni'. *Scientific American* (blog), 22 November 2011.

Melville, Hermann. *Moby Dick: Or, The Whale*. Edited by Tom Quirk. Illustrated. Penguin Classics, 2003.

Meurger, Michel. *Lake Monster Traditions, A Cross-Cultural Analysis*. Fortean Times, 1988.

Naish, Darren. 'Where Be Monsters?' *Fortean Times*, March 2000.

———. *Hunting Monsters*. Arcturus, 2017.

———. 'Sea Monster Sightings and the "Plesiosaur Effect"'. *Tetrapod Zooloy Blog* (blog), 28 April 2019.

Neff, Christopher. 'The Jaws Effect: How Movie Narratives Are Used to Influence Policy Responses to Shark Bites in Western Australia'. *Australian Journal of Political Science* 50:1 (2015), 114–27.

Nichols, Wallace J. *Blue Mind: The Surprising Science That Shows How Being Near, In, On, or Under Water Can*

Make You Happier, Healthier, More Connected, and Better at What You Do. Back Bay Books, 2015.

Nigg, Joseph. 'Olaus Magnus' Sea Serpent'. *The Public Domain Review* (blog), 5 February 2014.

Ogilvie, Brian W. *The Science of Describing: Natural History in Renaissance Europe*. University of Chicago Press, 2006.

Paré, Ambroise. *On Monsters and Marvels*. Translated by Janis L. Pallister. University of Chicago Press, 1982.

Pacoureau, Nathan, Cassandra L. Rigby, Peter M. Kyne, Richard B. Sherley, Henning Winker, John K. Carlson, Sonja V. Fordham, *et al*. 'Half a Century of Global Decline in Oceanic Sharks and Rays'. *Nature* 589:7843 (2021), 567–71.

Paxton, C. G. M. 'Unleashing the Kraken: On the Maximum Length in Giant Squid (*Architeuthis Sp.*)'. *Journal of Zoology* 300:2 (2016), 82–8.

Paxton, C. G. M., and D. Naish. 'Did Nineteenth Century Marine Vertebrate Fossil Discoveries Influence Sea Serpent Reports?' *Earth Sciences History* 38:1 (2019), 16–27.

Pennant, Thomas. *British Zoology*. Vol. 3. Printed by William Eyres, for Benjamin White, 1768.

Perathoner, Simon, Maria Lorena Cordero-Maldonado, and Alexander D. Crawford. 'Potential of Zebrafish as a Model for Exploring the Role of the Amygdala in Emotional Memory and Motivational Behavior: Amygdala in Fish'. *Journal of Neuroscience Research* 94:6 (2016), 445–62.

Pliny The Elder. *Natural History*. Translated by J. Healy. Penguin Classics, 1991.

Quammen, David. *Monster of God – The Man-Eating Predator in the Jungles of History and the Mind*. W. W. Norton & Company, 2003.

Rieppel, Lukas. 'Albert Koch's Hydrarchos Craze: Credibility, Identity, and Authenticity in Nineteenth-Century Natural History'. In *Science Museums in Transition*, 139–61. University of Pittsburgh Press, 2017.

Ronnberg, Ami, and Kathleen Martin, eds. *The Book of Symbols: Reflections on Archetypal Images*. Archive for Research in Archetypal Symbolism. TASCHEN, 2010.

Rosa, Rui, and Brad A. Seibel. 'Slow Pace of Life of the Antarctic Colossal Squid'. *Journal of the Marine Biological Association of the United Kingdom* 90:7 (2010), 1375–8.

Schama, Simon. *An Embarrassment of Riches: An Interpretation of Dutch Culture in the Golden Age*. Harper Perennial, 2004.

Seaver, Kirsten A. '"A Very Common and Usuall Trade": The Relationship between Cartographic Perceptions and "fishing" in the Davis Strait circa 1500–1550'. *The British Library Journal* 22:1 (1996) 1-26.

Szabo, Vicki Ellen. '"Bad to the Bone"? The Unnatural History of Monstrous Medieval Whales'. *The Heroic Age, A Journal of Early Medieval Northwestern Europe* 8 (2005).

———. *Monstrous Fishes and the Mead-Dark Sea: Whaling in the Medieval North Atlantic*. Vol. 35. The Northern

World: North Europe and the Baltic c. 400–1700 AD: Peoples, Economies and Cultures. Brill, 2008.

Worm, Boris, Brendal Davis, Lisa Kettemer, Christine A. Ward-Paige, Demian Chapman, Michael R. Heithaus, Steven T. Kessel, and Samuel H. Gruber. 'Global Catches, Exploitation Rates, and Rebuilding Options for Sharks'. *Marine Policy* 40 (2013), 194–204.

Zachos, Elaina. 'Why Are We Afraid of Sharks? There's a Scientific Explanation'. *National Geographic*, 29 June 2019.

Chapter Seven: Scaly Devils

Aldrovandi, Ulysse, and Bartolemmo Ambrosini. *Serpentum et Draconum Historiae Libri Duo*. Bononiae: C. Ferronium, 1640.

Blatchford, Thomas W. *Observations on Equivocal Generation: Prepared as Evidence in a Suit for Slander*. Albany: Printed by J. Munsell, 1844.

Bleichmar, Daniela, and Peter Mancall. '"Seeing the World in a Room"'. In *Collecting Across Cultures: Material Exchanges in the Early Modern Atlantic World*, 15–30. University of Pennsylvania Press, 2011.

Bontius, Jacobus. 'MS Sherard: "Jacobi Bontii Medici Arcis Ac Civitatis Bataviae Novae in Indiis Ordinarii Exoticorum Indicorum Centuria Prima, 1630"', 1630. Sherard Collection, Plant Sciences Library, Oxford.

———. '"Tropische Geneeskunde/On Tropical Medicine"'. In *Opuscula Selecta Neerlandicorum de Arte*

Medica, edited by M. Andel, Vol. 10. Sumptibus Societatis, 1931.

Carey, Daniel. 'Compiling Nature's History: Travellers and Travel Narratives in the Early Royal Society'. *Annals of Science* 54:3 (1997), 269–92.

Challender, Daniel W. S., Helen C. Nash, and Carly Waterman. *Pangolins: Science, Society and Conservation. Biodiversity of the World: Conservation from Genes to Landscapes.* Academic Press, 2019.

Clusius, Carolus. *Exoticorum Libri Decem: Quibus Animalium, Plantarum, Aromaticum, Aliorumque, Peregrinorum Fructum Historiae Describuntur.* Leiden: Plantin Press, 1605.

Cook, Harold. 'Global Economies and Local Knowledge in the East Indies: Jacobus Bontius Learns the Facts of Nature'. In *Colonial Botany: Science, Commerce, and Politics in the Early Modern World*, edited by Londa Schiebinger and Claudia Swan, 111–18. University of Pennsylvania Press, 2005.

———. *Matters of Exchange: Commerce, Medicine and Science in the Dutch Golden Age.* Yale University Press, 2007.

Dance, Peter. *Animal Fakes and Frauds.* Sampson Low, 1975.

Findlen, Paula. 'Jokes of Nature and Jokes of Knowledge: The Playfulness of Scientific Discourse in Early Modern Europe'. *Renaissance Quarterly* 43:2 (1990), 292–331.

———. *Possessing Nature: Museums, Collecting, and Scientific Culture in Early Modern Italy.* Berkeley, Los Angeles and London: University of California Press, 1996.

———. 'Inventing Nature. Commerce, Art, and Science in the Early Modern Cabinet of Curiosities'. In *Merchants and Marvels: Commerce, Science, and Art in Early Modern Europe*, 297–323. Routledge, 2002.

Jahme, Carol. *Beauty and the Beasts: Woman, Ape, and Evolution*. Virago, 2001.

Jong, Johan de. 'Drawings, Ships and Spices: Accumulation in the Dutch East India Company'. In *Centres and Cycles of Accumulation in and Around the Netherlands During the Early Modern Period*, edited by Lissa Roberts, 177–203. LIT, 2011.

Kircher, Athanasius. *Arca Noë*. Amsterdam: Apud Joannem Janssonium a Waesberge, 1675.

Koerner, Lisbet. *Linnaeus: Nature and Nation*. Harvard University Press, 2009.

Lawrence, Natalie. 'Exotic Origins: The Emblematic Biogeographies of Early Modern Scaly Mammals'. *Itinerario* 39:1 (2015), 17–43.

———. 'Monstrous Assembly: Constructing Exotic Animals in Early Modern Europe'. PhD, University of Cambridge, 2016.

MacGregor, Arthur. *Curiosity and Enlightenment: Collectors and Collections from the Sixteenth to Nineteenth Century*. Yale University Press, 2008.

Margócsy, Dániel. 'The Camel's Head: Representing Unseen Animals in Sixteenth-Century Europe'. *Netherlands Yearbook for History of Art / Nederlands Kunsthistorisch Jaarboek* 61:1 (2011), 62–85.

———. *Commercial Visions: Science, Trade and Visual Culture in the Dutch Golden Age*. University of Chicago Press, 2014.

Pieters, F. J. M. *Wonderen Der Nature in de Menagerie van Blauw Jan Te Amsterdam, Zoals Gezien Door Jan Velten Rond 1700*. Rare and Historical Books. ETI Digital, 1998.

Piso, Willem. *De Indiae Utriusque Re Naturali et Medica, Libri Quatuordecim*. Elzevir, 1658.

Pliny the Elder. *Natural History*. Translated by J. Healy. Penguin Classics, 1991.

Polo, Marco. *The Travels of Marco Polo*. Vol. 2. Edited by Guido Montelupo and translated by Henry Yule. CreateSpace Independent Publishing Platform, 2016.

Seba, Albertus. *Cabinet of Natural Curiosities / Das Naturalienkabinett / Le Cabinet Des Curiosites Naturelles*. TASCHEN, 2008.

Schmidt, Benjamin. 'Inventing Exoticism: The Project of Dutch Geography and the Marketing of the World'. In *Merchants and Marvels: Commerce, Science, and Art in Early Modern Europe*, edited by Pamela Smith and Paula Findlen, 347–69. Routledge, 2002.

———. 'Accumulating the World: Collecting and Commodifying "Globalism"'. In *Centres and Cycles of Accumulation in and Around the Netherlands During the Early Modern Period*, edited by Lissa Roberts, 129–54. Berlin and Zurich: LIT, 2011.

———. *Inventing Exoticism: Geography, Globalism, and Europe's Early Modern World*. University of Pennsylvania Press, 2015.

Sloan, Phillip R. 'The Buffon-Linnaeus Controversy'. *Isis* 67:3 (1976), 356–75.

Chapter Eight: Terrible Lizards

Bakker, Robert T. 'Dinosaur Renaissance'. *Scientific American* 232:4 (1975), 58–79.

Ballou, W. H. 'The Aeroplane Dinosaur of a Million Years Ago'. *The Ogden Standard-Examiner*, sec. Comic Section, 15 August 1920.

Balmford, Andrew, Lizzie Clegg, Tim Coulson, and Jennie Taylor. 'Why Conservationists Should Heed Pokémon'. *Science* 295(5564):2367 (2002).

Benton, Michael J. 'A Brief History of Dinosaur Palaeontology'. In *The Scientific American Book of Dinosaurs*, edited by G. S. Paul, 10–44. St Martin's Press, 2000.

———. *The Dinosaurs Rediscovered: How a Scientific Revolution Is Rewriting History*. Thames and Hudson Ltd, 2020.

Fallon, Richard. *Reimagining Dinosaurs in Late Victorian and Edwardian Literature. How the 'Terrible Lizard' Became a Transatlantic Cultural Icon*. Cambridge University Press, 2021.

———. 'Seen through Deep Time: Occult Clairvoyance and Palaeoscientific Imagination'. *Journal of Victorian Culture* 28:2 (2023), 143–62.

Fromm, Erich. *Anatomy of Human Destructiveness*. 1st edn. Holt, Rinehart and Winston, 1973.

Gomez, Jesse, Michael Barnett, and Kalanit Grill-Spector. 'Extensive Childhood Experience with Pokémon Suggests Eccentricity Drives Organization of Visual Cortex'. *Nature Human Behaviour* 3:6 (2019), 611–24.

Gordon, Elizabeth Oke Buckland. *The Life and Correspondence of William Buckland ... and First President of the British Association*. London: J. Murray, 1894.

Gould, Steven J. 'Dinomania'. In *Dinosaur in a Haystack*, by Steven J. Gould, 221–37. Harmony Books, 1995.

Halstead, L. B. 'Scrotum Humanum Brookes 1763 – the First Named Dinosaur'. *Journal of Insignificant Research* 5 (1970), 14–15.

Halstead, L. B., and W. A. S. Sargent. 'Scrotum Humanum Brookes – the Earliest Name for a Dinosaur?' *Modern Geology* 18 (1993), 221–4.

Hutchinson, Henry Neville. *Extinct Monsters and Creatures of Other Days: A Popular Account of Some of the Larger Forms of Ancient Animal Life*. New and enl. edn. Chapman & Hall, 1910.

Illustrated London News. 'Dinner in the Iguanodon'. 7 January 1854, vol. 24, no. 662.

Landers, Jackson. 'Paleontologist Jack Horner Is Hard at Work Trying to Turn a Chicken into a Dinosaur'. *The Washington Post*, sec. Health and Science, 10 November 2014.

Lyell, Charles. *Principles of Geology*. Edited by James A. Secord. Penguin Classics, 1997.

McPhee, Rod. 'PC REX Sir David Attenborough's BBC1 Dinosaur Show Presents Softer "Woke" Version of the T-Rex'. *The Sun*, 13 April 2022.

Mayor, Adrienne. *The First Fossil Hunters: Dinosaurs, Mammoths, and Myth in Greek and Roman Times*. Princeton University Press, 2000.

Naish, Darren. 'The Iguanodon Explosion: How Scientists Are Rescuing the Name of a "Classic" Ornithopod Dinosaur, Part 1'. *Scientific American* (blog), 15 November 2010.

———. 'The Explosion of Iguanodon, Part 2: Iguanodontians of the Hastings Group'. *Scientific American* (blog), 16 November 2010.

———. 'The Explosion of Iguanodon, Part 3: Hypselospinus, Wadhurstia, Dakotadon, Proplanicoxa . . . When Will It All End?' *Scientific American* (blog), 17 November 2010.

———. 'Robert Plot's Lost Dinosaur Bone'. *Tetrapod Zoology Blog* (blog), 16 December 2022.

O'Connor, Ralph. *The Earth on Show Fossils and the Poetics of Popular Science, 1802–1856*. University of Chicago Press, 2007.

———. 'Victorian Saurians: The Linguistic Prehistory of the Modern Dinosaur'. *Journal of Victorian Culture* 17:4 (2012), 492–504.

Plot, Robert. *The Natural History of Oxfordshire, Being an Essay toward the Natural History of England*. Oxford: Robert Plot, 1677.

Rieppel, Lukas. *Assembling the Dinosaur: Fossil Hunters, Tycoons, and the Making of a Spectacle*. Harvard University Press, 2019.

———. 'How American Tycoons Created the Dinosaur'. *Nautilus*, 4 September 2019.

Romano, Marco, and Marco Avanzini. 'The Skeletons of Cyclops and Lestrigons: Misinterpretation of Quaternary Vertebrates as Remains of the Mythological Giants'. *Historical Biology* 31:2 (2019), 117–39.

Seeley, Harry Govier. 'I. On the Classification of the Fossil Animals Commonly Named Dinosauria'. *Proceedings of the Royal Society of London* 43:258–65 (1888), 165–71.

Shapiro, Beth. 'Mammoth 2.0: Will Genome Engineering Resurrect Extinct Species?' *Genome Biology* 16:1 (2015), 228.

The Washington Post. 'Was Most Grotesque Animal'. 23 June 1912.

Villiers de l'Isle-Adam, Auguste. *Tomorrow's Eve*. Translated by Robert Martin Adams. University of Illinois Press, 2001.

Witton, Mark P. 'Why Protoceratops Almost Certainly Wasn't the Inspiration for the Griffin Legend'. *Mark P. Witton's Blog* (blog), 2016.

———. 'Dinosaur Fossils and Chinese Dragons: Ancient Association or Modern Wishful Thinking?' *Mark P. Witton's Blog* (blog), 26 March 2021.

Witton, Mark P., and Ellinor Michel. *Art and Science of the Crystal Palace Dinosaurs*. The Crowood Press, 2022.

Conclusion: Titans of Gaia

Byock, Jesse, and Snorri Sturluson. *The Prose Edda: Tales from Norse Mythology*. Penguin Classics, 2005.

Cellan-Jones, Rory. 'Stephen Hawking Warns Artificial Intelligence Could End Mankind'. *BBC News*, sec. Technology, 2 December 2014.

Dalley, Stephanie. *Myths from Mesopotamia. Creation, The Flood, Gilgamesh and Others*. Oxford University Press, 1989.

Głownia, Dawid. 'Socio-Political Aspects of Kaijū Eiga Genre: A Case Study of the Original Godzilla'. *Silva Iaponicarum* XXXVII (2013).

Hall, Stephen. 'Wolves and Brown Bear Numbers Are up in Europe, a New Report Shows'. World Economic Forum, 12 October 2022.

Harari, Yuval Noah. *Homo Deus: A Brief History of Tomorrow*. Harvill Secker, 2016.

Jacobson, Mark. 'What Does Godzilla Mean? The Evolution of a Monster Metaphor'. *New York Times*, sec. Vulture, 16 May 2014.

Jenkins, Richard. 'Disenchantment, Enchantment and Re-Enchantment: Max Weber at the Millennium'. *Mind and Matter* 10:2 (2012).

Larrington, Carolyn. *The Poetic Edda*. Oxford World Classics. OUP Oxford, 2014.

Ledger, Sophie, Claire Anna Rutherford, Charlotte Benham, Ian J. Burfield, Stefanie Deinet, Mark Eaton, Robin Freeman, Hannah Puleston, Kate Scott-Gatty, and Anna Staneva. 'Wildlife Comeback in Europe: Opportunities and Challenges for Species Recovery. Final Report to Rewilding Europe by the Zoological Society of London, BirdLife International and the European Bird Census Council'. ZSL, 2022.

Lovejoy, Arthur O. *The Great Chain of Being. A Study of the History of an Idea.* Harvard University Press, 1936.

Marotta, Mario. 'A Disenchanted World: Max Weber on Magic and Modernity'. *Journal of Classical Sociology* (2023).

Trischler, Helmuth. 'The Anthropocene: A Challenge for the History of Science, Technology, and the Environment'. *NTM Zeitschrift Für Geschichte Der Wissenschaften, Technik Und Medizin* 24:3 (2016), 309–35.

UNEP. 'Emissions Gap Report (EGR) 2022: The Closing Window – Climate Crisis Calls for Rapid Transformation of Societies'. United Nations Environment Programme, 2022.

Notes

Introduction: Making Beasts

Opening quote from Mary Shelley, *Frankenstein* (1888), Letter IV.

1. Monster definitions in Pliny's *Historia naturalis*, St Augustine's *De civitate Dei* and St Isidore's *Etymologiae*, respectively.

2. 'Monsters' were first distinguished with the idea of '*monstrare*' in Ulysse Aldrovandi's *Monstrorum Historia* (1642): '*Propter admirationem digito monstretur*', essentially the concept of wonder causing something to be pointed out or demonstrated. I would note that Aldrovandi and his contemporaries clearly distinguished between individual, one-off monsters, and monstrous kinds or species.

3. Gottschall offers a 'unified theory of storytelling' as a means by which we simulate and navigate the complexity of social life. He argues that storytelling is one of the many behaviours evolved 'to ensure our survival'. Gottschall's recent book *The Story Paradox: How Our Love of Storytelling Builds Societies and Tears Them Down* (Basic Books, 2021) examines the dark side of storytelling in the modern age of social media, in which stories can be used to get 'good people to act monstrously'.

4. One of Bettelheim's most powerful arguments is that we bring children up to believe everyone is good, despite the fact that they know very well that they are not totally good. Fairy tales, with all of their cruel, dark components, give the

child a place to work through and master these elements of themselves, without turning to the terrible conclusion that, because parts of them are unpalatable, they are therefore themselves monsters.

5   The original design of the Xenomorphs in *Alien* (1979) was based on the 'biomechanical' creatures depicted by surrealist artist H. R. Geiger in *Necronomicon* (1977). The quote from Levi Strauss is always ambiguously translated, the original French from 1963 is '*bonnes à penser*'. The English novelist and critic John Berger pointed out that we have always noticed correspondences between us and other animals. Aristotle, for example, described how 'in the great majority of animals there are traces of physical qualities and attitudes' akin to those in humans and 'just as in man we find knowledge, wisdom and sagacity, so in certain animals there exists some other natural potentiality akin to these'.

6   What's also intriguing is that according to Google, the uses of both 'beast' and 'creature' dipped in the twentieth century, but have seen a steady increase in the last two decades. Beastly creatures are having a cultural renaissance, perhaps due to a resurgence of interest in wilderness and wildness.

7   One of Becker's colleagues, Erich Fromm, commented that human experience is dominated by a 'paradoxical nature, the fact that he is half animal and half symbolic', and that we have the urge to expel the animal part. We are half beastly and half divine.

8   Quammen also points out that 'we have tolerated the dangerous problematic presence of big predators, finding roles for them within our emotional universe. But now, our own numerousness, our puissance, and our solipsism have brought us to a point where tolerance is unnecessary and danger of that sort is unacceptable'. The extermination of predators has been integral to colonial projects, Quammen argues, and

that 'you haven't conquered a people, and their place, until you've exterminated their resident monsters'. Two thirds of the world's thirty-one largest predator species are now listed as threatened. Worldwide, vertebrate populations have declined by sixty percent since 1970.

9 Many people today still intuitively understand evolution as a scale of development from 'simple to complex', and humans as the evolutionary apotheosis.

10 Joseph Campbell posited in *The Power of Myth* (1991) that a hero killing a dragon 'hears the song of nature. He has transcended his humanity and reassociated himself with the powers of nature, which are the powers of our life, and from which our minds remove us. You see, consciousness thinks it's running the shop. But it's a secondary organ of a total human being, and it must not put itself in control'. When the conscious mind is in full control, 'you get a man like Darth Vader in *Star Wars*'.

Chapter One: The Horned Sorcerer

Opening quote from Werner Herzog, *Cave of Forgotten Dreams* (2010).

1 This story is based as closely as possible on the written accounts that exist of these events, but I have taken some creative licence for enjoyment's sake. Max (nineteen) and Louis (sixteen) first entered the cave on 20 July 1912 with their brother Jacques (seventeen), having made exciting findings at other caves before. We begin later that year, on 10 October, when Max and Louis went further into the cave with their friend François Camel. The boys' father, Comte Henri Bégouën, was a French prehistorian, archaeologist and journalist.

2 The Upper Palaeolithic period, lasting between around 50,000

and 12,000 years ago, was the last period of the Palaeolithic or 'Old Stone Age' which started 3.3 million years ago. The Palaeolithic has been characterised by the first use of stone tools by *Homo sapiens*, though findings of tools from millions of years ago have raised the possibility that tool use began far earlier among closely related species such as *Australopithecus*. The hunter-gatherer Palaeolithic lifestyle was slowly abandoned during the following Mesolithic (Middle Stone Age) and Neolithic (New Stone Age) periods, when a settled, farming lifestyle arose. The Palaeolithic-Mesolithic transition in human development in Europe *roughly* coincides with the geological boundary between the Pleistocene and the current geological epoch, the Holocene, which began about 11,700 years ago with the end of the last Ice Age.

3   Henri did actually lose his trousers to a stalactite, I didn't make that up. The female and male bison are 61 and 63cm long, respectively, replicas of which can be seen at the Musée d'Archéologie Nationale (Paris). A third smaller and simpler bison was later found in the cave.

4   There are three caves in this system in all: Enlène (which was already well known), Tuc d'Audoubert and Trois-frères. This second discovery occurred on 21 July 1914 while the middle brother, Jacques, was returned from military service. The furthest tendrils of the Trois-frères complex reach within metres of the Tuc d'Audoubert chamber where the bison were found, now called the Salle des Bisons.

5   Louis and Max would continue to study the caves throughout their lives. Max even published an 'archaeological romance' novel, *Les Bisons d'argile* (1925, in English as *Bison of Clay* in 1926), narrating his fantasies of events inside the cave. The Bégouën family have fiercely protected the caves from public attention – Louis purchased Enlène in 1925 and closed it from public access. Only about 2,000 people in total have

visited the complexes, under supervision, so the Palaeolithic footprints and creations remain undisturbed.

6   Cave art, also known as parietal art, was generally made from a mixture of pigments, including iron oxides, manganese oxides and charcoal, and etching into the stone. They are often 'palimpsest' or overlaid on one another without obvious reason.

7   In fact, due to changes in the human environment, the human brain is thought to have decreased in size since the last Ice Age. Changes in brain function have also been linked to technological and behavioural changes in Stone Age humans, such as the development of hand-axe technology after 2 million years of using sharp stones. Animals are the most abundant kind of rock-surface images globally, occurring in more than 100 countries. It's also important to note that European animal cave art is by no means the earliest in the world. It's preceded by that on other continents, such as the pig depiction in the caves in the Maros-Pangkep karst of South Sulawesi, Indonesia, dated to be over 43,900 years old. Some experts posit that, given key similarities between cave paintings in different regions of the world, the practice might have arisen far earlier, even before human migrations out of Africa. Non-figurative paintings as old as 65,000 years – 20,000 years before modern humans arrived in Europe – have been found in Spain, suggested by some to have been made by Neanderthals.

8   It is possible that the original entrance to the cave has become obscured by tunnel collapse, but it would still not have been an easy journey, historically. Tuc d'Audoubert has exceptionally well-preserved footprints from this period, and San Bushmen trackers have been employed to decipher the tracks. They found that most footprints belonged to adult men, in particular eight men aged twenty-five to sixty years old.

9   Sediment analysis studies suggest that human overkill didn't cause the decrease in Ice Age megafauna, as coexistence persisted for significant periods of time, but rather that the disappearance coincided with the spread of forests.

10 Only about 11 per cent of the images are animals pierced by arrows.

11 In Freudian terms, the capacity to think and to imagine provided the ability to buffer raw feelings and impulses. Researchers have experimented recently with different kinds of light in caves to understand better the Palaeolithic experience and image-making – they even suggest that the origins of cinema exist in the dynamism created by the combination of firelight and cave images.

12 There is one other 'sorcerer' figure in the Trois-frères caves, an upright bovine creature playing what looks like a flute. At Lascaux there is what seems to be a bird-headed human figure being charged by a speared bison, from about 21,000–14,000 years ago. At Chauvet, north-east of Trois-frères, is the image named 'Venus and the Sorcerer': a part-man part-lion figure, encircling a female pubis. The oldest known therianthropes globally are hunting figures in the Leang Tedongnge cave in Sulawesi.

13 Archaeologists have recreated these headdresses with the skulls of modern red deer, that are flimsier than those of their Ice Age ancestors. They've worked out that the severed head of a deer was placed in a fire until the bone was charred, the upper half covered in clay to protect it from the heat. The skullcap was trimmed and bevelled using flint tools before two holes were bored, through which cords could be threaded to tie it onto someone's head. The antlers were also trimmed down to reduce the weight of the whole piece. The headdresses at Starr Carr were made before Britain became entirely isolated from the rest of Europe by rising sea levels, so it is likely that this hoard was not unique to Britain.

14   The earliest recorded eye-witness account of a shaman in Siberia was on New Year's Day in 1557, when the traveller Richard Johnson described seeing 'devilish rites'. The first visual record of a Siberian shaman was a 1692 engraving by Nicolaas Witsen (published in 1705), via which the term 'shaman' probably reached Europe.

15   In *Being Human* (2021) the writer Charles Foster gives a wonderful account of his time living as closely as possible as a Palaeolithic human and the way shamanism may have saturated daily experience.

16   The animal images could be interpreted in many ways. For example, some may have been totems for shamans rather than representations of animals. Evidence for music in ritual includes two collections of flutes dating to the Upper Palaeolithic that have been found at three sites in southern Germany: Geißenklösterle, Hohle Fels and Vogelherd caves as well as in the Isturitz caves in south-west France.

17   Later Mesolithic sites also have rock art showing human-animal hybrid shaman figures, suggesting that the hunter-gatherer cosmology persisted.

18   Robin Dunbar's 'social brain hypothesis' outlines that social group size and neocortex size are related in primates, predicting a group size of about 150 in humans. Beyond this, other mechanisms were required for cohesion. He developed this hypothesis to emphasise the transcendent nature of religious experience, enabling the development of larger societies by healing inevitable conflict and mediating individuality, though organised religion only appeared relatively late on in history.

19   The Gundestrup cauldron, for example, is a silverwork masterpiece made around the first century BCE, found in a peat bog in Himmerland, Denmark. It depicts a Celtic god that might have been called Cernunnos, a horned, torqued deity

that could pass to and from the spirit world. Cernunnos also appeared on the Pillar of the Boatmen, made about a century later under the Roman rule of Gaul and found under the foundations of Notre Dame.

Chapter Two: Dragons of Chaos

Opening quote from John Milton, *Paradise Lost* (1667), Book Seven, lines 211–12.

1   The reverberations of this 'Bang' are still detectable, 13.8 billion years later, in cosmic microwave background radiation. The universe is continually expanding outwards from the initial 'explosion' and may even collapse inwards at some point in a theoretical 'Big Crunch'.

2   Gunkel argued that the pattern he identified (though he was not the first to do this) was even detectable in the Biblical Book of Genesis. There has been considerable debate for and against Gunkel's theories, incorporating new discoveries such as the Ugaritic *Ba'al Cycle* from the thirteenth century.

3   'Cosmic serpents' have been widespread as creator gods in many mythologies, which were later inverted to become chaotic adversaries of creation. Zeus himself was sometimes represented as a serpent before he became a thunderous sky-god and serpent-slayer.

4   The *mušḫuššu* were protective spirits placed at entranceways to keep away evil. There were two Babylonian empires, Old and New Babylon. The first lasted c. 1894–1595 BCE and extended through Mesopotamia by 1755 BCE. Its capital, Old Babylon, was the largest city in the world and was ruled most famously by King Hammurabi (1810–1750 BCE). It was sacked by the Hittites in 1595 BCE and the kingdom was taken over by Kassites in 1570 BCE, who ruled for more than four centuries and made Babylon a cultural centre, with

Marduk as the primary god. Centuries of political struggle and war with neighbouring powers, including the Assyrians, followed. Eventually Babylon became an imperial power again under King Nebuchadnezzar II (r. 605/604–562 BCE). New Babylon fell in 539 BCE to Persian forces. During the *Akitu* festival, the king sequestered himself away for several days to represent the fight with Tiamat; he re-emerged and was publicly humbled so he could take on his sacred role afresh. A sacrificial lamb was also burnt representing Tiamat's consort son Quingu.

5   Assurbanipal was an Assyrian king who brought together Mesopotamia's first systematically organised library in the city of Nineveh. The tablets were discovered by English archaeologist Austen Henry Layard in 1849. They were deciphered by scholars looking for evidence of Mesopotamian history and the origins of Biblical stories. Mesopotamian documents are recorded in two languages, Akkadian and the older Sumerian (invented in Sumer around 3400 BCE).

6   The copy in Assurbanipal's library is the most complete version of the *Enūma Eliš* we know of and dates from the seventh century BCE. The story is much older though, dating to at least 1200 BCE, probably from Old Babylonia. The *Enūma Eliš* is a composite story drawing on earlier myths, such as the Mesopotamian *Atrahasis* flood story, which fed into later mythical traditions, including the Bible. 'Mesopotamia' comes from the Greek *mesos* (middle) and *potamos* (river), being situated between the Tigris and Euphrates rivers. This region was part of the 'Fertile Crescent', where settled agriculture began to develop.

7   My retelling is based on Stephanie Dalley's 1989 translation.
8   Assyriologist Jeremy Black notes that the 'rise of the cult of Marduk is closely connected with the political rise of Babylon from city-state to the capital of an empire . . . Marduk

became more and more important until it was possible for the author of the Babylonian Epic of Creation to maintain that not only was Marduk king of all the gods but that many of the latter were no more than aspects of him'. Assur, whom Marduk replaced, had in turn probably taken over from the God Ea or Enlil in older versions of the story. The particularly patriarchal message of the story may have been linked to the political situation during King Hammurabi's reign (1850–1750 BCE). He styled himself as the 'father to his subjects' and brought in some particularly strict legal changes which heavily restricted women's rights.

9   The German psychologist Erich Neumann suggests that this isn't a passive process, the order has to be fought for: 'To the hero, the clutching Earth Mother appears as a dragon to be overcome . . . seeks to hold him fast as an embryo, by preventing him from being born'. This has been echoed by other Jungian analysts such as Marie-Louise von Franz.

10 The Danish historian Thorkild Jacobsen emphasises the sense of chaos threatening constantly: 'in Mesopotamia, Nature stays not her hand; in her full might she cuts across and overrides man's will, makes him feel to the full how slightly he matters'. Cosmic order could only be maintained by the continual exertion of cosmic will and rule of law over individuals, families and the state.

11 Marduk was not the only god to keep the cycles of nature turning properly, of course, even in Babylon. Other myths, including that of Enki and Nunhursag, as well as Tammuz and Ishtar, portray these deities' roles in seasonal cycles.

12 This quote is commonly attributed to Eric Hoffer, though it is not traceable to an original source.

ENCHANTED CREATURES

Chapter Three: The Minotaur and the Labyrinth

Opening quote from Jorge Luis Borges, *The Aleph* (2000), page 102.

1. A bullfight is usually about twenty minutes long, and occurs as a 'tragedy in three acts', called *tercios*. The details of the whole affair are complex, ritualised and full of superstition.
2. Bullfighting still occurs in Spain, France, Portugal, Mexico, Colombia, Venezuela, Peru and Ecuador. Humane Society International states that 180,000 or 250,000 bulls are killed in bullfighting annually, though estimates vary widely. At the time of writing, bullfights were recently banned in Mexico City and another ban is being pushed through in Colombia, generating a backlash from enthusiasts. The controversy around this blood sport is not new. Pope Pius V banned deadly bullfights as far back as 1567, on pain of excommunication. The underground bullfighting community persisted, until it was allowed out into the open again when the Pope's successor removed the ban and bullfights even became part of holy feast days. Today, the opening of the bullfighting season is Easter Sunday.
3. These paintings are: *La Minotauromachie* (Picasso, 1935, etching and engraving; Museum of Modern Art, New York); *Minotaure dans une barque sauvant une femme* (Picasso, 1937, ripolin, gouache and pen and India ink on board; private collection) and *Barque de naïades et faune blesse* (Picasso, 1937, oil and charcoal on canvas; private collection) respectively. Aside from the Minotaur being held at bay in *La Minotauromachie*, gentle female power features a number of times in Picasso's Minotaur paintings, another example being *Blind Minotaur Guided by a Girl in the Night* (from the *Vollard Suite*, Picasso, 1934, aquatint, etching, and drypoint with scraping and burnishing; the Louis E. Stern Collection).
4. John Richardson described Picasso's philandering and his

sex-soaked history, going to brothels from the age of thirteen in Southern Spain. The French artist Françoise Gilot had an intense relationship with Picasso from 1944–1952. She produced a series of fifty works from 1962–3 called the Labyrinth Series, exploring the myth of the Minotaur and the Labyrinth from a psychological perspective. She died eight days before I wrote this, at the age of 101.

5   In 1968, the photographer Gjon Mili visited Picasso at Golfe-Juan in France's Côte d'Azur and took a series of photographs of the artist (wearing a bull's head intended for bullfighters' training) for *LIFE Magazine* which have become iconic images of Picasso's Minotaur obsession (now in The LIFE Picture Collection). With the sea as a backdrop, the photographs evoke the Minotaur roaming the shores of Crete.

6   Knossos was first discovered in 1878 by the Cretan merchant and antiquarian Minos Kalokairinos. He uncovered two storerooms but was prevented from continuing his excavations by the landowner. Lured there by the promise of finding ancient Cretan coins and seals to add to the Ashmolean Museum's collection in Oxford, Evans purchased the plot of land and began digging. He was also searching for early writing systems to build an image of a nature-loving, matriarchal society. Evans interpreted his findings at Knossos through the lens of what he expected to be there, 'restoring' the palace in his own image of Minoan culture. Many of the iconic artworks of 'Minoan culture' he identified were in fact from an entirely different time period.

7   The first reference to Minos, three generations before the Trojan war, is in Homer's *Iliad* and *Odyssey*, dated around the eighth century BCE. Minos was supposed to have ruled for an impossibly long time, so it might have been a name bestowed on a number of real kings. One of the most exquisite artefacts from Knossos is the Bull's Head Rhyton, a ritual drinking

vessel combining the animal with the intoxicating drink of the god Dionysus.

8 This retelling was based on several of my much-loved childhood books of mythology, especially Roger Lancelyn Green's *Tales of the Greek Heroes* (1958) and Edith Hamilton's *Mythology: Timeless Tales of Gods and Heroes* (1942).

9 Minos's own mother, Europa was a beautiful Phoenician princess who had been borne across the sea and bedded on the shores of Crete by Zeus in the form of a bull. So it was a cruel irony that Minos's wife had also fallen for a bull. Pasiphaë herself was the daughter of the Sun God, Helios, and the witch-nymph Circe.

10 Theseus proceeded to do fairly badly after this triumph. He either lost or abandoned Ariadne on the island of Naxos after they stopped over there, *en route* to Athens. She was picked up by the god Dionysus, who fell in love with her while she was sleeping. Theseus also forgot to switch the dour black sails, with which the tribute of Athenian youths and maidens had sailed from Athens, for white ones, the signal of a successful venture that he had promised to his stepfather, King Aegeus of Athens. Looking out anxiously for Theseus's return and seeing black sails, Aegeus threw himself into the sea in despair, thinking Theseus was dead.

11 The Minotaur's story was also told by later Latin authors such as Catullus and Ovid. Modern renditions include Jorge Luis Borges's *House of Asterion*; the play *Asterion*, which ran at The Getty Villa in 2016, directed by Katharine Noon; and David Elliott's 2017 *Bull*, a darkly comedic verse novel for young adults.

12 Momigliano points out that even ancient sources from the late Classical period used as 'evidence' of Minoan Crete, such as the histories of Herodotus or Thucydides, were also a sort of early 'Cretomania'. Two scripts were used on Crete: Linear

A, which has not been translated, and Linear B, which was later used on mainland Greece and has been translated.

13 Mythographer Joseph Campbell describes how 'the bull was the animal of the moon: the waning and waxing god, by the magic of whose night dew the vegetation is restored; the lord of tides and the productive powers of the earth, the lord of women, lord of the rhythm of the womb'. The historical novelist Robert Graves also suggests that 'Minos' might have been the 'royal title of a Hellenic dynasty which ruled Crete early in the second millennium, each king ritually marrying a Moon-priestess of Cnossus and taking his title of "Moon-being" from her'. Even the word 'Crete', he suggests, might originate from the Greek *crateia*, meaning 'strong or ruling goddess'. This would suggest that the myth encodes a patriarchal as well as political takeover.

14 The separate threads of Theseus's story from earlier writers and tales of the Cretan monster coalesced only in the fifth century BCE, a thousand years after Crete's fall, when they were retold by Greek and Roman authors for hundreds of years subsequently. The story was revivified in the wars with Persia in the fifth century BCE, when the hero Theseus was resurrected to fight a monstrous enemy, this time from the exotic East.

15 Asterion's bull-headedness also parodied Minos's selfishness above his dedication to the divine role as ruler. Seneca's depiction is from his play *Phaedra*.

16 Ruth Padel argues that 'Freud unearthed the unconscious and psychical repression at a time, and in a language, eerily parallel to Evans's discovery at Knossos'. It was a time of 'human psyches getting themselves organized and labelled by science according to patterns of Greek myth'. The name 'Daedalus' means 'skilfully wrought' in Greek.

17 In one version of the story, the Labyrinth itself is the palace

that Minos built at Knossos, where he 'spent the remainder of his life in the inextricable maze . . . at the very heart of which he concealed Pasiphaë and the Minotaur', trapped in the maze of his shame.

18 Stephen King is well known to have disliked Kubrick's cinematic portrayal but *The Shining* film has obsessed critics, tortured by the impossibility of understanding its 'real' meaning. There are many different ways to read it, entwining theorists in an unending maze of detailed analyses of Kubrick's visual clues. It could be anything from Holocaust nightmare to social commentary on the American elite to a mythical retelling. But it is perhaps this obscurity and multifaceted resonance that gives the film its terror.

19 Borges's story can be read as a metaphor for human existence and the longing for redemption. He inverts the hero–monster opposition to turn this battle into the final, freeing climax for which the Minotaur can only wait.

Chapter Four: Snake Women

Opening quote from Marina Warner, *No Go the Bogeyman* (1998), Chapter 3, page 90.

1 Many of these experiments were intended to shed light on human ailments such as depression and bipolar disorder.

2 Trichromacy refers to the possession of three types of cone cell in the retina, each able to detect a different set of wavelengths of light. Combined, these enable trichromats to distinguish every wavelength of light in the visible spectrum. Primate trichromacy evolved separately in prosimians (such as lorises and lemurs), Old World primates (catarrhines) and New World primates. (platyrrhines). Venomous snakes evolved later than constrictors and were even more dangerous. Unsurprisingly, primates that evolved in places where there are

3   venomous snakes are significantly better at detecting snakes. Most other mammals are thought to be dichromats, having only two types of cone cell in their retinas.

3   In one study in 2020, a series of animal images were shown to seven- to ten-month-old infants that were naïve to snakes. Electrophysiological recordings revealed that specific neuronal responses were greater and of higher amplitude when looking at a snake compared to when looking at other animals, especially in the occipital region of the brain. This suggests an evolved specific brain response to snakes which might aid in rapid detection. A 2016 study found that human subjects could detect degraded ('mosaic') images of snakes better than degraded images of other animals – functionally equivalent to being able to detect camouflaged snakes better than other camouflaged species, such as birds or cats.

4   In this study, Isbell found that 2.7 centimetres of exposed gopher snakeskin was sufficient for a response among the four groups of vervets tested. A 2014 study showed that a particular neuronal response in adult women was specific to snakes, different to that induced by other reptiles such as crocodiles, and was not related to disgust.

5   The earliest cave art we know of, from about 70,000 years ago in the Blombos Cave in South Africa, features cross-hatched designs which look like snakeskin. Another nice example is the wooden snake figurine from 4,400 years ago, excavated in a Neolithic site in Finland in 2020.

6   I wasn't sure that I was entirely with Narby on his conclusions but the understanding of the human connection with nature beyond materialistic explanations is a valuable idea.

7   The pomegranate, for example, is a widespread symbol of fertility. Likewise, breadfruit in Polynesian myth, peaches in Japanese mythology and apples in Norse mythology are all symbols of plenty and youth.

8   Other myths feature fruit as an irresistible temptation too. For example, in Greek myth, the pomegranate seeds that Hades tricked Persephone into eating trapped her for six months a year in the underworld as his queen. There was also the golden 'apple of discord' coveted by the three top goddesses Hera, Athena and Aphrodite, which seeded the Trojan War. The hedonic, wild god Dionysus was also associated with figs and, of course, grapes.

9   Michelangelo, *The Fall and Expulsion of Adam and Eve* (1509, fresco, Cappella Sistina, Vatican) and Lucas Cranach the Elder, *The Fall of Man* (1500, woodcut, British Museum). Likewise, in Hugo van der Goes's *The Fall of Adam* (1470, oil on wood, Kunsthistorisches Museum, Vienna, Austria) and *A Serpent with a Woman's Head Lurks in the Tree of Knowledge above Adam and Eve* by Masolino da Panicale (1380, chromolithograph, Wellcome Collection), woman-headed serpents lurk around the Tree of Knowledge, watching Adam and Eve.

10 Some scholars had very personal reasons for giving the story a certain slant. Stephen Greenblatt describes how, while many theologians accepted marital sex as a healthy pre-Fall human condition, the fourth-century philosopher St Augustine had different ideas. He depicted a pre-Fall Adam and Eve having arousal-free, immaculate intercourse, not unlike a couple of coral polyps releasing their gametes dispassionately into balmy water. This serene exchange became disturbed and disrupted by violent passions after they tasted the forbidden fruit. Ironically, the Saint had a history of steamy adolescent adventures in the brothels of Carthage and was riddled with guilt (and who knows what else). Putting a spin on scripture was a way of abdicating the responsibility for these illicit excursions and furiously repressing his urges: Eve made him do it.

11 Other references to Lilith can be found in the Dead Sea

Scrolls, the Babylonian Talmud, the Zohar and the Book of Adam and Eve, among others.

12 John Collier, *Lilith* (1889, oil on canvas, Atkinson Art Gallery, Southport); Dante Gabriel Rossetti, *Lady Lilith* (1868, oil, Bancroft Collection, Wilmington Society of Fine Arts, Delaware).

13 In his *Theogany*, Hesiod describes 'the goddess fierce Echidna who is half a nymph with glancing eyes and fair cheeks, and half again a huge snake, great and awful, with speckled skin, eating raw flesh beneath the secret parts of the holy earth', and 'grim Echidna, a nymph who dies not nor grows old all her days'. In contrast, Lamia was a beautiful queen beloved of Zeus, so his jealous wife Hera stole her children and turned her into a monster. In her grief, Lamia turned to murdering children, her face became distorted and horrible, and Zeus gave her the power to take her eyes out of her head and replace them at will. She was used as a warning tale for naughty children. Later, *lamiae* were pictured as beautiful succubi who would murder young men.

14 In the Underworld of Homer's *Odyssey*, Odysseus relates how 'pale fear seized me, lest august Persephone might send forth upon me from out of the house of Hades the head of the Gorgon, that awful monster'.

15 In the Latin poet Lucan's *The Civil War* he identified the Gorgons as having been banished to Libya, as an explanation for why there were snakes there. In Hesiod's *Theogony*, Medusa's coupling with Poseidon occurred 'in a soft meadow amid spring flowers'. The violent rape by Poseidon was actually a later reimagination by Ovid.

16 Chrysaor or Khrysaor was depicted as a stony-hearted man with a golden sword or a winged boar with golden tusks. He might have sired the half-woman half-snake monster Echidna and the three-headed giant Geryon.

17   Manasa was worshiped in Bihar, Bengal, Jharkhand, Lower Assam and other parts of North-eastern India. The Venus of Willendorf figurine from Austria dates to about 28,000–25,000 BCE (currently at the Natural History Museum, Vienna). She's one of about 120 such figurines or fragments that have been found, and many have been hypothesised to be fertility symbols or Earth goddesses, though we have no way of proving this.

18   There are plentiful other examples of chthonic female monsters overcome by gods and heroes in the making of a new order in Greek and Roman mythology: the Python at Delphi bested by the god Apollo; Heracles's slaying of the many-headed Hydra at Lerna; Odysseus's narrow escape from the cave-dwelling Scylla in Homer's *Iliad* and Anaeas's victory over the odorous Harpies in Virgil's *Anaeid*.

19   The fourteenth-century writer Jean d'Arras compiled the most famous version of Mélusine's myth in which she was turned into a serpent hybrid for incarcerating her father in a mountain (read into that what you will). He described how she was 'euery satirday tourned unto a serpent fro the nauyll dounward' and instructed to never let any man see her in this condition. She managed to get a husband after this unfortunate transformation, but one day he 'sawe Melusyne within the bathe, vnto her nauell in fourme of a woman kymbyng her heere, and fro the nauel dounward in lyknes of a grete serpent, the tayll as grete & thykk as a barell, and so long it was that she made it to touche oftymes (. . .) the rouf of the chambre'. After this, she fled, presumably after shrinking down to human form so she could fit through the door.

20   Milton referenced Ovid's description of Scylla, who was a beautiful naiad that attracted the attentions of Glaucus, a youth loved by the witch Circe. The envious Circe poisoned

the water where Scylla bathed so that when Scylla entered it, her lower body became horribly malformed with a sea-monster tail and dogs' heads sprouting from her thighs.

21   Freud pointed out that Medusa herself was castrated when her head was cut off.

22   Joseph Campbell poignantly comments: 'This is one of the glorious things about the mother-goddess religions, where the world is the body of the Goddess, divine in itself, and divinity isn't something ruling over and above a fallen nature . . . Our story of The Fall in the Garden sees nature as corrupt; and that myth corrupts the whole world for us. Because nature is thought of as corrupt, every spontaneous act is sinful and must not be yielded to. You get a totally different civilization and a totally different way of living according to whether your myth presents nature as fallen or whether nature is in itself a manifestation of divinity'.

Chapter Five: Grendel

Opening quote from William Shakespeare, *The Tempest* (1610–11), Act 5, Scene 1, lines 274–5.

1   The *Beowulf* manuscript contains several other medieval texts, including an account of St Christopher; *The Marvels of the East* (or *The Wonders of the East*), illustrated with strange beasts and monsters; the *Letter of Alexander to Aristotle*; and a partial copy of the Old English poem, *Judith*. Sir John Cotton (d. 1702), bequeathed the *Beowulf* manuscript to the nation, and it entered the British Library's collection. In some of Grendel's modern guises across literature, comic books and film, the story has been inverted so that Grendel is a victim of military power or violence, with just cause for his retaliation – the monster is created by powerful men, a projection of their own aggression.

2. The Norman Conquest (1066–71) was the invasion of England by thousands of Norman, Breton, Flemish and French troops led by William the Conqueror. The violent cultural trauma of the Norman Conquest would radically change the island's social structure and language. Paul Kingsnorth's *Wake* (2014) is a fantastic reimagining of a fenlander's experience of this time.
3. Caliban has variously been interpreted as a monster, a slave or an 'Indian', born to a witch from Algiers in Africa who worships a Patagonian god. He represents the liminal status of 'natives' from a colonial European perspective, as not-quite-human. That he did 'gabble like a thing most brutish', according to Prospero, furthers the impression. Caliban's name may be a transformation of *canibal*, a token of the traditional belief that 'cannibals' lived in exotic, uncivilised lands.
4. According to some Biblical interpretations, Cain might have been the progenitor of the mysterious Nephilim giant race.
5. Christine Alfano argues that 'Grendel's mother disrupts gender conventions; to Anglo Saxons, this made her *atoll*, "terrible" (line 1332), but to contemporary translators, it makes her "monstrous"'.
6. St George's myth, though based on a man born in Turkey or Israel, was almost entirely fictitious. He acquired his dragon quite late on in the story's development.
7. In the Sumerian version of *The Epic of Gilgamesh*, this story is said to be set in the Zagros Mountains in south-west Iran; in the Akkadian version, in Lebanon. This episode might even relate to a historical timber raid bringing precious building material from far away to the clay plains of Mesopotamia. There is an Old Babylonian clay mask of Humbaba/Huwawa in the British Museum from 1800–1600 BCE inscribed with a cuneiform legend foretelling the power of King Sargon.

8. Marina Warner points out that we allow wildness in children, in their diminutive, harmless bodies. Their unrestrained appetites and emotions make them 'little monsters'. She describes how, in Maurice Sendak's *Where the Wild Things Are* (1963), the boy Max leaves what he sees as the punitive confines of domestic life after being sent to bed without dinner for being naughty and threatening to eat his mother. Dressed in a wolf suit, he goes on to cavort as king of the Wild Things in an alternate forest world. The fantasy comes to an end and he returns home to a wholesome supper waiting for him.

9. Jennifer Neville points out that our definition of the 'natural' world now excludes 'supernatural' and 'human' elements – but no parallel word existed in Old English. It's likely that the weather conditions experienced by Anglo-Saxons were far tougher than they are now, and they were far less insulated from them.

10. German journalist Elmar Lorey records 280 known cases of werewolf convictions between 1407 and 1725 (peaking 1575–1657). Contrast this with 12,000 recorded cases of executions for witchcraft, with about 60,000 estimated to have actually occurred. Werewolf convictions equalled only 2 per cent of the recorded witchcraft executions or a mere 0.5 per cent of the estimated executions.

11. 'Windigo Psychosis' appears in the *APA Dictionary of Psychology* as a 'severe culture-bound syndrome occurring among northern Algonquin Indians living in Canada and the north-eastern United States. The syndrome is characterized by delusions of becoming possessed by a flesh-eating monster (the windigo) and is manifested in symptoms including depression, violence, a compulsive desire for human flesh, and sometimes actual cannibalism'.

12. In much the same way, badgers are now being blamed for bovine TB in the UK. This is despite the scientific evidence

showing that killing badgers disperses badgers and might actually spread TB.

13 Scientists from the University of New South Wales have monitored the increase in arid space as a result of dingo culls. A 2021 study found that the dingo fence has created knock-on ecological effects which have decreased vegetation cover. Similar processes might be occurring in other parts of the world. A 2020 study found that poisoning dingoes with Compound 1080 led to increased average dingo body mass due to selection for larger, more poison-resistant bodies.

14 Pioneer of wilderness science George Stankey argues that Romanticism and Transcendentalism, along with the increasing scarcity of wilderness, helped to shift the Judeo-Christian ambivalence towards it. Fantasy writer Ursula le Guin comments on the effect of this domestication of the wild on our fantasy literature, saying the 'only world we know of, now, that isn't shaped and dominated by human beings, is "long ago." "Far away" won't do any more, unless we leap to a literally other world, another planet, or into an imagined future'. Bill Cronon offers a fantastic analysis of the cultural construction of wilderness: 'Wilderness is the natural, unfallen antithesis of an unnatural civilization that has lost its soul. It is a place of freedom in which we can recover the true selves we have lost to the corrupting influences of our artificial lives. Most of all, it is the ultimate landscape of authenticity'. It has become an imagined Eden, where sublime, transcendental connection can still be made – for the (usually economically) privileged few.

15 Gardner's Grendel is a personification of nature, a forest creature, so the novel can also be seen as an ecocriticism.

16 Another parallel was Gardner's cavernous, book-lined study in which he shut himself away to write feverishly: not unlike the lair in which Grendel kept apart from humans. In addition,

Gardner had accidentally killed his seven-year-old brother with a tractor when he was young, so his *Grendel* can be seen as a metaphorical working through of this trauma.

Chapter Six: Leviathans

Opening quote from John Steinbeck, *The Log from the Sea of Cortez* (2001), Chapter 4.

1. Many thanks to Katharina Kraus and Nick Jardine for their help with this translation. Bishop Walkendorf was the Bishop of Nidrosia or Nidaros, the medieval name for Trondheim, Norway. The painting on the town wall went on to inspire many subsequent images in books and other formats, beginning with Conrad Gessner's *Historia Animalium* (1551–87). The image even became the basis for the depiction of an Amerindian water god, Mishipizhiw, by a seventeenth-century French explorer. Pretty good for a piece of graffiti.
2. Walrus products were regularly sold in European markets – but, being so large, walrus carcasses were not brought back on ships, they were butchered at the kill site, so very few people had seen a whole one.
3. Albrecht Dürer, *Head of a Walrus* (1521, brown pen and ink, British Museum). Dürer made this sketch on a tour of northern Europe that year, though he didn't record seeing any live walruses, so he might have drawn a preserved specimen. He added the description, 'that stupid animal of which I have portrayed the head was caught in the Netherlands sea and was twelve brabant ells long with four feet'. One 'brabant ell' was 69.2 centimetres, so twelve 'brabant ells' was approximately 8.3 metres. This is clearly an exaggeration, because walruses reach a maximum of 3.6 metres.
4. In the early sixteenth century, rulers in Sweden and Norway led a shift towards Protestantism. As a Catholic ecclesiast,

Magnus wanted to forge greater ties with the Vatican in defence.

5   The name *Morse*, used commonly in England from the late fifteenth century, was borrowed from the Russian *morsz*, Lapp *mor'sa*, or Finnish *mursu*. The Icelandic names for the walrus were *hrossh-valur, rosm-hvalur* or *rostungur*, becoming *hross-hvalr, rosm-hvalr* and *rostungr* in Old Norse, and later *rosmal* or *rosmar* in Norwegian. Many place-names in Norway echo this, such as *Rosmalvik* or *Rosmalen*.

6   Matthew Paris inscribed this legend off the north-west coast of Scotland on his map in *Abbreviatio Chronicorum Angliae* ('Abbreviated Chronicles of England').

7   Most maps in the Medieval period were not really depictions of geographical space. They were a varied set of systematic, symbolic representations of the world based on Classical knowledge and scripture, called *mappae mundi*. This began to change from the thirteenth century, with the creation of nautical maps for navigation. Waldseemüller's 1516 *Carta Marina* map was a much-updated version of his 1507 *Universalis Cosmographia*. Laurentius Fries, in a revised 1522 edition, moved the *morsus* into the seas off Greenland, perhaps as a result of new information or the Strasbourg head.

8   Whaling was dominated by the Basques for many centuries from the eleventh century, using mainly bay whaling. Catches were tiny compared to modern standards, around two to six whales per year in the sixteenth and seventeenth centuries. Later Arctic whaling expeditions by the Dutch Noordsche Compagnie (Northern Company) and the English Muscovy Company were often manned by Basque whalers. There was considerable bloodshed over Arctic whaling bases between different countries because the rewards were so great.

9   Isidore of Seville drew this idea for his *Etymologies* from the New Testament Book of Jonah 2:3: 'He heard me from the

10. Likewise, William Caxton interpreted the appearance of whales and a *morss piscis* in the Thames as 'Pronostycacions of warre and trouble to ensue soone after'.
11. Scrimshaw is artwork made by etching onto bones and teeth, typically by whalers.
12. A new species of shallows-dwelling vertebrate has recently been identified in Peru that might have been larger than a blue whale, *Perucetus colossus* – a basilosaurid whale from the middle Eocene epoch.
13. Plastic rubbish is still making its way to the bottom of deep-sea trenches, though!
14. Pennant was describing the great white shark in particular. There's some debate as to whether this orca boat-ramming is a vendetta or just a fad. In 1987, for example, a female orca took to wearing a dead salmon on her head. Within the space of the summer, the fishy millinery had been adopted by several other nearby pods. The trend disappeared as quickly as it appeared, but might have been revived recently.
15. In a 2013 meta-analysis using data such as stock estimates and catch records, it was estimated that between 6.4 and 7.9 per cent of sharks are killed per year, ascribed to an 18-fold increase in global fishing pressure on rays and sharks since 1970.
16. Despite differences in brain structures between fish and mammals, fish have brain areas analogous to the mammalian amygdala and hippocampus, for example.
17. A 2010 study estimated that Greenland shark need only 0.03 kg of prey per day, and, far from being top predators, are actually more of the 'float around and see what comes along' kind of hunters.

Chapter Seven: Scaly Devils

Opening quote from the caption accompanying Francisco Goya's 1799 etching, *Los Caprichos no. 43: The sleep of reason produces monsters* (the Metropolitan Museum of Art in New York).

1. Jacob de Bondt was latinised to Jacobus Bontius. De Bondt's original manuscript notes are in the Plant Sciences Library, Oxford, Sherard Collection.

2. Known now as the Dutch East India Company, the 'Vereenigde Oostindische Compagnie' (VOC) was chartered in 1602 and became the first joint-stock company in the world. It amassed such military and financial power that it was able to overwhelm competing European countries in Asian trade. The modern stocks and shares system originated with the VOC mechanism for funding the delays between fleets sailing out and cashing in on returning cargos. It enabled the Company to establish fort colonies around Indonesia and keep a monopoly on the valuable seaborne spice market, previously dominated by the Spanish and Portuguese. Eventually, in 1799, corruption and rising running costs led to the VOC going bankrupt.

3. I have taken some poetic licence with de Bondt's notes for dramatic effect but have kept as closely as possible to the spirit of the original.

4. There are currently eight recognised species of pangolins, four in Asia and four in Africa. All are categorised as 'Vulnerable to Extinction' or 'Endangered' by the International Union for Conservation of Nature (IUCN) Red List, while the Chinese pangolin (*Manis pentadactyla*) and the Sunda pangolin (*Manis javanica*) are 'Critically Endangered'.

5. Sunda pangolins can even swim between islands in Indonesia, but they are largely arboreal. Bontius reported that the animal was also called *tamach* locally.

6   The third-century Roman author Aelianus described how 'Indians' kept 'red Apes' away from their cities 'because they are oft-times mad in lust toward women', so they'd 'hunt and destroy them as being adulterous beasts'. Even as late as 1844, Dr Thomas Blatchford in Albany published evidence in defence of one Betsey Gifford, who had been accused of improper relations with a dog. Blatchford argued that a dog could not sire a hybrid offspring, but that orangutangs were the only animals that might ever be 'able to impregnate the female of our own species besides her own appropriate lord'. Writer Carol Jahme explores stories of female primatologists working in the field. Rape by orangutangs was said to be a threat, one which the American actress Julia Roberts apparently narrowly avoided when filming in Borneo in 1996. On this theme, some dubious attempts to create human–chimpanzee hybrids (humanzees) were attempted in the Soviet Union in the early twentieth century too.

7   Armadillos were already familiar from the Americas by the seventeenth century. Aristotle laid out his theory of how creatures were organised in *The History of Animals*, written c. 350 BCE.

8   Menageries had existed among nobles for hundreds of years, but by the sixteenth century they had become accessible to the public. Well-stocked animal shows were quite exceptional. Transporting animals long distances in this period was no mean feat, so only 150 species of large mammal were known in Europe in the late seventeenth century. Jan Velten's private album of sketches was recently found in the Artis Library in Amsterdam.

9   Collections were meant to be 'microcosms' of the world, relying on the concept of 'metonymy', where an object could conceptually substitute for something else in the wider world or an abstract concept. They could be arranged to maximally

juxtapose different things to increase sensory surprise, or be tightly organised encyclopaedias of the world. The emphasis shifted from the Renaissance to the Enlightenment, moving away from 'rooms of wonder' towards increasingly systematic collections.

10   Policing these trafficking routes is very difficult, given the scale and geographic area over which it occurs. Seizures can contain material (mainly skins and scales) from thousands of animals at once – nearly 200,000 animals were estimated to have been trafficked in 2019.

11   The Battle of Prague was the last battle of the Thirty Years War (1618–48). The hydra was taken by General Hans Christoff von Königsmarck, and after his death, passed through merchants to Hamburg.

12   *Red Dragon* was the psychological horror-prequel to *Silence of the Lambs* (1991). Dolarhyde believed that each time he killed a victim, it brought him closer to becoming the Red Dragon. Turning yourself into a dragon-devil and figuratively smiting God is a rather inventive way for a serial killer to resolve his father issues.

13   By 1735, two years after Seba's catalogue was published, the owner was urgently trying to sell the hydra for only 2,000 thalers. After Linnaeus gave his verdict on it, he rapidly left Hamburg to avoid the ire of the seller, whose merchandise he had conclusively devalued. The hydra was not heard of again.

14   Pliny wrote that the dragon was the natural foe of the elephant. The dragon had the advantage of flight while the elephant ccould crush the dragon to death. He located dragons alongside elephants in both India and Ethiopia.

15   This inscription is on the Hunt-Lenox globe from 1510, the third-oldest known terrestrial globe, now housed at the New York Public Library.

16   Aside from Linnaeus, other naturalists were also working in

increasingly taxonomic ways, such as the French polymath, Georges-Louis Leclerc Comte de Buffon. The shift between what could be called the 'symbolic' and scientific approaches was far from clear-cut.

17 A 'Jenny Haniver' was a ray carefully cut and dried into the shape of a 'dragon'. They were common museum objects through to the nineteenth century.

Chapter Eight: Terrible Lizards

Opening quote from an interview with Larry Niven's friend Arthur C. Clarke: Claudia Dreifus, 'A conversation with Arthur C. Clarke; An Author's Space Odyssey and His Stay at the Chelsea', *New York Times*, 26 October 1999.

1 Buckland described the *Ichthyosaur* eye as 'an optical instrument of varied and prodigious power', either 'a telescope' or 'a microscope', which is clearly evident in the Crystal Palace model.

2 Erich Fromm argued that caring about nature was essential for human wellbeing, but that it was only possible in a healthy society. The term was later used by E. O. Wilson in his book *Biophilia* (1984), who added a possible genetic basis for the human tendency to focus on other lifeforms.

3 Some of the details of the evening are shaky, such as who exactly was invited, and whether, as the pictures show, everyone actually dined inside the *Iguanodon*. Or even where the dinner was held. But as with many myths in science history, the story that was spun around the event is the most engaging – and the most telling.

4 The Iguanodonts have a long and complex history. They have been pictured as fat-bellied lizards with horns on their noses by the Victorians, as twentieth-century Godzilla-like bipeds, and now as elegant, spike-thumbed quadrupeds. The group

has been used as a catch-all for a wide array of orthodont (regularly-toothed) dinosaurs over time. Many of these species have been misidentified and assumed to be related when in fact they were not in the same genus. Almost despite themselves, so the apocryphal story goes, the Mantells decided that the teeth must come from a vast herbivorous lizard, and Gideon searched avidly for other specimens to reinforce the theory. This idea was greeted by many a derisive snort among the intelligentsia. But in 1834, a quarry owner in Maidstone, Kent contacted Gideon about a limestone slab that had been blown open, containing what looked like *Iguanodon* fossils that Mantell could use to prove his case.

5   The notorious 'Bone Wars' in the late nineteenth century between Edward Drinker Cope (1840–97) and Othniel Charles Marsh (1831–99) were a bitter rivalry which led to many new discoveries but also to many destroyed specimens and much incomplete science. The American dinosaurs were shaped in the mould of industrial giants by American tycoons, who also ran museums, educational institutions and the media.

6   Other scholars have followed Adrienne Mayor's lead, fleshing out some of her predictions. Marco Romano, a postdoc at the Museum of Natural History in Berlin, and Marco Avanzini from the Science Museum in Trento, Italy, published their compendium of all the accounts of giants scattered across the Southern European landscape reported by Classical writers, or second-hand by Medieval and Renaissance scholars. Aside from cyclops skulls imagined from elephant skulls unearthed on the hills of Sicily and Sardinia, and dragon tongues conjured from swordfish bones, they found widespread evidence of gigantic extinct humans. Pliny the Elder, for example, recorded that on the island of Crete, the bones of the hero Orion and another skeleton about 20 metres long, thought to

7. be a giant called Oto, had been found. Palaeontological artist Mark Witton argues against these kinds of interpretations. He demonstrates, for example, that griffon imagery long predated the fossil findings to which Mayor ascribes their origins.

7. There was some controversy in the twentieth century about whether this was in fact an actual binomial which predated the convention of the Linnaean system, whether it had precedence over the name *Megalosaurus*, and whether it should be actively suppressed. Darren Naish has pointed out that the identification as a human scrotum was a mis-labelling in Brookes's publication: in fact, Brookes's text identified the bone as part of a femur, but the plate opposite was labelled as '*Scrotum humanum*'. Subsequent writers took the picture and its label at face value. Naish and colleagues tried to find the original bone but the whereabouts of the *Scrotum humanum* remain a mystery.

8. Richard Fallon pointed out to me that occult palaeontology and the psychometry on which it was based (the theory that objects contain impressions of light waves etc. they have been exposed to, allowing mediums to see images of objects' histories) were even practised into the twentieth century.

9. Owen constructed the word from the Greek *deinos* (terrible) and *sauros* (lizard).

10. Lyell did not support the idea of sudden, catastrophic extinction, of which the dinosaurs would become emblematic. His 'uniformitarian' model of very gradual changes over geological time – that could be observed in the layers of the fossil record, for example – strongly contrasted with the 'catastrophism' of the Biblical Flood.

11. Henry Neville Hutchinson's 'Law of Anticipation' theorised that successive forms which appeared and went extinct made way for better lifeforms, a process of gradual improvement through which 'Nature was dimly groping after more perfect types'.

12   The image was captioned with: 'The reconstruction of the "Father of all the Birds" showing its bird like head and the moveable plates which served as its gliding planes'. The article began: 'when most of the earth was a steaming swamp, Nature carried on what was certainly her most fantastic experiments in animals making. This was the time of the dinosaurs, gigantic reptilian creatures whose weird, nightmarish shapes were strongly suggestive that Mother Nature had an extreme case of creative indigestion after a course of cosmic Welsh rarebit . . . Ages afterward she had learned her lesson and the dinosaurs were wiped out'.

13   This was also the period during which 'dinosaur' was reinstated as a technically accurate category. For most of the twentieth century, the term 'dinosaur' was seen as scientifically inaccurate, as just a popular term describing two distinct groups. But in the 1980s, further taxonomic work revealed that Owen's original definition did in fact hold up to evolutionary history.

14   The *Woolly Mammoth Revival Project* was launched in 2015, with the hope of reconstructing a woolly mammoth genome from DNA fragments recovered from preserved tissue. The fragments were inserted into the genome of an Indian elephant, which is the mammoth's closest living relative. The hybrid animals were to roam the Pleistocene Park, 50 square miles in the Siberian Arctic, founded in 2012 by Sergey Zimov. The project has not yet been successful though. We can only really bring extinct *traits* back to life, not extinct animals for which there are no extant living cells.

15   *Pyroraptor* was a genus that existed in the Late Cretaceous in what is now southern France and Spain. It appeared in *Jurassic World Dominion* (2022), directed by Colin Trevorrow.

Conclusion: Titans of Gaia

Opening quote from Stephen King, *The Shining* (2007), Chapter 17.

1. 'Godzilla' is actually an anglicised version of the Japanese word *Gojira*, which is a combination of two Japanese words: *gorira* (ゴリラ), meaning 'gorilla' and *kujira* (鯨), meaning 'whale'. He's a whale of a gorilla.
2. Such as *The Island of Lost Souls* (1932) directed by Erle C. Kenton, *The Island of Dr Moreau* (1977) directed by Don Taylor, and *The Island of Dr Moreau* (1996) directed by Stanley Richard and John Frankenheimer.
3. Hesiod elaborated this theory in his didactic poem, *Works and Days* from around 700 BCE.
4. The *Völuspá* is the most famous poem of the *Poetic Edda*, a collection of anonymous Norse poems (for a translation, see Larrington, 2014). The most notable manuscript version is the Icelandic *Codex Regius* (c. 1270, now in the Árni Magnússon Institute for Icelandic Studies). The *Völuspá* was also used in the thirteenth-century Icelandic *Prose Edda*.
5. It's hard to put together these Biblical images with the taxidermy hydra we met in Chapter Seven – a stuffed snakeskin with a few weasel paws sewn onto it.
6. The nature of other *kaiju*, such as Mothra and King Ghidorah in the Japanese films, might also be related to political events such as Japan's 1965 treaty with South Korea and China's nuclear developments, respectively. All this political meaning is stripped from the American remakes to reduce the anti-American sentiment.
7. Oppenheimer related this quote in the 1965 TV documentary *The Decision to Drop the Bomb*. The original quotation from the *Bhagavad Gita* means 'I am death, the destroyer of the worlds'.
8. Koonin was Undersecretary for Science in the US Department

of Energy under President Obama from 2009 to 2011.

9   The original quote from Christopher Nolan's *The Dark Knight* (2008) is: 'he's the hero Gotham needs, but not the one it deserves right now' – Batman being the only hero capable of helping Gotham, but entirely unappreciated.

10 Eliot imagined the poem in 1914, but completed it in 1921, after a breakdown precipitated by his father's death in 1919. It was edited by the poet Ezra Pound and published first in October 1922 in *Criterion*, the magazine that Eliot edited, then a few days later in *The Dial* and many times subsequently. Irritated by its overwhelming success compared to his other works, Eliot dismissed *The Wasteland* as just 'the relief of a personal and wholly insignificant grouse against life; it is just a piece of rhythmical grumbling'.

11 *Alien* (1979) directed by Ridley Scott; *28 Days Later* (2002) directed by Danny Boyle; *Daybreakers* (2009) directed by Michael and Peter Spierig.

12 Max Weber is said to have introduced the term during a lecture in 1918, using the German word *Entzauberung*, which can be translated into English as 'disenchantment'. The literal meaning is 'de-magication'.

Index

Aboriginal myths 108
Adam 110, 113–14, 121, 128, 143, 149–50, 333n. 10
AI (artificial intelligence) 270
Aldrovandi, Ulysse 216, 218
Alfano, Christine 143–4
Algonquian peoples 153, 338n. 11
Alien (film) 12, 269
Amsterdam 178, 207, 213
Anastasiadou, Maria 116
Anglo-Saxons 136, 139–45, 150, 175
Anning, Mary 238
Anthropocene 262–4, 266
Antlers (film) 153
Anu 57, 59–61
apocalypse 258–64, 270, 272–3
Apsu 57–9, 66, 69
Arctic 167, 168, 171, 173–4, 211
Ariadne 86, 96, 329n. 10
Aristotle 15, 203, 206, 318n. 5, 344n. 7
armadillos 223, 344n. 7
Arthurian legends 147–8, 267
Aspidochelone 176–7
Assur 64, 68, 326n. 8
Assurbanipal, King 55–6, 325n. 5
Asterion 84–6, 90, 330n. 15
Athena 116–19, 125

atomic bombs 260–1, 262, 264–5
Atrahasis 258, 325n. 6
Augustine, St 4, 333n. 10
Augustus, Emperor 240

Babylon 53–4, 62–4, 68, 324n. 4
badgers 156, 338n. 12
Barnum, P. T. 224
basilisks 122, 216, 219, 224
Bégouën family 23–9, 52, 319n. 1, 320n. 3–5
Benchley, Peter 187–8
Beowulf 134–48, 158–62, 235
Berger, John 155
bestiaries 176
Bettelheim, Bruno 10, 273, 317n. 4
Bible 109, 111–13, 175, 176, 177, 203, 204, 215, 216
Big Bang 51–2, 63, 324n. 1
Bintley, Michael 151
birds 6–7, 202, 234, 251
Blake, William 215
Book of Revelation 259–60
Borges, Jorge Luis 77, 95, 331n. 19
Boston Dynamics 270
brain: amygdala 35–6, 104–5
  in childhood 232
  and fear 35–6, 104–7

353

brain—*contd*
  fish 342n. 16
  prehistoric man 321n. 7
  social brain hypothesis 323n. 18
  trance states 42–4, 46, 48
Breuil, Abbé Henri 28, 29, 32–3, 38
Brookes, Richard 241–2, 348n. 7
Buckland, William 236, 238, 242, 244
bulls 81–90, 327n. 1–2

Cain and Abel 143, 337n. 4
Caliban 141–2, 337n. 3
Campbell, Joseph 65, 88, 127, 319n. 10, 330n. 13, 336n. 22
cannibalism 153
Catholic Church 168
caves: prehistoric paintings 24, 26–40, 43
  and shamanism 42–5, 47
Cellini, Benvenuto 129
centaurs 224
Cernunnos 47, 323n. 19
chaos 52–4, 63–4, 67–74, 175, 257
Chauvet Cave 30–1
children, love of dinosaurs 231–3
Christianity 47–8, 109–12, 130, 142–3, 147, 175–7, 186, 216, 259–60, 268
Circe 335n. 20
classification of animals 223–4
climate change 262–3
Clottes, Jean 43
Clusius, Carolus 206
Cocidius 47
coelacanth 182
collections 208–10, 344n. 9
Collier, John 114
Cook, Jill 34–6, 45

Covid-19 pandemic 269
Cranach, Lucas the Elder 112
creation myths 51–74
Crete 82–90, 116
crocodiles 199–200, 201
Cronon, Bill 157, 339n. 14
cryptozoology 182–3
Crystal Palace Dinosaurs 229–31, 236, 237–8, 243, 248
Cuvier, Georges 236, 241

Daedalus 84–5, 92, 330n. 16
Dante Alighieri 90, 244
Darwin, Charles 246
de Bondt, Jacob 199–206, 211
deep sea 189–92
deer 40–1, 322n. 13
Dent, Harvey 266
Devil 175–6
dingoes 156–7, 339n. 13
dinosaurs 229–53
disenchantment 272–3
DNA 108–9, 251
dodos 6–7, 252, 266
dragons 3, 7, 9, 12, 49–74, 147, 216–20, 222, 239, 245
drugs, psychedelic 46–7
Dunbar, Robin 46
Dürer, Albrecht 167, 340n. 3
Dutch East India Company 199–200, 204, 207, 222, 343n. 2

Ea 57–62, 326n. 8
Echidna 115, 120, 121, 126, 334n. 13, n. 16
elephants 172, 218, 251, 252, 345n. 14
Eliot, T. S. 72, 266–7, 351n. 10
Enkidu 149
entropy 68–70

Enūma Eliš 56–68, 119, 170, 325n. 6
Epic of Gilgamesh 119–20, 149, 337n. 7
Evans, Arthur 82–4, 87, 328n. 6, 330n. 16
Eve 104, 110–13, 121, 125, 128, 130, 143, 149–50, 333n. 10
Evenk people 41
Evens people 41
extinctions 245–8, 258

The Fall 109, 110–14, 336n. 22
Fallon, Richard 242
fear 35–8, 104–7, 268–9
Fenrir 259
fertility goddesses 120, 335n. 17
Field, Eugene 246–7
films 93–4, 124–5, 144–5, 187–9, 250–3, 256–8, 260, 264–6, 269–71, 274–5
floods 258
Fontcuberta, Joan 220–1
fossils 180, 182–3, 238–43, 245–6, 249
Freud, Sigmund 66, 87, 92, 96, 126, 189
From Dusk Till Dawn (film) 124–5
Fromm, Erich 232, 318n. 7, 346n. 2

Gaia 53, 63
Garbati, Luciano 129, 130
Garden of Eden 109, 110–14, 121, 149–50, 175, 223, 267
Gardner, John 137, 158–62, 339n. 15–16
Genesis 263
genetics 251–2, 257–8
geology 246
George, St 147, 216, 337n. 6
Gervase of Tilbury 151–2

Giallongo, Angela 121–3, 128, 129
Gilgamesh 119–20, 149
Gilot, Françoise 328n. 4
Godzilla 256–7, 260–1, 264–6, 350n. 1
Golding, William 153–4
Gorgons 104, 115–19, 121–2, 125, 126, 130, 334n. 15
Gould, Stephen J. 234
Goya, Francisco 199
Graves, Robert 330n. 13
Great Exhibition, London (1851) 237
Greenblatt, Stephen 112, 113
Gregory XIII, Pope 216
Grendel 131–48, 151, 158–62, 266
griffins 7, 218, 240, 348n. 6
Gundestrup cauldron 323n. 19
Gunkel, Hermann 52

Hawking, Stephen 270
Hawkins, Benjamin Waterhouse 237
Hayek, Salma 124–5
Haynes, Natalie 128–9
headdresses 40, 322n. 13
Heaney, Seamus 137, 144
Hemingway, Ernest 79, 80
Henson, Jim 97
Hera 125, 334n. 13
Hercules 117
Herzog, Werner 23, 30–1
Hesiod 53, 258, 334n. 13, n. 15, 350n. 3
Heuvelmans, Bernard 182–3
Hoffer, Eric 73
Holland, Tom 130
Homer 116, 328n. 7
Honda, Ishiro 257, 260, 261, 264
Horner, Jack 251
Hrothgar, King 134, 135, 140

Humbaba 149, 155
Hutchinson, Henry Neville 245, 247, 348n. 11
Hydrarchos 179–81
hydras 3, 9, 213–16, 218, 219–20, 345n. 11, n. 13

International Wildlife Museum, Arizona 224
Isbell, Lynne 105–7, 109
Ishtar 64, 326n. 11
Ishtar Gate 54–5
Isidore of Seville, St 4, 176, 341n. 9

Jacobson, Mark 260
Japan 260–1
Java 199–204, 206
Jaws (film) 187–9
Jonah 176
Jörmungandr 53, 244, 259
Jung, Carl 65, 189
Jurassic Park (film) 234, 250–1, 252–3

kaiju films 257, 260, 261, 264–5, 271, 350n. 6
kangaroos 157
Keats, John 126
King, Stephen 93–4, 255, 331n. 18
Kircher, Athanasius 223
Klein, Melanie 66
Knossos 82–90, 328n. 6–7
Koch, Albert 179–81
Koonin, Steven 263
Kraken 182
Kratos 69
Kubrick, Stanley 93–4, 331n. 18

Labyrinth 81, 83–98, 330n. 17
Lamia 104, 115, 120, 121, 123, 125, 126, 334n. 13
The Last of Us (TV series) 148
'Lazarus species' 182–3
le Guin, Ursula 146, 339n. 14
Legendary Studios 256, 264
Leo X, Pope 166
Leonardo da Vinci 12
Leviathan 177, 179–80, 193
Lewis-Williams, David 43–4
Lilith 113–15, 124, 125, 128, 333n. 11
Linnaeus, Carl 215, 223–4, 345n. 13
Lion-man 39
Lovecraft, H. P. 148
Lucifer 160, 176, 267
Lyell, Charles 246, 348n. 10

Mad Max films 269
Magnus, Albertus 169, 171–5
Magnus, Olaus 167–9, 192
mammoths 24, 32, 39, 172, 239, 240–1, 349n. 14
Manasa 120, 335n. 17
Mantell, Gideon 236, 238, 242, 347n. 4
manticores 3, 8, 266
Marduk (Storm God) 53, 59–65, 67, 69, 72, 74, 325n. 8
Marmery, Nikki 128
The Matrix (film) 270–1
Mayor, Adrienne 239–40
Medusa 104, 115–19, 120–2, 123, 125, 126, 128–30, 266, 334n. 15, 336n. 21
Mélusine 104, 115, 125–6, 335n. 19
Melville, Herman 178–9, 189
mermaids 224
Mesopotamia 54–69, 113, 119–20, 149, 258, 325n. 6
MeToo movement 129

Michelangelo 112
Milton, John 51, 126, 160, 267, 335n. 20
Minoans 82–90, 116, 328n. 6
Minos, King of Crete 83–5, 90, 92, 328n. 7
Minotaur 81–98, 266
Moby Dick 178–9, 189
Momigliano, Nicoletta 87–8
Monbiot, George 37
morse 168–70, 172–3, 341n. 5
Mother Nature 53, 119–21, 127

Naga 108
Naginis 108
Naish, Darren 183, 235, 348n. 7
Narby, Jeremy 108–9
Natural History Museum, London 180, 181, 234–5
Neumann, Erich 65
Neville, Jennifer 140
Nietzsche, Friedrich 71–2
Nin, Anaïs 96–7
Niven, Larry 229
Norman Conquest 337n. 2
Norse myths 244, 258–9

oceans 165–93, 211
O'Connor, Ralph 243–4
Odysseus 334n. 14, 335n. 18
Olympus 53, 240
Oppenheimer, Robert 261, 350n. 7
orangutans 344n. 6
orcas 186–7, 342n. 14
Ovid 90, 117, 334n. 15, 335n. 20
Owen, Richard 236, 242–3

Pagans 45
Palaeolithic art 26–41, 43, 120

Pan 47
pangolins 200–8, 210–13, 217, 222–4, 266, 275, 343n. 4–5
Paris, Matthew 171, 341n. 6
Pasiphaë 84–5, 88–90, 329n. 9
pelican fish 191
Pennant, Thomas 186
Perseus 118–19, 129
Peter Damian, St 113
Peyote 46–7
phoenix 6, 223, 266
The Physiologus 176
Picasso, Pablo 73, 80–2, 87, 327n. 3–5
Piso, Willem 204–5
Pliny the Elder 4, 171, 172, 216, 345n. 14, 347n. 6
Plot, Robert 241
Plutarch 87, 89
Pokémon 232
Polo, Marco 216–17
Poseidon 84–5, 117, 334n. 15
psychedelic drugs 46–7

Quammen, David 14–15, 177, 318n. 8
Questing Beast 148
Quingu 59–60, 62, 67

Ragnarok 258–9
Rainbow Serpent 108
religion 46–8
Richardson, John 81
Rieppel, Lukas 249–50
robots 270
Romanticism 30, 267, 339n. 14
Rossetti, Dante Gabriel 114–15
Royal Society of London 224

Satan 48, 112, 259

Satyrs 47
Scales, Helen 190
Scylla 335n. 20
sea monsters 165–93, 211
Seba, Albertus 213–14, 345n. 13
Sendak, Maurice 338n. 8
Seneca 90
Shakespeare, William 65, 125, 133, 141–2, 179
shamanism 40, 41–5, 47, 323n. 14–17
sharks 184–9, 192, 342n. 15, n. 17
Shelley, Mary 1, 11, 72, 159
The Shining (film) 93–4, 331n. 18
Simpson, Liz 91
Sloane, Sir Hans 241
snakes and snake women 101–30, 275
Sorcerer 29, 31, 32–3, 38–41
Soylent Green (film) 274
Spielberg, Steven 187–9, 250–1
squid, giant 181–2, 192
Star Carr 40, 41, 322n. 13
Steinbeck, John 165
Stonehenge 45
Stumpf, Petr 152

Tammuz 64, 326n. 11
Tasmanian tiger 155–6
therianthropes 29, 39, 45, 322n. 12
Theseus 86–7, 89, 92, 96, 329n. 10, 330n. 14
Thor 53, 259
Thoreau, Henry David 157
thylacines 155–6, 252
Tiamat 53, 57–64, 66–7, 69, 71, 74, 121, 235, 244, 275
Tiberius, Emperor 240
Titans 53, 241, 257
Tolkien, J. R. R. 137–9, 145–6, 147, 260

trance states 42–4, 46, 48
Trois-frères cave 27–32, 40–3

unicorns 170, 213, 218, 223

vampires 2, 125
Velten, Jan 208, 344n. 8
Verne, Jules 182
Villiers de l'Isle-Adam, Auguste 247
Volp River 23–8

Waldseemüller, Martin 172
Walkendorf, Bishop 166–8, 340n. 1
walruses 165–73, 176, 340n. 2–3, 341n. 5
Warner, Marina 103, 144
wastelands 150, 266–7
water 66, 170–1
Weber, Max 272, 351n. 12
Wells, H. G. 257
Wendigo 153, 338n. 11
werewolves 2, 151–2, 338n. 10
whales 173–9, 180, 184, 186–7, 189, 341n. 8, 342n. 10–12
Wilde, Oscar 82
wildness/wilderness 134–62, 338n. 8, 339n. 14
Williams, Thomas 151
Williers, Bill 224
witches 123, 152, 338n. 10
wolves 151–2, 155, 275
Wordsworth, William 72
Wynd, Viktor 224

Zemeckis, Robert 144–5
Zeus 53, 121, 324n. 3, 334n. 13